Divided Spirits

CALIFORNIA STUDIES IN FOOD AND CULTURE

Darra Goldstein, Editor

Divided Spirits

TEQUILA, MEZCAL, AND
THE POLITICS OF PRODUCTION

Sarah Bowen

UNIVERSITY OF CALIFORNIA PRESS

University of California Press, one of the most distinguished university presses in the United States, enriches lives around the world by advancing scholarship in the humanities, social sciences, and natural sciences. Its activities are supported by the UC Press Foundation and by philanthropic contributions from individuals and institutions. For more information, visit www.ucpress.edu.

University of California Press
Oakland, California

Library of Congress Cataloging-in-Publication Data

Bowen, Sarah, 1978–.
    Divided spirits : tequila, mezcal, and the politics of production / Sarah Bowen.
        p.   cm.—(California studies in food and culture ; 56)
    Includes bibliographical references and index.
    ISBN 978-0-520-28104-2 (cloth : alk. paper)
    ISBN 978-0-520-28105-9 (pbk. : alk. paper)
    ISBN 978-0-520-96258-3 (ebook)
    1. Mescal.   2. Mescal industry.   I. Title.   II. Series: California studies in food and culture ; 56.
    HD9393.6.A2B69   2015
    338.4'76635—dc23

                                                    2015006369

Manufactured in the United States of America

24 23 22 21 20 19 18 17 16 15
10 9 8 7 6 5 4 3 2 1

In keeping with a commitment to support environmentally responsible and sustainable printing practices, UC Press has printed this book on Natures Natural, a fiber that contains 30% post-consumer waste and meets the minimum requirements of ANSI/NISO Z39.48–1992 (R 1997) (*Permanence of Paper*).

To all of the farmers, workers, and small producers
who make tequila and mezcal

Contents

Illustrations

Acknowledgments

First, I express my gratitude to all of the kind and generous people who welcomed me into their homes, offices, and distilleries. Every story that was shared with me has contributed to the richness of my understanding of tequila and mezcal and the institutions that regulate them.

My research in Mexico was supported by the Rural Sociological Society, the Land Tenure Center at the University of Wisconsin-Madison, the Centro de Estudios y Programas Interamericanos at the Instituto Tecnológico Autónomo de México, and the Department of Sociology and Anthropology at North Carolina State University. My research in Europe, which served as an important comparison with my work in Mexico, was supported by a Fulbright Institute of International Education Grant to the European Union, by the Center for European Studies at the University of Wisconsin-Madison, and by the French development and research organization CIRAD.

I am indebted to the many people who helped make my research in Mexico possible. Doña Guadalupe Michel welcomed me to the first place I lived in Mexico, more than ten years ago. Doña Lupita's house provided a wonderful place for conversation and served as my introduction to many Mexican foods, traditions, and telenovelas. Professors Peter Gerritsen and

Ana Valenzuela Zapata offered their guidance at early stages of this project and became valued collaborators and friends. My ongoing collaborations with Marie Sarita Gaytán, which began when we met while doing field-work in Jalisco, have been fruitful and fun, and I continue to learn from her. Representatives of the Tequila Regulatory Council facilitated my access to interview contacts and statistical data. Alejandro Macías Macías shared his calculations on agave prices with me. Cati Illsley was one of the first people I talked to when I began studying the mezcal industry, and I am grateful for the depth of her knowledge and for her commitment to social justice and environmental sustainability. Jorge Larson Guerra and the National Commission for the Knowledge and Use of Biodiversity (CONABIO) generously allowed me to use their map in this book. I appreciate the willingness of Pedro Jiménez and David Suro to go above and beyond in answering my many questions, and I thank David for sharing his beautiful photos with me.

I am also thankful for the scholars who have shaped my thinking about food systems and development. Many people gave me valuable feedback throughout this project, including Keera Allendorf, Brad Barham, Jane Collins, Kathy DeMaster, Michaela DeSoucey, Marie Sarita Gaytán, Peter Gerritsen, Jess Gilbert, Cristina Grasseni, Jill Harrison, Pete Nowak, Heather Paxson, Michael Schulman, Amy Trubek, and Jonathan Zeitlin. I am especially grateful to Jane Collins, at the University of Wisconsin-Madison, for her guidance during the earliest stages of my research and for her insightful advice throughout this process. My interactions with Gilles Allaire, François Boucher, Tad Mutersbaugh, Marie-Christine Renard, Gerardo Torres Salcido, Denis Sautier, and others associated with the SYAL (local agrifood systems) network in Latin America and Europe influenced and deepened my thinking about ideas related to terroir, embeddedness, and local development. I appreciate the valuable comments and questions I received at seminars and workshops organized by Matthew Booker and Chad Ludington, Neil Caren and Andrew Perrin, Rudi Colloredo-Mansfeld, and Cristina Grasseni and Heather Paxson. David Lobenstine's apt sugges-tions helped make this book clearer and easier to read. I also thank Jim Bingen and two anonymous reviewers for their useful feedback.

I appreciate the assistance of the excellent team at the University of California Press. I thank Kate Marshall, my editor, for her vision and her faith in this project. Stacy Eisenstark, Jessica Moll, and Tom Sullivan did a great job of guiding me through the process of publishing this book.

My colleagues and graduate students in the Department of Sociology and Anthropology at North Carolina State University, and those associated with Voices into Action: The Families, Food, and Health Project, supported me throughout the process of writing this book. I thank Michaela DeSoucey, Kim Ebert, and Sinikka Elliott for their advice and encouragement over the years, and Brett Clark, now at the University of Utah, for encouraging me to write this book. I thank Annie Hardison-Moody, in the Department of Youth, Family, and Consumer Sciences, for helping me find the time I needed to finish this book. The graduate students in my seminar on sociology of food pushed me to better articulate my conclusions about alternative markets and neoliberalism. My graduate research assistant, Dayne Hamrick, helped analyze legislative documents and newspaper articles and assisted with the coding of some of my interviews. He also carefully assisted with the proofreading of this manuscript in its final stages. Another graduate student, Lillian MacNell, did the GIS analysis for the map of the DO regions.

I am most grateful for the support of my family over the years. My parents, Curt and Karen Bowen, fostered my love of reading and writing and my curiosity about new places. I am thankful for their unwavering belief in me. My sisters, Betsy and Alissa Bowen, visited me at all of my research sites. They support me in many ways and make me laugh like no one else. My children, Simon and Anna Nance, inject a sense of adventure into every day. They give me hope for the future, and I look forward to one day sharing my favorite places in Mexico with them. Finally, I thank Mark Nance, my partner and fellow traveler. He convinced me that I could write a book, and he read multiple drafts of every chapter. By commenting on my work, taking care of Simon and Anna during my travels, and making our house a great place to come home to, he made it possible for me to write this book.

Abbreviations

CIGC	Comité Interprofessionnel du Gruyère de Comté (Interprofessional Committee for Gruyère from Comté)
CNIT	Cámara Nacional de la Industria Tequilera (National Chamber of the Tequila Industry)
COMERCAM	Consejo Mexicano Regulador de la Calidad del Mezcal (Mexican Regulatory Council for the Quality of Mezcal)
CONABIO	Comisión Nacional para el Conocimiento y Uso de la Biodiversidad (National Commission for the Knowledge and Use of Biodiversity)
CRM	Consejo Regulador del Mezcal (Mezcal Regulatory Council)
CRT	Consejo Regulador del Tequila (Tequila Regulatory Council)
DGN	Dirección General de Normas (General Directorate of Standards)
DO	denominación de origen (denomination of origin)

INAO	Institut National des Appellations d'Origine (National Institute for Appellations of Origin)
NAFTA	North American Free Trade Agreement
NOM	Norma Oficial Mexicano (Official Mexican Standard)
oriGIn	Organization for an International Geographical Indications Network
PDO	Protected Designation of Origin
PGI	Protected Geographical Indication
SAGARPA	Secretaría de Agricultura, Ganadería, Desarrollo Rural, Pesca, y Alimentación (Secretary of Agriculture, Livestock, Rural Development, Fisheries, and Nutrition)
UNESCO	United Nations Educational, Social, and Cultural Organization
USDA	United States Department of Agriculture
WIPO	World Intellectual Property Organization
WTO	World Trade Organization

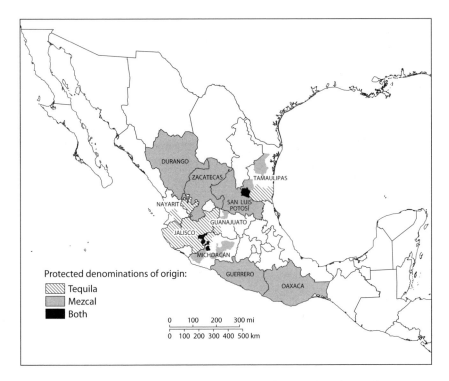

Territories protected by the denominations of origin for tequila and mezcal.

Plants used in the production of mezcal

This version of the map was produced by the National Commission for the Knowledge and Use of Biodiversity (CONABIO, according to its Spanish acronym) specifically for this book. At this scale, it is not possible to depict the distribution of particular species. The brief descriptions give additional information on distribution, and the common and indigenous names suggest the cultural importance and richness of varieties within species.

Agave angustifolia
doba-yej (zapoteco: maguey de flor), *hamoc* (seri), *juya cuu* (mayo: mezcal del monte), bacanora, espadilla, espadín
This species is both wild and cultivated; it has the widest distribution.

Agave salmiana subsp. *crassispina*
mbänuada (otomí), bronco, cimarrón, manso, verde
This subspecies is exclusive to the highlands of San Luis Potosí and Zacatecas.

Agave rhodacantha
quixe, mexicano
This species is found only in the foothills of the highlands from Sonora to Oaxaca.

Agave maximiliana
lechuguilla, manso, tecolote
This is one of the species used to produce raicilla in western Jalisco.

Agave lophanta
estobillo, lechuguilla, mezortillo
This species is found in the slopes of the eastern Sierra Madre.

Agave durangensis
cenizo
Used to make both pulque and mezcal, this species is found in scrublands and in pine and oak forests in the mountains of Durango and Zacatecas.

Agave tequilana
azul, azul listado, pata de mula, sigüin, bermejo, moraleño, zopilote
Tequila is made exclusively from the blue variety; other varieties are found in western Mexico.

Agave inaequidens
hocimetl (náhuatl), lechuguilla, alto, bruto
Used to make pulque and mezcal, this species grows among pine and oak groves in volcanic regions in central Mexico.

Agave marmorata
du-cual (zapoteco), *pitzometl* (náhuatl), curandero, tepeztate
This species is found in arid lands in southern Mexico.

CONABIO

COMISIÓN NACIONAL PARA EL
CONOCIMIENTO Y USO DE LA BIODIVERSIDAD

Agave potatorum
tobalá (zapoteco), *papalometl* (náhuatl: maguey mariposa), *yauiticushi* (mixteco)
Found in Oaxaca, this is a wild and highly valued species of agave.

Agave americana
t' ax' uada (otomí), *teometl* (náhuatl), americano, serrano
This species is used to make mezcal in northeastern Mexico.

Agave americana var. *oaxacensis*
dua-bzog (zapoteco), *yavi cuan* (mixteco), arroqueño, maguey de coyote, de pulque, de rayo, sierra negra
This is a domesticated variety found in Oaxaca. Valued for its fibers and as a living fence, it is also used in mezcal.

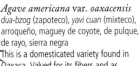

Agave cupreata
papalometl (náhuatl: maguey mariposa), *yaabendisi* (mixteco), ancho, chino, cimarrón, papalote, tuchi
This species is found in the mountains of Guerrero, Michoacan, and Puebla.

Agave karwinskii
bicuixe, tobasiche (zapoteco), barril, cirial
This species is found in the arid regions of the Tehuacán Valley and the central valley of Oaxaca.

Ilustración: Rafael Ruiz   Design: Rosalba Becerra   CONABIO. 2015. Prepared for the University of California Press and Sarah Bowen for the book *Divided Spirits: Tequila, Mezcal, and the Politics of Production*.

1 The Promise of Place

In May 2012, more than one hundred people crammed into a conference room at the Hotel El Ejecutivo in Mexico City, to debate proposed changes in the regulation of mezcal, a spirit distilled from the roasted heart of Mexico's native agave plant. It was a diverse group that included governmental officials, retailers, producers from all over Mexico, and even a group of American bartenders, whom I had come with. To casual observers, it likely sounded like another dry debate over governmental regulations. In late 2011, the Mexican government had unveiled proposals that would reserve the use of the word *agave* for producers inside government-designated regions, including specific territories reserved for tequila and mezcal. Proponents of the proposals argued that the latter would protect consumers by ensuring the quality and safety of distilled agave spirits. But the proposals made international headlines because the debate was about something much more profound. Critics contended that the proposals would protect the big tequila and mezcal companies that had pushed for them, and that they threatened small producers throughout Mexico, many of whom had been making distilled agave spirits for generations but which were not included in the protected regions.

Opponents organized quickly and convened two forums, one in Guadalajara and the other in Mexico City, in order to hear from those who had been excluded from the drafting of the original proposal. At the Mexico City forum, which I attended, the group spent a full day trying to collectively develop an alternative set of standards. A gentleman in a dark suit took the floor. "These are artisanal producers, who come in sandals," he said authoritatively. "If we include a thousand rules, the government is going to come and shut them down."[1] The tension in the room was palpable as everyone waited to see how the small mezcal producers, identifiable by their cowboy hats and, in some cases, the aforementioned sandals, would react. One raised his hand. "No one can take away our rights," he said. "We are all equal, and it is our right to defend what we do. And we are proud of it. . . . You need to have a little bit of respect, for us, the producers. We all know that the big companies have always gone above the laws; they have trampled us, but we are no longer in the sixteenth century. We are educated, and we want to do things in the best possible way."[2] Many people applauded, while the governmental officials at the front of the room shifted awkwardly in their seats. Jorge Cruz, the owner of a high-end tequila company, was the first to respond. "I have more trust in a producer who is wearing sandals than in a person who is wearing the cowboy boots of an industry executive," he said.[3]

The sentiments expressed in that meeting reflect a larger debate in Mexico, one with roots that reach deep into Mexico's colonial past. It is a debate about what constitutes Mexico's national "spirit"—a discussion of Mexico's national liquor industries, and also a conversation about the past and future of Mexico's people. What is mezcal? Who has the right to produce mezcal, and how should that right be protected? What does mezcal have to do with being Mexican?

THE ORIGINS OF MEZCAL AND TEQUILA

For centuries, people in Mexico have battled over the right to make and sell mezcal and tequila, two of its most iconic products. The word *mezcal* comes from the Nahuatl words *metl* (meaning "agave") and *ixcalli* (meaning "cooked" or "baked"). Colonial settlers used the word *mezcal* to refer to the agave plants that indigenous populations in Mexico had consumed as food and in fermented beverages for thousands of years.[4] There are more than two hundred species of agave, a stubborn succulent that thrives in dry climates and is endemic to Mexico. Eventually, the meaning of *mezcal* shifted to refer to distilled agave spirits, which likely originated in the Colima volcanoes region in western Mexico. Scholars debate whether indigenous populations started distilling before the arrival of colonial settlers, but they agree that distillation became widespread in the seventeenth century. Mezcal producers (also known as *mezcaleros*) collected wild agave, roasted the agave hearts (*piñas*) in earthen pits, and then chopped the piñas and fermented the mash. This process could take several weeks. They then slowly distilled the fermented juice in wood-fired stills. Distilled spirits were subject to frequent and ongoing periods of prohibition by colonial authorities, which drove production into isolated rural regions. As distillation techniques spread southward into indigenous communities, and northward into mining centers and along trade routes, the mezcaleros adapted their techniques to each region.

Today, at least twenty species of agave are commonly used in the production of mezcal, with some studies finding upward of forty-two species.[5] The type of agave, production practices, and equipment used to make mezcal vary between regions. Of course, most people are familiar with the most famous version of mezcal: tequila, named after the town of Tequila in central Jalisco. In the late nineteenth century, the *tequileros* (the producers in and around Tequila) began to expand and industrialize, differentiating themselves from the mezcaleros in other parts of Mexico. Tequila is now made in huge factories, while thousands of small mezcaleros continue to make mezcal using methods similar to those employed by their ancestors.

PROTECTING AND DEFINING MEXICO'S SPIRITS

In the second half of the nineteenth century, people began referring to "mezcal from Tequila" simply as tequila. Recalling his travels through Mexico in 1854 and 1855, French writer Ernest Vigneaux noted that "just as [the town of] Cognac has given its name to French brandies in general, Tequila has given its name to the spirit mezcal."[6] After a "mezcal brandy" from Tequila and a "Tequila wine" were recognized, respectively, at the 1893 Chicago World's Fair and in San Antonio in 1910, the name of the drink became synonymous with the name of the town.[7]

In the twentieth century, as the market for tequila grew, the tequileros sought protection from imposters outside Jalisco who were fraudulently attempting to pass off their products as tequila. In 1949, Mexico established the first official quality standard for tequila. The standard stated that tequila could be made only from one variety of agave (*Agave tequilana* Weber), cultivated in the state of Jalisco. But in practice, it did little to protect the tequileros from people who were trying to produce tequila abroad. In an attempt to solve this problem and legally establish tequila as Mexico's national spirit, tequila became, in 1974, the first product outside of Europe to be protected by a denomination of origin (DO). DOs, established by national governments in the places where they are produced, confer on particular places the right to produce a food or drink. They also set rules governing how those foods or drinks must be produced. The DO for tequila gave distilleries in Jalisco and parts of four other states the exclusive right to produce tequila.[8] In 1994, the Mexican government established a DO for mezcal, defining the territory where mezcal could be produced, despite the fact that *mezcal* is a generic term for distilled agave spirits. According to the DO, mezcal can be legally produced only in eight states: in all of Durango, Guerrero, Oaxaca, San Luis Potosí, and Zacatecas; and in parts of Guanajuato, Michoacán, and Tamaulipas.[9]

Advocates of the DOs and the corresponding quality standards argue that they protect Mexico's cultural heritage, expand market opportunities, and ensure the reputation and safety of Mexico's national spirits. However, my research shows that in practice, the institutions that regulate tequila and mezcal adopt a narrow and technical understanding of quality, one that focuses on maximizing economic efficiency and meeting the standards required for export markets. The regulations have not taken into account the perspectives of agave farmers, workers, and small tequila producers and mezcaleros. In addition, they exclude all of the producers who live outside the regions delineated by the DOs. One study found evidence of a history of mezcal production in twenty-four of thirty-one Mexican states and the Federal District of Mexico,[10] but the DOs for tequila and mezcal include territories in only ten states.

The debates that I document and analyze in this book are intensely Mexican. At the same time, conflicts over tequila and mezcal mirror debates about the production (and protection) of foods and drinks that are unfolding throughout the world. In recent years, traditional foods and drinks have emerged as profitable and politically salient alternatives to the perceived homogenizing effects of globalization. Initiatives like the Slow Food movement and DOs attempt to "rescue eating establishments, dishes, and products from the flood of standardization" engendered by the industrial food system.[11] In doing so, they strive to support the rural communities, farmers, and processors involved in the production of traditional products. And yet, as my research shows, efforts to regulate Mexico's iconic spirits illustrate the limitations of relying on alternative markets to protect food cultures and the livelihoods of those who produce them. My work demonstrates how cultural symbolism can be manipulated to perpetuate and deepen long-standing inequalities along global commodity chains.

In this book, I investigate the process of using DOs to protect and certify Mexican spirits. I do so by telling the stories of tequila and mezcal: the stories of the people who make them, the institutions that regulate them, and the retailers and consumers who buy and sell them. This book chronicles my work over the past ten years, a project that took me into the living rooms and kitchens of agave farmers and day laborers and to the glitzy offices and gleaming factory floors of tequila companies. It also took me to small mezcal distilleries and trendy mezcal and tequila bars from Oaxaca City to New York. In total, I visited more than thirty distilleries—from tiny family mezcal distilleries perched on mountain bluffs and almost hidden by the surrounding forest, to huge industrial tequila factories. And I participated in mezcal and tequila tastings, agave farmers' meetings, academic conferences, and forums organized by governmental organizations and the Tequila Regulatory Council (CRT). This book uses the stories of these places and these people to investigate the politics of protecting local products in a global market.

FOOD FROM SOMEWHERE

In a modern global food system characterized by "distance and durability,"[12] we can get tomatoes in the middle of winter; but many people have never had the sublime experience of biting into a ripe garden tomato on a hot August day. Agribusiness firms rely on global sourcing strategies, and contract arrangements are used to integrate farmers into what is essentially an industrial enterprise, in which hybrid seeds are combined with chemical inputs, and information technology is used to coordinate multiple production sites spread across the globe.[13] And in a context in which our food comes to us from "a global everywhere, yet from nowhere . . . in particular,"[14] people are trying to find ways to connect with the people—and the places—that produce their food.

Today, within just a few miles of my house in North Carolina, I have my pick of more "farm-to-table" restaurants than I could count on one hand. At these places, rotating chalkboard menus offer seasonal specialties, like fried pickled shrimp from the coast paired with an aioli made with ramps harvested in the mountains, or a salad that combines watermelon from the local farmer's market with farmstead goat cheese from a few counties over. The number of farmers' markets in the United States has exploded in the last twenty years; according to the U.S. Department of Agriculture, there are now more than eight thousand, scattered in tiny towns and big cities all over the country.[15] On-farm dinners and farm tours offer city dwellers the opportunity to see how working farms operate. Community-Supported Agriculture, another model, allows consumers to "invest" in a farm, paying upfront and then getting a weekly delivery of produce. Where I live, there are also community-supported fisheries, where customers get weekly deliveries of fresh fish and shellfish from the North Carolina coast. Even the grocery stores where I shop are trying to connect customers with the farmers who grow their produce. They hang huge color photographs of farmers over the coolers where I buy otherwise indistinguishable bags of apples or lettuce, inviting me to "meet my neighbors" who grow and make my food.

The posters at my grocery store are an example of how people who do not literally "know their farmer,"[16] as the Department of Agriculture tells us we should, can still have a sense of "knowing their food": by hearing the story of how their food was grown. In contrast to the "food from nowhere" regime,[17] which operates on invisibility, obscuring the social and environmental bases of food production, the "food from somewhere" regime renders the food supply more visible, in response to increased consumer demand for traceability.[18] The "food from somewhere" regime is characterized by wealthy consumption niches, complex new forms of auditing and inspection, and emblematic new products, from certified organic to fair trade. This new set of relations operates globally, in that it makes "local production conditions visible over global-scale distances," as in the case of Kenyan organic green beans that are audited by European certifiers and then sold through Swiss food cooperatives.[19]

In this context, the French notion of *terroir*—literally translated as "region" or "earth" and understood as evoking the relationship between a product and the land, soil, and specific place that it comes from—has become increasingly salient. Terroir conveys the taste of place. As Starbucks put it in advertisements for their single-origin coffees, terroir is the idea that "geography is a flavor." As a legal concept, DOs, which originated in France but have now been exported around the world, are based on the belief that the environmental and cultural characteristics of particular places—their terroir—are translated into the tastes of the foods and drinks produced there and, moreover, that they deserve to be protected.

Because DOs link the production of agricultural goods to particular local places, but allow these goods to be traded in global markets and require protection by national and global institutions, DOs embody what some scholars refer to as *glocalization*. This term emphasizes how local cultures and global institutions mutually shape each other.[20] Many scholars have focused on how DOs embed food systems in their social and ecological contexts, drawing on Karl Polanyi's notion of economic embeddedness. Sociologist Elizabeth Barham argues that "by insisting upon a strong link in production to the ecology and culture of specific places, [DOs] re-embed a product in the natural processes and social context of its territory."[21] Another rural sociologist, Henk Renting, and his colleagues argue that DOs constitute "short food supply chains" that have the capacity to "resocialize or respatialize food" by increasing the transparency of the people, places, and processes associated with particular foods.[22] Advocates of DOs maintain that focusing on terroir opens up possibilities for an engagement with the "place of food" that goes deeper than simply measuring the distance between producers and consumers.[23]

TERROIR, TRADITION, AND COMTÉ CHEESE

When people want to show how protecting terroir can benefit farmers and rural regions, there is one case that they often return to: Comté cheese. Although many Americans have not heard of it, Comté is France's best-selling DO cheese, outpacing even the famous Roquefort. Produced in eastern France, in the rolling hills and valleys of the Jura Mountain region near the Swiss border, Comté is an aged cheese made in huge wheels from cow's milk pooled from dairy cooperatives known as *fruitières*. In 2007, I traveled to France to learn more about Comté and the people who made it. I spent five months living in Poligny, a small town in the heart of the Jura region, where I interviewed people involved with the production of Comté cheese: farmers, cheesemakers, *affineurs* (the people who care for and age the cheese), governmental officials, and people who worked at the Interprofessional Committee for Gruyère from Comté (CIGC, according to its French acronym), the collective organization that sets the rules with which producers must comply. The stories I heard gave me an appreciation for just how powerful a development strategy built around terroir could be.

Although cheese has been produced in the region for close to a thousand years, for most of that time cheese was mainly made for local consumption.[24] After World War II, farmers and cheesemakers began looking for a way to protect themselves from imposters from other regions. In 1958, Comté became only the second French cheese name (after Roquefort) to be recognized with an "appellation of origin" (France's version of the DO).[25] The CIGC was formed in 1963 to regulate the Comté label and determine the rules of production.

Because of its reputation as one of France's most traditional cheeses, Comté is adored by French and European governmental officials, academics, and retailers. However, this wasn't always the case. Some older farmers told me that in the 1970s, the French government, like the U.S. government, began pushing a strategy of industrialization, encouraging concentration among the cooperatives in order to increase efficiency and foster economies of scale. Cheese producers in other parts of France followed suit; but the Comté producers and the CIGC decided to pursue the opposite path, instead gradually adding rules to create obstacles to industrialization. For example, they required that Comté be produced with raw milk and prohibited the use of corn silage in the cows' feed; later, they established rules that the milk had to come from within 25 kilometers (about 15.5 miles) of the fruitière and that each cow had to have a minimum of one hectare (about 2.5 acres) of pasture.

The Comté producers' forward-thinking efforts paid off. Largely because of the strict rules, concentration has proceeded more slowly among Comté's farms and cheesemakers than among other French cheese producers. Today, about twenty-seven hundred dairy farmers are organized into 150 fruitières.[26] The cooperatively managed fruitières produce the majority of Comté cheese, accounting for about 85 percent when I was there.[27] After the fruitières collect the milk from the dairy farmers, cheesemakers make huge, ninety-pound wheels of Comté. The cheese is then aged for a minimum of four months by one of sixteen affineurs.[28]

Comté producers believe that the large number of small fruitières accounts for the diversity of flavors in their cheese. The CIGC has tried to preserve this link to terroir, which consumers are willing to pay big money for. One fancy New York cheese shop, where Comté sells for twenty-five dollars a pound, advertises that they handpick each wheel of Comté from a specific fruitière in order to capture "the essence of raw, mountain pasture-fed cow milk."[29] In France, an affineur whom I interviewed confirmed the cheese shop's claim, explaining, "We allow our clients to choose not only the age of the cheese but also the providence of the cheese. Our clients become loyal to a taste that is very specific and tied to a particular village."[30]

Focusing on terroir has turned out to be a highly profitable strategy, and it was possible only because the Comté producers went against the dominant advice in France (and around the world) in the 1980s. The affineur said that the owner of his company had been one of the first people in the region to promote the link between the terroir and the taste of the cheese. Now, he said, almost everyone in the industry recognized that their job was to "translate" the terroir of particular places. He explained, "When we are working with raw milk, we give the milk the right to express its entire life, until the moment that it becomes cheese. We do not intervene in order to steer it into a specific taste. . . . The more slowly we refine the cheese, the more it is going to express the specific characteristics from its region of origin."[31]

This collective belief in terroir frames the individual interests of the farmers, cheesemakers, fruitières, and affineurs in ways that are mutually reinforcing. Comte's link to terroir also helps prevent industrial cheese-makers from intruding into the industry. French cheese producers are not immune to the pressures of industrialization and globalization. Industrial cheese companies have encroached on other French cheese supply chains.[32] But in the Comté case, the rules impede an industrial model and discourage the large companies from getting involved. Another affineur told me, "Because of the terroir and the aging process, Comté has a thousand faces. This is the strength of Comté, and it allows us to resist takeover from the big companies."[33]

Comté's success is largely due to the CIGC's efforts to preserve the link to terroir. Comté is France's highest-volume DO cheese, with almost sixty thousand tons produced in 2013.[34] Comté farmers receive a price for their milk that is consistently higher than the average milk price in France.[35]

There are other positive outcomes associated with the Comté DO. One study found that because Comté cheese is made mainly by small farmers and cheesemakers, it generates five times more jobs per liter of milk than Emmental, an industrial cheese without DO protection.[36] Rates of migration away from the Comté region are much lower than in other parts of France, owing not only to the price premiums and additional jobs associated with the production of Comté but also to revenue deriving from tourists who come to see the fruitières, the caves where the cheese is aged, the Comté museum in Poligny, and other places along the "Comté trail."[37]

In addition to creating jobs in the region, the Comté DO has had a positive effect on the local environment. Because of the strict specifications that farmers are required to meet, dairy farms in the Comté region are more extensive—meaning, in the words of the CIGC, that instead of focusing on maximizing yields, they focus on "quality, taking into account soil characteristics and the diversity of plant species and microflora"—than in other parts of France.[38] One fruitière can have as many as 160 different prairie species (grasses, flowers) for the cows to consume.[39] Because farmers and cheesemakers believe that the diversity of native plant species in the cows' diet is an important contributor to the quality of Comté cheese, the DO has helped maintain biodiversity in the region.

I left Poligny inspired by what DOs could do—for farmers, rural regions, and local environments. It wasn't all that surprising that the archetype for a successful DO would come from France, which has the oldest and best-developed system of DO protection in the world. Comté is exceptional in France as well; Comté producers have consistently sought to differentiate their cheese through a stronger commitment to quality, tradition, and terroir than we see in other French DOs. But because the cultural and political systems that undergird DO protection in France have been so influential, it's important to start with France when thinking about how policies to protect DOs have developed and evolved over time.

CREATING THE TASTE OF PLACE IN FRANCE

The idea of terroir has a long history in France. In the seventeenth century, French agriculturalist Olivier de Serres wrote that "the fundamental task in agriculture [was] to understand the nature of the terroir, whether it is the land of your ancestors or land recently acquired."[40] In 1789, French historian Pierre Jean-Baptiste Le Grand d'Aussy discussed how the diversity of French cuisine was fundamentally rooted in "what nature has seen fit to allow each of our provinces to produce."[41] In his culinary classic *La Physiologie du Goût* (The Physiology of Taste), Jean-Anthelme Brillat-Savarin writes that the ability to trace certain tastes to their natural origins is a "point of perfection." He asks, "Have we not plenty of *gourmands* who are able to indicate the latitude under which a wine has ripened, as certainly as a pupil of Biot or Arago can foretell an eclipse?"[42]

All of these descriptions frame terroir as an objective reality: the way the attributes of the physical environment—soil, weather, and topography—created the distinctive tastes of French wines and cheeses. However, as anthropologist Amy Trubek explains in *The Taste of Place: A Cultural Journey into Terroir*, it was ultimately France's food culture, more than the natural environment, that created the *goût* (or taste) of terroir. Starting in the early twentieth century, a group of influential French tastemakers, including journalists, cookbook writers, and chefs, along with taste producers like cheesemakers and winemakers, began working to advance the notion of terroir. By creating a "language of taste" that linked places, tastes, types of agriculture, and quality, these tastemakers shaped how people tasted wine and food. They also worked to protect and define certain forms of agriculture and French cuisine. Trubek writes, "These men and women observed their world and decided to champion certain practices (small farms, regional dishes) and values (tradition, local taste) in order to make sure that they did not disappear. . . . What they did was to create a vision of agrarian rural France and convincingly put it in people's mouths."[43]

The 1855 Bordeaux wine classifications had been the first attempt to link the quality of wines to their place of origin, but these were developed by wine brokers (to rank wines for the Exposition Universelle de Paris), not by the state.[44] The 1883 Paris Convention on Intellectual Property and the 1891 Madrid Agreement for the Repression of False or Deceptive Indications of Source of Goods represented the first efforts to create forms of international protection for place-based goods.[45] Around the turn of the twentieth century, French winemakers began lobbying the French state for stronger protections.[46] The first law tying production of a food or drink to a particular place, passed in 1905, aimed to protect against fraud.[47] Winemakers from Champagne were the first to use it. This marked the beginning of the concept of *appellation d'origine* (appellation of origin), a system that first protected and promoted French wine and which was eventually extended to cheese and other products.

Over the years, French laws on appellations of origin have been modified to become more specific and address perceived shortcomings of the 1905 law. A revision made in 1908 clarified that protection should be granted to products with a "local and constant" association with a region.[48] In 1919, another iteration stated that delimitations were to be made based on "local, loyal, and constant" associations between places and products.[49] But the law was enforced through court cases, which dragged on and were not very effective. In 1935, a revised law established the concept of *appellation d'origine con-trôlée* (controlled appellation of origin, the term used today), a change in nomenclature that signaled an increase in control and regulation of the process.[50] Furthermore, although the earlier laws had considered only provenance, the 1935 law clarified that the appellations protected not only the geographical origin of a product but also the characteristics that contributed to its quality and authenticity.[51] Geneviève Teil, a French researcher, argues that as regulations regarding the viticultural and wine-making process were gradually developed, the French state was careful not to define restrictions excessively, in order to "leave room for desirable technical innovations which could arise in the future."[52] At the same time, geographer Warren Moran notes that in some cases the appellation laws for French wines went "as far as specifying the spacing of the vines and the methods of trellising and pruning."[53]

The National Institute for Appellations of Origin, established in 1935 and part of the French Ministry of Agriculture, was charged with monitoring and determining the "conditions of production."[54] French law stipulates that controlled appellations of origin protect the name of a place (country, region, or locality) used to designate a product that originates in that place, when "the quality and characteristics" of that product are "due to the geographical environment, including both natural and human factors."[55] Many national, regional, and international agreements are based on the French model. Spain adapted its wine statute to protect *denominaciones de origen* (denominations of origin) for wines in 1932, and extended protection to other agricultural products in the 1970s.[56] Italy established a similar classification—*denominazioni di origine* (denomination of origin)—for dairy products in 1954 and for wine in 1963.[57]

In 1958, the Lisbon Agreement established the most comprehensive multilateral agreement on DOs to date. It created an international system of registration and protection of DOs, adopting a definition of DOs that was similar to the French definition.[58] The Lisbon Agreement provided for the registration of DOs that were "recognized and protected as such, in their own country of origin."[59] Nine countries signed the original agreement in 1958; today, there are twenty-eight "contracting parties."[60]

At that time, even in France and other parts of Mediterranean Europe, there were relatively few DOs, although many of the world's most famous DOs—champagne, of course, and also Roquefort, Rioja wine, and Parmigiano-Reggiano cheese—have been protected since before the establishment of the Lisbon Agreement. Starting in the 1990s, however, the taste for terroir began to take off, first in France and then around the globe. In France, a surge of interest in what French historian Jacques Revel called *patrimonialisation*—the effort to trace and commemorate all things related to French history and heritage—developed and extended to natural places, landscapes, and traditional foods.[61] Elizabeth Barham explains that the movement stemmed from French consumers' "malaise" with modernization and globalization, as well as from escalating concerns over recent food safety scares.[62] But the surge of interest in terroir was also "a conscious and active social construction of the present by various groups concerned with rural areas in France."[63] Public intellectuals, urban consumers, and agricultural organizations banded together to protect rural landscapes, traditional foods, and other elements of national and regional heritage.[64] According to geographer Daniel Gade, these efforts to rescue "authentic agricultural products" with "strong identities" could be seen as a "salvage effort akin to preserving a language or plant species from extinction."[65] France led the world in the effort to protect and promote traditional and authentic foods and drinks, and this effort centered on the notion of terroir.

For consumers, terroir helped anchor French consciousness to its rural roots.[66] Amy Trubek describes taste as a form of local knowledge in France, explaining that the French still retain a powerful connection to the land of their ancestors, and that they evoke the taste of terroir in order to "remember an experience, explain a memory, or express a sense of identity."[67] For French farmers and food producers, and for the French state, promoting and protecting the link to terroir is also an economically salient strategy. French farms are relatively small: 129 acres, on average, or about one-fourth the size of an average American farm.[68] As a group, however, French farmers are economically and politically powerful. France is the biggest agricultural producer in the European Union, with 18 percent of Europe's total agricultural output.[69] France also receives the biggest share of the European Union's agricultural subsidies. In debates over the regulation of food and agriculture, both within the European Union and globally, French farmers play an important role.

French farmers have made their crusade against the homogenizing forces of globalization a central part of their discourse. In 1999, a group of French farmers made international headlines when, led by activist farmer José Bové, they dismantled a McDonald's that was being built in the southwestern French town of Millau. The farmers, producers of Roquefort cheese, were protesting the United States government's decision to impose a 100 percent import tax on certain European "luxury" goods in retaliation for the European Union's ban on hormone-treated U.S. beef. They framed their campaign as representing fair trade, the right to good food, and the local, in contrast to mass-produced, globalized "food from nowhere."[70] "My struggle remains the same," declared Bové as he handed himself over to French police: "the battle against globalization and for the right of people to feed themselves as they choose."[71] As French studies scholar Sarah Waters notes, the farmers that Bové represented were a marginal, obscure farmer's union, but they managed to mobilize a campaign with broad appeal because of their symbolic power. Waters argues, "Where globalization was experienced as ceaseless change and upheaval, peasant farming was presented as a symbol of tradition and continuity, one that anchored the French to their past and to a shared cultural legacy."[72] Explained Philippe Folliott, the mayor of a town in the region, "Roquefort is made from the milk of only one breed of sheep, it is made in only one place in France, and it is made in only one special way. . . . It is the opposite of globalization. Coca-Cola you can buy anywhere in the world and it is exactly the same."[73]

Bové and his fellow farmers counterposed an image of terroir and tradition—"a whole symbolic universe linked to peasant farming" against images of the evils of globalization, ever-expanding markets, the increasing dominance of multinational corporations, and mass agricultural production.[74] But while Bové and others framed terroir as antithetical to globalization, it is precisely because of terroir's value in the global marketplace that DOs are so popular—and so controversial.

THE WAR ON TERROIR

Because of its economic and symbolic power, terroir has emerged as a key issue within international trade negotiations.[75] From its origins as an obscure clause in the 1947 General Agreement on Tariffs and Trade, terroir has moved to the forefront of transatlantic trade negotiations.[76]

The economic stakes associated with terroir are high: by granting a monopoly over the right to use a name like "champagne" or "Roquefort," DO protection can confer substantial rents to producers. Further, in the face of global pressure to cut agricultural subsidies and eliminate trade barriers, DO protection gives governments the opportunity to provide economic support to farmers.

International conflicts over the regulation of DOs have ramped up since 1994, when, under the 1994 Agreement on Trade-Related Aspects of Intellectual Property, the World Trade Organization legally defined "geographical indications," the generic term used to refer to the various institutions that protect terroir (e.g., appellation of origin, denomination of origin).[77] (Although international debates generally refer to "geographical indications," I have chosen to use the term used in Mexico, *denominations of origin,* throughout this book, in order to maintain consistency.) In bilateral and multilateral trade negotiations, the United States and its allies have argued that enforcing protection of DOs violates principles of free trade and threatens to incur exorbitant costs, while the European Union frames its position in terms of DOs' potential to protect local food cultures and offer a stronger quality guarantee to consumers.[78] Some arguments have gotten quite heated. In 2014, more than half of the members of the United States Senate, on both sides of the aisle, joined together to urge the Department of Agriculture and the United States Trade Representative to fight the European Union's attempts to prevent American dairy producers from using cheese names like "Parmesan" and "feta." "They are trying to take our nouns from us," said the executive director of the Wisconsin Cheese Makers Association. "They are trying to create new barriers to trade by stealing their [cheese] names back."[79] Not so, argued the Europeans. The Italian deputy minister of economic development stated that DOs were "meaningful tools to protect freedom of enterprise and freedom of consumers." He contended that the regulation of DOs had allowed countries like Italy and France, and later the European Union and the World Trade Organization, to "combine historic craftsmanship in food and wine with a modern capitalist economy."[80]

The European Union's position rests on being able to argue that DOs are not merely a form of French or European exceptionalism. In other words, the European Union needs to show that DOs are not just a way to protect European goods at the expense of the rest of the world. So, in recent years the European Union has, as legal scholar William Kerr puts it, begun to "beat the development drum," arguing that DOs are a viable rural development strategy not only for European farmers but also for farmers around the world, especially in developing countries.[81]

BENEFITS OF PROTECTION

Empirical analyses have focused on the impacts of DO protection in three main domains: for farmers, rural regions, and the environment. First, economists argue that DO protection confers a "reputation rent," a price premium that consumers pay for DO products on the basis of the collective reputation of the product and the region. They debate why consumers would be willing to pay a premium; some argue that it is due to the quality standards that DO producers are required to meet, while others claim that consumers' bias for goods from a particular place explains their preferences for DOs.[82] Others contend that consumer demand for DOs is linked to perceptions of DOs' authenticity, heritage, and traceability.[83] In any case, economists explain that price premiums are a necessary, but not sufficient, condition of successful DOs.[84] One analysis, of 134 observations collected from twenty-two studies, found that, on average, DO protection conferred a 15 percent price premium over standard products.[85] A comparison of thirteen European DOs with their standard counterparts came to a similar conclusion, finding that DO protection was associated with price premiums in almost all cases.[86] However, both studies also observed considerable variability in the extent of price premiums, with some DOs receiving substantial premiums and others receiving none.

Second, scholars argue that the benefits of DO protection extend beyond the farm and the processors, to rural regions more broadly. Researchers have shown how DOs create employment opportunities, both directly (for the people involved in the production of the DO) and indirectly (through associated industries like tourism).[87] One study found that the labor-intensive practices associated with production of Parmigiano-Reggiano cheese created more employment opportunities than existed for comparable, industrial cheeses.[88] DO protection can also promote the clustering of synergistic activities in a region. For example, the region around Parma, Italy, is home not only to Parmigiano-Reggiano cheese but also to another famous DO, Parma ham, made from pigs that are fed a blend of grains and whey from Parmigiano-Reggiano cheesemakers.[89]

Finally, a third perspective focuses on the environmental benefits of DO protection, with a particular emphasis on how DOs help preserve biodiversity. For example, one study showed how, in France, the DOs for Ardèche chestnuts and calvados (an apple-and-pear brandy) have helped protect local varieties of chestnuts, apples, and pears, as well as traditional practices for managing the trees.[90] A comparison of eight European DOs found positive results in reference to biodiversity conservation and maintenance of cultural landscapes, although the study also found that processes of agricultural intensification, which negatively affected the environment, were present and possible under DO protection.[91]

If success is measured in terms of the political and economic power of DOs, then the "terroirists," as some jokingly call them, have succeeded. In 1992, the European Union established a pan-European system of regulating "protected designations of origin" (PDOs, which are virtually identical to the French definition of controlled appellation of origin) and "protected geographical indications" (PGIs, which are not as strict).[92] Since then, 867 PDOs and PGIs for food products have been registered in the European Union, as well as more than 1,900 for wines and spirits, which are protected under separate legislation.[93] The total value of all of the registered PDOs and PGIs for wines, spirits, and agricultural products in Europe exceeds €50 billion, with France and Italy alone accounting for 60 percent of this value.[94] The Organization for an International Geographical Indications Network (oriGIn), founded in 2003, is a nonprofit advocacy organization that now represents more than four hundred associations of DO producers and other DO-related institutions from 40 countries.[95] One report found that 167 countries actively protect DOs as a form of intellectual property.[96]

Because of the proliferation of European DOs,[97] most of the existing research on DOs has focused on European cases. And yet policy makers argue that DO protection represents a viable development strategy for countries all over the world. The International Trade Center, a joint agency of the World Trade Organization and the United Nations, conducted a comprehensive study of DO protection around the globe and concluded that while DOs will not work in all contexts, DOs are "an integral form of rural development." According to the International Trade Center report, DO protection "offers a valuable framework for powerfully advancing commercial and economic interests while potentially integrating local needs that are anchored in cultural tradition, environment, and broad levels of participation."[98]

TRANSLATING TERROIR FOR THE WORLD

Europe has invested a lot in spreading the gospel of terroir around the world. The European Union now allows producers from non-European countries to apply to the European Commission for protection of their goods as PDOs or PGIs.[99] The European Union and individual European countries like France and Italy have also directed considerable resources to the promotion of DOs in developing countries, as I had the opportunity to observe several years ago.

While I was still a graduate student, I was invited to teach one of the sessions for an intensive course on DOs that had been organized by a group of French and Swiss governmental organizations. The course, held in an old castle in a picturesque small town on the shore of Lake Geneva in Switzerland, brought together governmental officials and representatives of producers' organizations from many countries: Brazil, Honduras, India, Indonesia, Kenya, Mongolia, Serbia, and South Africa. Over an intensive two-week period, European experts gave presentations on the legal, economic, social, and organizational aspects of DO protection. Participants in the course also went on field trips to study Switzerland's DOs, visiting a mill and bakery that made Valais rye bread and talking with producers of Gruyère cheese.

My session came at the end of the course, and I was nervous about how it would go. The other presenters were experts in their fields, people who had been studying DOs for years, while I was just a graduate student. But I shared what I had learned so far about the challenges that the tequila producers and agave farmers were facing: the farmers' struggle to get a fair price for their agave, how tequila was becoming increasingly indistinguishable from other industrial liquors, and how the Mexican government didn't seem to be doing much on behalf of the farmers or the small distilleries. Afterward, as we ate a delicious lunch overlooking the castle gardens, and over cocktails at the closing dinner that night, people kept coming up to me and telling me how much they had appreciated my presentation. The other sessions had been so positive, they said. They were worried that what had worked in France or Switzerland wouldn't translate as well in their countries, where the farmers were smaller and poorer and the governments were strapped for organizational and financial resources.

My research in Mexico, and conversations that I have had over the years with producers and governmental officials from all over the world, have convinced me that we need to be careful when thinking about how the "taste of terroir" might apply to developing countries. But if anything, efforts to promote and protect products that are linked to terroir have only ramped up in recent years. In 2014, the intensive course on DOs was offered for the eleventh time, with participants paying forty-five hundred euros to attend. The Food and Agriculture Organization of the United Nations has made promoting DOs one of its main foci. The organization has hosted seminars around the world (in Chile, Costa Rica, Guinea, Morocco, Serbia, and Thailand), bringing together high-level governmental representatives and researchers in order to determine how governments and stakeholders can work together to promote regional products. It also published a guide and even created an online tool to help stakeholders determine the best way to set up protective arrangements for their products.

All these efforts appear to be paying off. In the last twenty years, many countries have passed legislation on DOs, with Brazil and Peru establishing policies on DOs in 1996, followed by South Korea and India in 1999, Columbia in 2000, and Chile in 2005, to name just a few. The European Union's list of protected products now includes Columbian coffee, rice from Thailand, Darjeeling tea from India, and several products from China, including apples, tea, and garlic.[100] In 2013, the African Intellectual Property Organization, an organization representing sixteen countries, recognized its first three DOs: for Oku honey and Penja pepper from Cameroon and for Ziama Macenta coffee from Guinea.[101] A comparison of DOs around the world concluded with the observation that the growing popularity of DOs reflects "not only the high economic stakes involved" but also the perception—by both producers and governmental officials— that DOs are a "useful rural development strategy."[102] Luis Fernando Samper, an official at the Columbian Coffee Federation and the former president of oriGIn, argued that that DOs were "the best legal tool for the protection" of foods and drinks that derive from developing countries.[103]

A MODEL FOR DEVELOPMENT, OR BUSINESS AS USUAL?

Not everyone is so sanguine about the presumed benefits of DO protection. Legal scholar William Kerr cautions that while the European Union's strategy of promoting DO protection in developing countries may be a good negotiating tactic, it is "cynical manipulation of developing countries at worst and naïve meddling in the affairs of poor countries at best."[104] According to Kerr, although short-term rents may accrue to producers of established DOs in the European Union, "the case for similar rents accruing to producers in developing countries is weak."[105] He concludes that this approach may thus "lead to developing countries wasting their limited resources chasing an illusive dream."[106]

Kerr is not the only person to warn that DOs are not a panacea. Sociologist Michaela DeSoucey argues that DOs are a form of gastronationalism, a process in which states make strategic claims about the idea of nation as a protector of cultural patrimony within a neoliberal and globalizing context. She sees gastronationalism as "part of a broader identity project unfolding across Europe and the world that is responding to potential losses of control of production and national industries, accelerated by global moves toward open trade." As states engage with their citizens by promoting national belonging and pride, says DeSoucey, "gastronationalism ties to, and potentially substitutes for, attention paid to other changes" that are associated with globalization, such as income inequality, the erosion of the welfare state, and increased migration.[107] In other words, gastronationalism potentially represents a way for nation-states to distract consumers, interest groups, and industries away from deeper changes and broader inequalities, by highlighting a collective national identity centered on the cultural traditions and places associated with certain foods and drinks.

Other scholars have analyzed the process by which decisions about DO protection are made and the underlying power relations. Marion Fourcade, a sociologist, argues that the rigid system of qualifications that characterizes the logic of terroir—the rationale upon which DOs are based— emerged out of "political conflicts over the economic advantages" derived from wine commerce.[108] According to Fourcade, the DO system relies "on an elusive quest for quality to create market rents for wines," by anchoring status distinctions through nature.[109] Geographer Kenneth MacDonald notes that the process of qualifying certain products as culturally unique often leads to the reorganization of practices, environments, and communities in order to meet the multiple and often contradictory demands of the different people and institutions involved in the production and consumption of these goods.[110] Tad Mutersbaugh, another geographer, argues that, in general, values-based standards (including organic and fair trade certifications and DOs) constitute a form of policy rent that helps high-capacity producer groups increase their income-earning potential relative to other, less organized groups.[111] Dwijen Rangnekar, a law scholar, contends that DOs necessarily involve a contradiction: they seek to preserve and celebrate cultural processes that have stabilized in a particular place, but they "inherently involve transformation through the importation of a global institution."[112]

Some critics argue that DOs, instead of representing an alternative to the standardizing and commodifying tendencies of the global marketplace, exemplify neoliberal regulation. Geographer Julie Guthman states that, in keeping with neoliberalism's "fetish of market mechanism," DOs and other values-based labels "not only concede the market as the locus of regulation" but also "employ tools designed to create markets." They are governed by a complex array of institutions, at a variety of scales, that "subscribe to notions of audit and transparency as 'action at a distance.'" They also "extend property rights to practices where none previously existed, entail forms of enclosure that produce scarcity, attach economic values to ethical behaviors, and, finally, devolve regulatory responsibility to consumers."[113] Guthman argues that because these labels fundamentally shift responsibility for the social and environmental consequences of food production from the state to individual consumers, they are "a far cry from the politics of social protection" associated with Polanyi's double movement.[114] Other scholars agree that DOs epitomize the characteristics of neoliberalism: privatization, marketization, and regulation of formerly public goods.[115]

Scholars and policy makers also raise questions about whether DOs are a viable tool for addressing inequality and persistent poverty, especially in developing countries. Many note that little research has examined the effect of DOs on social and economic differentiation within regions and along supply chains. As anthropologist Sarah Besky aptly puts it, "justice," as defined by DO regulations, comes in the form of new property rights that protect the name of the DO. "But who [is] this justice for?" asks Besky.[116] Market success does not guarantee that the benefits of protection will trickle down to others in the region or even to everyone along the supply chain.[117] Small farmers and processors may be unable to meet the requirements of certification, and this could actually increase concentration along supply chains and push small producers out of business.[118] In addition, there is potential for the most powerful groups within the supply chain to appropriate images of tradition and place for their own benefit, to the exclusion of others.[119] Furthermore, wage laborers are often made invisible by DO regulations and conceptualizations of terroir.[120] And scholars note that evaluations of the impact of DOs need to consider gender relations, including "who grows and produces what" in diverse family and social structures.[121]

Existing research on the distribution of the benefits of DO protection supports this skepticism. A recent comparison of thirteen European DOs found that although almost all of them were associated with a price premium, the farmers who produced the raw materials often received no premium.[122] The study found that products with certain characteristics tended to generate higher premiums for farmers.[123] But researchers also noted that the evidence was conflicting and offered few straightforward lessons on what worked better for farmers.[124] A comparison of twenty-one European DOs found that although several conferred substantially higher prices on farmers, the "contrasting circumstances of other products" made it difficult to draw any conclusions on the ability of DO protection to foster rural development or improve farm incomes.[125]

Unfortunately, much of the existing research on the costs and benefits of DO protection has focused on European cases. We have good reason to expect that circumstances might be worse for farmers in developing countries, where farmers have fewer economic resources, are less likely to be organized into a cooperative, receive less support from the state, and must contend with the legacies of colonization. A study of Chontaleño cheese, a DO cheese from Nicaragua, found that DO protection introduced new competitive pressures that reinforced local and foreign elites (industrial dairy farmers and cheesemakers) and made the situation worse for small farmers and cheesemakers.[126] In Peru, with $2.4 million in aid from the United States, the Peruvian government launched a project to promote Chulucanas ceramics, protected as a DO since 2006.[127] But instead of revitalizing community pride in the techniques practiced by artisans in Chulucanas, the

DO weakened bonds of collective identity and led to increased distrust, price wars, and wage exploitation.[128] Sarah Besky's research on Darjeeling tea, India's first and most famous DO, finds that, in the Darjeeling case and in discussions of DOs in general, wage laborers are ignored. Instead, Darjeeling tea producers and governmental officials have reframed "an industrial plantation crop with a less than savory colonial past," produced by Nepali workers on huge tea plantations, into an artisan product with an authentic terroir.[129] They did so by recasting the exploitative labor relations of the plantations as part of a "palatable national heritage of craft production."[130] Besky argues that this seductive imagery serves to obscure and downplay the repressive, hierarchical aspects of tea production, in which female workers continue to labor for very low wages and depend upon plantation owners not only for money but also for food, medical care, schools, and housing.[131] This case, and others, are stark reminders of the need to seriously consider the impact of colonial legacies and global inequalities on contemporary social and economic relations.

THE MEXICAN MODEL

Despite emerging evidence that suggests that the benefits of DO protection often fail to trickle down to farmers, workers, and communities, people in many developing countries are rushing to jump on the DO bandwagon. As they look to share in the benefits of the consumer craze for authentic, local products, many are looking to Mexico for answers. As the first protected DO outside of Europe and one of the largest and most famous, tequila stands as a model for agricultural producers and governments around the world who aim to protect their own unique goods and help ensure the livelihoods of the people who make them. While the French tastemakers were the first to protect the link between taste and terroir, the tequila producers were the first to show that it could be done outside of Europe. However, my analysis of tequila and mezcal highlights the limitations of relying on labels and alternative markets to protect cultural traditions or ensure a fair and sustainable food system. Because the agave farmers and small tequila producers have been systematically excluded from the process of defining the traditions that they want to protect, multinational liquor companies have appropriated notions of authenticity and quality for their own benefit. In some cases, they have even taken away from small producers the right to produce these drinks.

A NOTE ON NAMES

I use pseudonyms to refer to everyone interviewed for this book. Although I considered asking for permission to use people's real names, in the end I concluded that I needed to protect people's identities. People have been arguing over the production and regulation of tequila and mezcal for generations, with debates sometimes getting quite heated and, in a few cases, even becoming violent. The owner of a tequila distillery was murdered in 1997; and although his killing remains unsolved, many people believe that he was killed by someone who did not agree with his outspoken opinions about tequila regulations. More recently, a visible opponent of some of the industry's regulations told me that he was careful not to make his travels too public.

I refer to distilleries and organizations by name in this book, but in order to protect the identities of the people I interviewed, I have avoided linking quotes to the names of any distilleries or companies. I do occasionally refer to people by their actual names when the information is in the public record (for example, when I am citing a newspaper quote or referring to industry statistics). I have done my best to give as much contextual detail as possible for the people I interviewed—for example, about their regions and the size of their distilleries—while still protecting their identities. To protect people's identities, the photos in the book do not correspond with the narrative; for example, I did not match photos of distilleries with quotes from producers from those distilleries.

2 From the Fields to Your Glass

Like many people, I don't have a clear memory of my first taste of tequila. I am sure that the first tequila I tried was cheap, probably mixed into a margarita that I bought during a happy-hour special at one of the dive bars that I frequented in college. I do remember the first time I really tried to savor tequila, a few years later. During graduate school, after spending a semester at a university in southern Jalisco, I made the first of what would be many trips to Tequila. After taking a bus from Guadalajara to Tequila, a friend and I headed straight for La Rojeña, which Cuervo boasts is the oldest distillery in the Americas. (Their industrial distillery on the other side of Guadalajara, where they produce the bulk of their tequila, is not open for touring). Our guide led us around the grounds of Cuervo's beautiful hacienda, showing us the masonry ovens where they roasted the agave, the copper stills in the distillation room, and the stacked wooden barrels in which they aged the tequila. At the end, we sampled several tequilas of different ages, including an *añejo,* a tequila that had been aged for at least one year in oak barrels.[1] I was surprised by how sweet the añejo was. Not bad, I thought, taking a deep whiff of the oaky scent and swirling the amber-colored liquid around in my glass before sipping.

My first taste of mezcal was unforgettable, but not in a good way. A few months after I got back from that trip to Jalisco, some friends, hearing that I liked tequila, brought me some mezcal that they had picked up during a vacation in Oaxaca. I didn't know anything about mezcal, but I immediately noticed its smoky smell. We knew that mezcal was stronger than tequila and that some people referred to it as "Mexican firewater," and it was late at night before we finally got up the nerve to try it. It tasted like artificial smoke and burned going down my throat. No one liked it, and we never even got to the worm floating around in the bottom of the bottle.

Since then, I have tasted hundreds of mezcals and tequilas. I sampled an *extra añejo* tequila at an official tasting in an expensive Guadalajara hotel, and I savored a *blanco* alongside a meal of grilled steak and tortillas at the edge of an agave field in the Amatitán-Tequila valley. After the inauspicious beginning of my relationship with mezcal, I discovered traditional, small-batch mezcals. I have sipped mezcals from dried-gourd *jicarras* and plastic cups, on visits to distilleries in the highlands of Michoacán and Guerrero, and from a plastic bottle passed back and forth in the back of an old truck heading through the Oaxaca hills. My palate and my preferences have evolved over time. If I'm drinking tequila, I prefer blancos over the sweeter *reposados* and añejos, because the spicy, vegetal taste of the agave is much more pronounced in blancos. I have grown to love traditional mezcal, which is more interesting and complex than tequila, with smokier, richer aromas and flavors. Because mezcals are rarely aged, the taste of the agave is front and center: spicy, vegetal, earthy, and complex. As Eric Asimov, the *New York Times*'s wine critic, notes, "The flavors of a great mezcal are unmediated by oak or long aging. They offer no vanillas or chocolates, honeys or heathers. Instead, you get a briny, vegetal burst, with Tabasco-like hints of vinegar, salt, oily smoke and earth, and an uncompromising purity."[2]

Distilled agave spirits are among the fastest-growing liquor categories in the world. Between 1995 and 2008, tequila production tripled, peaking at more than 300 million liters in 2008 and then stabilizing at around 250 million liters.[3] The market for mezcal is much smaller, but is growing even faster. Between 2005 and 2014, production of certified mezcal increased from about 400,000 liters to almost 1.5 million.[4] Both tequila and mezcal have developed cultlike followings, with celebrities launching their own brands and devoted fans making pilgrimages to Jalisco's Tequila Express, Oaxaca's "Capital of Mezcal," or the trendy tequila and mezcal bars popping up all over the United States.

Tequila and mezcal share the same origins; tequila is actually just the name for Mexico's most famous mezcal. But over time the growing global demand for tequila—and more recently, for mezcal—has shaped the trajectory of these spirits and of the people who make them.

THE BIRTH OF MEZCAL

Mexico is the center of origin for the genus *Agave,* which includes more than 200 species, 150 of which are found in Mexico.[5] As described by Ana Valenzuela Zapata and Gary Paul Nabhan in *¡Tequila!: A Natural and Cultural History,* agave plants are "the sword-leaved succulents" that Anglo-Americans recognize as "century plants" and most Mexican-Americans call "maguey."[6] Although the plants look like giant cacti, agave is more closely related to flowering plants like hyacinths and asparagus.[7] Agave plants require a long time to grow and flower; most species take between eight and twenty years to mature.[8] Indigenous populations in Mexico have relied on agave for thousands of years, using it for food and to make textiles, rope, paper, and *pulque,* a fermented agave drink.[9]

The European settlers who traveled to western Mexico in the sixteenth century noted that the indigenous populations were making fermented agave beverages, which the Europeans referred to as "mezcal wine." A description from 1580, of what is now southern Jalisco, noted that there was "in this province a tree called *mexcatl* [mezcal] that the Spanish call maguey. From it are made wine, vinegar, honey, string, rope, wood for houses, needles, nails, thread, [and] balsam for injuries."[10] An account of Michoacán from the same period described "the wine the natives of this region use," made from agave, "of which there is an abundance."[11]

Many scholars have tried to discern exactly when and where distilled agave spirits originated. The first mezcal wines were made via fermentation, a process in which yeasts convert sugars into alcohol. When a substance with sugar is combined with yeast, the yeast "eats" the sugar. It multiples itself and changes the sugar into alcohol and carbon dioxide gas, producing bubbles.[12] Distillation is a process in which heat is used to extract and concentrate alcohol. The first distilled agave spirits likely originated in the Colima volcanoes region in western Mexico.[13] Scholars continue to debate whether indigenous populations in Mexico may have started distilling before the arrival of colonial settlers. Recently, a group of Mexican scientists conducted a series of experiments using vessel replicas, techniques, and materials (including agave ferment) available in Colima between 1500 and 1000 B.C.E.[14] Based on their experiments, they argue that it is possible that distillation began before European contact, a hypothesis first proposed more than a century ago.[15] However, the earliest documented reference to distilled agave spirits dates to 1619. While stationed in what was then known as Nueva Galicia (which today encompasses parts of Nayarit, Jalisco, Sinaloa, and Zacatecas), Spanish cleric Domingo Lázaro de Arregui wrote that the "the roots and leaf bases [of the agave plant] are eaten roasted," explaining that by "squeezing them thus roasted, they extract a must from which they obtain wine by distillation, clearer than water and stronger than firewater."[16] Mezcal was born.

THE DIFFUSION OF DISTILLATION

Early mezcal producers collected wild agaves and roasted the agave piñas in earthen pits. They crushed the piñas by hand, with wooden mallets, and then fermented the agave mash in pits in the ground. They then likely used a version of what archaeologist and ethnobotanists call the "Filipino still," an adaptation of the stills introduced by Filipino settlers to make coconut wine in the sixteenth and seventeenth centuries.[17] The Filipino still consists of an earthen, stone, or wooden base; two metal pans; and a hollow tree trunk. A fire is built in the base, below the tree trunk. One of the metal pans, placed below the tree trunk and directly above the fire, holds the fermented mash. The other pan sits atop the hollow trunk. Cool water continually runs in and out of the top kettle. When the heat from the mash rises and hits the cool top created by the water, condensation occurs. The resulting condensation (mezcal) drips into an agave leaf that runs into a piece of bamboo that is cut into the tree trunk and into the collection container.

Figure 1. Filipino-style still in a small mezcal distillery, Jalisco. Photo by Sarah Bowen.

Later, the Arab still,[18] introduced by Spanish colonists for sugarcane distillation, was adapted to produce agave spirits. Patricia Colunga-García Marín and Daniel Zizumbo-Villarreal, Mexican scientists who have done extensive research on the origins of mezcal and tequila, explain that the rich and diverse mezcal culture in Mexico emerged "with the different adaptations of the Filipino still, the later adoption of the Arab still . . . and the blending of both the Asian and the Arab techniques."[19] During the seventeenth century, colonial authorities prohibited production of distilled agave and coconut spirits, which drove production into isolated sites in the foothills of the Colima volcanoes.[20] Demand from the mining regions also prompted the diffusion of distillation techniques northward, along trade routes, to mining centers in central and northern Mexico (including regions in Jalisco, Zacatecas, Durango, and Sonora).[21] Distillation practices also spread southward, to rural areas and indigenous communities in Michoacán, Guerrero, and Oaxaca. The Filipino still was quickly adopted because it was small, easy to transport, and made of local materials. It could have been installed, used to distill a batch of ferment, and then dissembled and moved very quickly, with only the hollow tree trunk left behind as evidence.[22]

MEZCAL AND THE COLONIAL STATE

The production of mezcal was the subject of constant conflict in the early colonial administration. Ignacio Gómez Arriola, a researcher at Mexico's National Institute of Anthropology and History, writes that "despite the contradictory and fluctuating prohibitions imposed by the Viceroy, the taxes generated by [mezcal] provided a significant source of income for the Crown."[23] Juan Canseco y Quiñones, the governor of Nueva Galicia between 1636 and 1640, decided to regulate the production and sales of mezcal wine, creating a state store and taxing all sales.[24] The store soon closed, but it was ordered to reopen in 1673.[25] The income from the store was used to bring water to Guadalajara and make repairs to the Palacio de Gobierno.[26]

After 1750, sales of mezcal increased, extending not only to Guadalajara but also throughout Nueva Galicia.[27] In 1750, Nicolas Rojas established a distillery on the ranch of San Martín, and the Cuervo-Montaño family began a distillery on another hacienda in the same year.[28] The roots of Tequila Cuervo go back to 1758, when a distillery on the Cuervo-Montaño hacienda was deeded to José Antonio Cuervo.[29] Other distilleries were established on the haciendas of the region over this period, and the cultivation of agave spread.[30] In the late eighteenth century, the Spanish naturalist José Longinos Martínez, passing through the Amatitán-Tequila valley, described the town of Amatitán as "an Indian village, with grain crops and a great quantity of mezcal, a species of agave."[31] Of Tequila, he wrote that "thousands of barrels of mezcal wine were manufactured in Tequila and shipped off every year."[32]

In 1785, the Spanish king, Carlos III, established a ban on the production and sale of alcoholic drinks in New Spain, in order to encourage the importation of Spanish liquors.[33] The ban was not very effective, however, and lasted only ten years. In 1795, the Spanish government granted José María Guadalupe Cuervo, the son of José Antonio, the first license permitting the legal establishment of a mezcal distillery.[34] By this point, vast expanses of hacienda land in the Amatitán-Tequila valley had been dedicated to the cultivation of agave.[35] One description, from 1791, stated that Tequila was known "for all kinds of [agave] plantings . . . annually worth more than $2,000 pesos, whose *vinos* ["wines," which in this case refers to mezcals] are consumed in Guadalajara, Tepic, Bolaños, and the port of San Blas."[36]

Until this point, most mezcal production took place on the haciendas.[37] Small distilleries were situated close to the agave plantations and near the water sources that were necessary to make mezcal.[38] Starting in the early nineteenth century, distilleries began to concentrate in the town of Tequila.[39] After Mexico became independent from Spain in 1821, distilleries in Tequila began making and commercializing mezcal on a larger scale. By 1840, the largest distillery in the Tequila region, part of the hacienda of San Martín, was producing more than four hundred barrels per week, or almost 1 million liters per year.[40]

In his 1864 study of agave and the products made from it, Manuel Payno wrote that mezcal was being produced "on a grand scale in Guadalajara and San Luis Potosí." He further noted that the mezcal from Guadalajara was "generally known as Tequila and is consumed throughout the country."[41] As late as the mid-nineteenth century, records indicate that the Pinos Hills region of western San Luis Potosí and southeastern Zacatecas, which supplied mining districts in Guanajuato and Zacatecas, may have produced more mezcal than the Tequila region.[42] However, the mezcal producers in and around Tequila were beginning to expand and differentiate themselves from producers in other parts of Mexico.

TEQUILA GOES GLOBAL: THE PORFIRIATO

During the reign of Mexican president Porfirio Díaz (1876–1911), also referred to as the Porfiriato, tequila began its transformation into the globally recognized and industrially produced symbol that it is today. In the early nineteenth century, distilleries had begun moving from the countryside to the town of Tequila, establishing themselves separately from the productive structures of the haciendas.[43] During the colonial period, dis-

Figure 2. Horse-drawn tahona in a tequila distillery, Jalisco. Photo by Sarah Bowen.

tilleries in Jalisco began using *tahonas,* large stone wheels pulled by animals (donkeys, mules, oxen, or horses), to crush the roasted agave hearts instead of crushing the agaves by hand.[44] In the Tequila region, copper serpentine stills had also largely replaced the Filipino stills.[45]

Under the regime of President Díaz, following the path of capitalist development that was taking place in Mexico, distillers in Jalisco adopted "a differentiated [and modernized] process."[46] Small quantities of mezcal from Tequila had been distributed to Sinaloa, Sonora, and California via the port of San Blas starting in the early nineteenth century, and a 1857 edition of a Spanish-language newspaper advertises *mezcal de Tequila* (mezcal from Tequila) for sale in Los Angeles.[47] However, tequila exports, especially to the United States, really took off in the 1870s. In 1873, 80 percent of mezcal exports were destined for the United States; a governmental publication from 1875 boasted that, once north, tequila fetched "the price of gold."[48] Anthropologist Guadalupe Rodríguez Gómez writes that during this period, "access to export markets was one of the principal objectives of the [tequila] producers."[49] The large consumer market and strategic location provided by Tequila's proximity to Guadalajara gave it an advantage over other parts of Mexico, and the completion of the Guadalajara–Mexico City Railway line in 1888 furthered Tequila's advantage and allowed the distilleries to consolidate domestic and foreign markets.[50]

In the 1870s, in response to the growing demand for tequila and in anticipation of the completion of the railway, a handful of powerful distillers began investing in technological innovations that would allow them to ramp up their production of mezcal.[51] Tequila historian Ignacio Gómez Arriola characterized the late nineteenth century as "a fertile period of development and industrial innovation" in Tequila.[52] As evidence of the industrialization that took place in Tequila, a publication from 1875 describes the "columns of smoke" rising above the town. The publication notes that the smoke came from "the *tabernas,* the principal source of wealth in Tequila," which breathed "enormous quantities of steam."[53] The Mexican government encouraged the tequileros to industrialize; the dominant belief at the time was that modernization was good for the industry and good for Mexico.

The two primary innovations of the tequila industry in the late nineteenth century were continuous evaporation stills and masonry ovens.[54] Continuous evaporation stills, also known as column stills, were invented by Martín Martínez de Castro in 1881 for distillation of agave spirits.[55] The new stills were more efficient and allowed for more precise temperature control during the distillation process, although they also required more water.[56] An 1887 study of mezcal production in Jalisco characterized the older stills as "primitive and inefficient," noting that the modern system was "based on scientific principles."[57] In 1891, Mariano de la Barcéna, Jalisco's former interim governor, praised the "factories with improved stills, which can produce on a large scale."[58] The adoption of continuous stills helped differentiate the distilleries in Tequila from those in other regions.[59] As the distilleries adopted a more efficient distillation process, they needed a new method for cooking the agave. Up until this point, agave had been roasted underground; the process took at least four days and required large quantities of wood.[60] Masonry ovens, heated by steam boilers and adopted in the tequila industry starting in the 1890s, cut the cooking time in half and distributed the heat more uniformly.[61]

Among the tequileros, Jesús Flores, who had acquired the Cuervo family's distillery, led the charge to modernize.[62] Flores was the first producer to bottle his mezcal in individual (half-liter) glass bottles, instead of barrels, in 1880.[63] In 1887, Flores was also one of the first producers in Jalisco to start using column stills.[64] An 1887 description of the industry also credits Flores as having introduced "a pressure screw that extracts all of the juice out of the [agave] fibers." The description notes that Flores distilled the fermented agave juice "in stills heated by steam coils, with everything powered by a steam-driven motor."[65] By the end of the nineteenth century, his distillery was lauded as a "model factory, resembling a European [factory], and perhaps the best in Tequila."[66]

Flores's primary competitor was Cenobio Sauza. Born landless, Sauza moved to Tequila in 1858 to work in a distillery that had been established by José Antonio Gómez Cuervo around 1830.[67] He worked his way up, first rising to the rank of director of the distillery and then becoming a regional distributor of mezcal.[68] He bought his first distillery in 1873 and then began acquiring agave fields and investing in upgrading his distillery. In 1888, he installed two column stills.[69]

Supported by the government and buoyed by their own faith in modernization, Flores, Sauza, and other tequileros embraced the industrial model. At the same time, the technological innovations that they adopted were already altering the taste of the mezcal. A description from the late nineteenth century claimed that the modern system—in particular, continuous stills and masonry ovens—produced mezcals "that [were] chemically purer." But the writer admitted that the old system had preserved "a certain taste and aroma . . . that characterize[d] the classic flavor for the majority of consumers."[70] According to one article, the masonry ovens "suppressed the smoky flavor of the agave piñas" and represented the key innovation that differentiated tequila from mezcal.[71]

Until the late nineteenth century, most tequila companies did not have extensive landholdings or grow their own agave.[72] Instead, they bought agave from the haciendas and larger farms in the area.[73] As demand for tequila increased, the distillery owners began buying up smaller distilleries and acquiring land. Jesús Flores, Cenobio Sauza, and other local elites expanded their plantations of agave, engaging in what sociologist Rogelio Luna Zamora called "the speculation and pillaging of land" in the

Tequila region.[74] This led to an enormous concentration of ownership of the agave plantations. In 1890, out of a total of 60 million plants in Jalisco, Cenobio Sauza had more than 5 million (spread out over twenty-five hundred to three thousand hectares of land); several other elites in the region had between 2.5 and 5 million agaves each.[75] By this point, the hacienda land in the Amatitán-Tequila valley was almost completely planted with agave.[76] A description of the region from 1893 noted that the tequila producers had "dedicated themselves assiduously to the cultivation of [agave], which now [constituted] the wealth of some of the haciendas."[77] And in 1896, making full use of the loopholes permitted to elite landowners by President Díaz, Cenobio Sauza obtained the last agave fields in Jalisco that were still held by the indigenous population.[78]

By the end of the nineteenth century, the Cuervo and Sauza distilleries together produced more tequila than all other distilleries in the area combined. The Tequila region had emerged as the clear center of mezcal production in Mexico. (The first distilleries in Los Altos, the highlands west of Guadalajara, were also established at this time, but remained small and marginal until later.) Jalisco produced 68 percent of Mexican mezcal in 1896, with most of this coming from the Tequila region. In comparison, Guanajuato produced just 12 percent, San Luis Potosí produced 6 percent, and Colima produced 5 percent.[79] In 1899, a traveler to Jalisco wrote that "tequila [was] without a doubt, Mexico's best national beverage."[80] Tequila's international reputation grew after mezcals from Tequila were recognized at the 1893 Chicago World's Fair and in San Antonio in 1910.[81] After this, the name of the drink and the town where it was made became synonymous. The tequila industry was on the path to becoming distinct from the mezcal produced in other parts of Mexico.

REVOLUTION AND TEQUILA

President Díaz's obsession with modernizing Mexico had benefited elites like Jesús Flores and Cenobio Sauza, but not workers or landless peasants. Hispanic studies scholar Tim Mitchell describes the concentration of land, capital, and power that Mexican elites enjoyed at the dawn of the twentieth century as "the culmination of a process began centuries earlier:

de-Indianization, colonialization, fragmentation, privatization, more de-Indianization, and commercialization."[82] The increased inequality, widespread poverty, and dominance of foreign interests associated with the Porfiriato incited the Mexican Revolution (1910–1920). The revolution, in turn, had profound effects on the tequila industry. On the one hand, the years following the revolution secured tequila's position as Mexico's national spirit. Sociologist Marie Sarita Gaytán argues that "amid competing ideas about the nation's path toward modernity and a revitalized sense of patriotism, new expressions of nationalism were established, among them tequila as a populist symbol of *lo mexicano* (Mexicanness)."[83] On the other hand, the havoc caused by the revolution and the land reform that followed it, as well as the Cristero War (1926–1929) shortly thereafter, had a destabilizing effect on the tequila industry. Of the eighty-seven distilleries operating in Jalisco in 1910, only thirty-two remained in 1930.[84] In the town of Tequila, just half of the sixteen distilleries that were in operation in 1919 survived until 1929.[85]

After the revolution, the land held by the haciendas and other rich landowners was restructured into collective landholding units called *ejidos*. In the Amatitán-Tequila valley, land redistribution took place between 1927 and 1942.[86] Without their massive landholdings, the tequila companies became dependent on the new *ejidatarios* for their agave. Blue agave takes eight years to mature after planting, and many ejidatarios initially chose to plant corn or other staple crops instead of agave, either because they had no experience with agave, or because they couldn't afford to wait so long for the harvest.[87] The amount of land planted with agave plummeted from a high of 46,000 hectares in 1900 (before the revolution) to 2,603 hectares in 1940 (after the land reform).[88] The shortage nearly destroyed the tequila industry; total tequila production fell from almost 10 million liters in 1901 to just under 2 million liters in 1930.[89]

The tequila companies devised new contract arrangements to help finance the cultivation of agave by the ejidatarios and other small farmers.[90] The supply of agave began to recover, but demand for tequila surged during World War II, and the supply of agave could not keep up.[91] The intermediaries who controlled the bottling plants and railways engaged in the massive adulteration of tequila, sometimes watering it down on the very trains that carried it north to the United States.[92]

PROTECTING AND MARKETING MEXICO'S
NATIONAL SPIRIT

As adulteration continued, the tequileros pushed the Mexican government to take action.[93] In 1949, the Mexican government established the
first official quality standard for tequila. The standard stipulated that
tequila was to be made from 100 percent *Agave tequilana* Weber (blue
agave) grown in the state of Jalisco.[94] But as the tequila industry continued to grow in the 1950s and 1960s, agave shortages prompted the largest
tequila companies to push for what Rogelio Luna Zamora calls "the legal
adulteration of tequila," by changing the laws to allow for smaller and
smaller proportions of agave.[95] In 1964, the companies convinced regulatory authorities to permit the production of tequila made from 70 percent
blue agave and 30 percent generic sweeteners.[96] This type of tequila is
known as *tequila mixto,* because it mixes an agave spirit (tequila) with
other sweeteners. Luna Zamora notes that the new rule was motivated by
the convergence of two phenomena: the shortage of agaves at the time,
and the increased demand (primarily in the United States) for cocktails
like the margarita and the tequila sunrise.[97] Another revision to the regulations, made in 1968, allowed flavorings and colorings to be added to
tequila and permitted the cultivation of agave outside the state of Jalisco,
as long as the agave "maintained the characteristics of the plants cultivated in Jalisco."[98] Just two years later, in 1970, yet another revision was
passed; this one reduced the minimum percentage of agave sugars to 51
percent.[99] Over this period, tequila companies worked to control the price
of agave, keeping it below one peso per kilogram for decades.[100]

The tequila distilleries further industrialized their methods of production in order to achieve greater economies of scale. Around 1950, they
switched to mechanical shredders, which used steel blades and conveyer
belts to shred the agave.[101] All of the distilleries had shifted to masonry
ovens by 1930; starting in 1960, some began using more even efficient
steel autoclaves to cook their agave.[102] While it took at least forty-eight
hours to roast the agave in a masonry oven, the autoclaves required only
twelve hours.[103]

The ownership of the tequila companies also began to shift. Until the
1960s, the distilleries were still owned by Jalisco's elite families. In 1967,

Figure 3. Field of blue agave (*Agave tequilana* Weber), Jalisco. Photo by Sarah Bowen.

the doors of the industry opened up to foreign capital, when distillery owner Roberto Ruíz created an association with Seagram's, a Canadian liquor company.[104] Many of the other tequileros reacted with fear, worrying that the entry of firms like Seagram's—and the "specter of imperialism" that came with such foreign influence—would undermine the character of the industry and negatively affect Jalisco's economy.[105] But foreign capital proved alluring, and distilleries began establishing alliances and selling shares to foreign firms in rapid succession. The Mexican bottling company Distribuidora Bega, partly owned by a subsidiary of Kentucky Fried Chicken, and Heublein, an American liquor producer and distributor, acquired partial ownership of Cuervo in 1970.[106] Pedro Domecq, a Spanish sherry and brandy company, became the principal shareholder of Tequila Sauza in 1976 and acquired full ownership in 1988; Sauza was sold to Fortune Brands/Beam Global in 2005.[107] Foreign firms also invested in smaller distilleries, and, starting in the late 1960s, an increasing number of distilleries began operating as *maquiladoras*, companies that produced tequila for foreign distributors and bottlers, who then sold it under their own labels.[108]

In the 1960s, with the revisions to the standard, the tequila companies had made a series of decisions that had the effect of weakening tequila's ties to its region of origin. It was somewhat ironic, then, that in the 1970s these same companies began petitioning the Mexican government to establish a piece of landmark legislation that would tie tequila production to a particular place. The denomination of origin (DO) for tequila, established in 1974 and the first of its kind outside of Europe, restricted production to Jalisco and parts of several other states—Guanajuato, Michoacán, Nayarit, and, after a controversial revision in 1977, Tamaulipas.[109]

The DO consolidated the power of the Jalisco-based tequila distilleries by designating them as the (nearly) exclusive producers of tequila, but it could not prevent the collapse of the tequila industry in the 1980s. With the debt crisis that began in Mexico in 1982 and the "lost decade" that followed, domestic sales of tequila declined precipitously, falling more than 60 percent just between 1984 and 1986.[110] The concurrent expansion of the export market allowed the larger tequila companies to hang on, but the industry's problems were compounded by another severe agave shortage, one that more than doubled the real price of agave between 1986 and 1987.[111] Total tequila production decreased by almost 30 percent between 1984 and 1986. Almost half of the tequila companies closed.[112] Small companies without access to the export market were in the greatest danger, but even the big tequila companies were affected: Sauza and Cuervo each had to suspend operations in one distillery.[113]

NEOLIBERALISM AND THE TEQUILA BOOM

In response to the debt crisis and as part of a broader global shift, the Mexican government embraced neoliberalism. Especially under the administration of President Carlos Salinas (1988–1994), the government enacted a series of reforms focused on deregulating (and reregulating) various sectors of the economy in order to open up the market and create a more favorable business climate for foreign investors. The government liberalized the financial system, privatized public enterprise, lowered tariffs and nontariff barriers on imported goods, and ended Mexico's revolutionary history of land reform by allowing private investors to purchase ejido lands.[114] It also revamped its procedures for establishing and enforcing quality standards and DOs. The 1992 Federal Law on Metrology and Standards aimed to provide greater transparency, public participation, and authenticity in the development and enforcement of norms and standards in Mexico.[115] The Mexican Institute of Industrial Property, created in 1993, took over management of Mexican DOs, as well as brands and patents.

These changes had important effects on the tequila industry. In 1994, a revised quality standard for tequila replaced earlier versions. Before the 1992 changes to the Mexican regulatory system, the federal government had been responsible for verifying compliance with Mexican quality standards. Responsibility now shifted to private organizations, accredited by the state. The Tequila Regulatory Council (CRT, according to its Spanish acronym), a private, nonprofit organization, was established in 1994 to verify compliance with the tequila standard.[116] The CRT stated that it was created "due to the Mexican government's interest in transferring functions of the establishment of standards, verification, and certification . . . to the private sector."[117] The new procedures represented a significant ramp-up in quality control; a CRT inspector was assigned to every tequila distillery.

In 1994, the United States and Canada officially recognized Mexico as the exclusive producer of tequila and mezcal; the European Union followed suit in 1997.[118] The CRT established branches outside of Mexico—currently located in Washington, D.C., Geneva, Madrid, and Shanghai—in an effort to monitor and prevent infringement of the DO and the quality standard.[119] In 2002, the CRT signed an agreement with the Mexican government that allows CRT personnel to be present as observers and representatives of the tequila industry in all customs offices. The CRT initiated a permanent training program to police the transport of pseudo-tequilas into the United States and hired customs certifiers to work in forty-eight border-control offices.[120] The combination of increased quality control by the CRT and its strategic partnerships with government agencies contributed to improvements in tequila's reputation and a decline in the production of uncertified tequila.

In what became known as the "tequila boom," annual production of tequila tripled between 1995 and 2008, from 104 million liters to 312 million liters. It has since leveled off at around 250 million liters per year.[121] The market for high-end tequilas has grown even faster. Production of 100 percent agave tequila grew 949 percent between 1995 and 2008 (compared to 67 percent growth for mixto tequilas); and in 2008, production of 100 percent agave tequila surpassed that of mixto tequilas for the first time since the CRT began keeping records of the two categories.[122] U.S. imports of superpremium tequilas have increased faster than all other categories in recent years.[123]

The overall consensus within the industry is that stricter quality standards, the CRT's enforcement efforts, and savvy domestic and international marketing campaigns have all contributed to the growth of the tequila market. Tequila is hailed as a model for producers in developing countries who are trying to make a name for themselves and find their niche in the global marketplace. But the farmers, workers, and communities in Jalisco have largely failed to benefit from the tequila boom. And the DO and the quality standards have not prevented tequila from becoming an increasingly generic spirit, one that has little in common with the *mezcal de Tequila* that became famous more than a century ago.

BEYOND TEQUILA

The trajectory of mezcal production outside the Tequila region is far more varied. Small mezcal producers in Oaxaca, Guerrero, Michoacán, and other parts of Mexico were largely cut off from the foreign capital and technology that transformed the tequila industry starting in the nineteenth century. As a result, mezcal production in these places "maintain[ed] the features and essence of the artisanal process."[124] The exclusion of Oaxaca and other parts of western Mexico wasn't coincidental. Marie Sarita Gaytán argues that in contrast to the inhabitants of Jalisco, a state dominated by the haciendas, the indigenous population in Oaxaca was more self-sustaining; historian William Taylor stated that they held enough land "to escape the paternalism and peonage of hacienda life."[125] While Tequila's close proximity to and relationship with Guadalajara ensured a steady

flow of investment into Jalisco, the large indigenous population and preva-
lence of communal land rights in Oaxaca made it less attractive to investors, both local and foreign.[126] Gaytán argues that tequila became Mexico's
national spirit in part because it was not associated with indigenous populations. She states that, compared to pulque and the mezcal produced in
small distilleries in Oaxaca and elsewhere, "the mezcal of Tequila, Jalisco,
was the least linked to indigenous culture, the lower classes, and the back-
wardness associated with local and small-scale production."[127]

Thus, when the tequila distilleries began adopting innovations like
masonry ovens and continuous stills in the late nineteenth century, Oaxaca
and many other mezcal-producing states largely "escaped the process of
modernization."[128] In these places, most mezcaleros remained small and
marginal, hidden in the highlands and other rural areas, making mezcal
mostly for their families and people in their villages. In 1885, a French
miner who traveled to Sonora provided a description that could have
applied to small mezcal distilleries in any number of states. He wrote, "It is
a mobile distillery. When the wild agaves are depleted within a radius of
two or three miles around a spring [a source of water], the producer carries
his still to another spring, digs another hole for cooking the agave, and
exploits [the resources of] his new region, with the help of a few workers
and a half-dozen donkeys. The quality of the mezcal varies, according to
the type of soil where the agave grows."[129]

Prohibition and taxation also stifled the development of the mezcal
industry. Over time, state and federal governmental institutions increasingly sought to control and eliminate clandestine mezcal production,
which led to increased corruption and evasion of taxes, in turn contributing to additional controls and driving small producers further into the
highlands and into obscurity (and in some cases, out of business).[130] In
1920, in response to a controversial tax on mezcal, a group of small mezcaleros in Oaxaca published their opposition to the decision. They argued
that the tax had been created on the pretext of establishing a dry state, but
was really "only looking to squeeze every last cent out of the pueblos."
Moreover, they said that given the lack of alternative industries in the
region, many villages were reduced "to outright begging or theft."[131] One
historical account of mezcal production in Oaxaca charged that even as
the titles of the officials who enforced the regulations changed, they always

acted in the same way: they wanted "more and more money; their hunger for money was gluttony."[132] Writer William Foote states that during the post–World War II recovery period, the Mexican government "levied alcohol taxes amounting to 300 percent of the price of mezcal."[133] In Guerrero, where prohibition lasted until 1986, one researcher concluded that almost every mezcalero could tell stories about the persecution, abuse, and corruption that resulted from prohibition.[134] At the same time, the mezcaleros in Guerrero, Oaxaca, and Michoacán persisted. Ulises Torrontera, the author of several well-known books on mezcal, writes that the most significant aspect of the history of mezcal production is "the extraordinary resistance of the *indios* [the indigenous populations] . . . to preserve a technology that they made theirs, [that was] so intimately related to their daily religious, social, and cultural life that it survives even today."[135]

MEZCAL'S UNEVEN INDUSTRIALIZATION

The distilleries in Oaxaca were not immune to the wave of modernization that swept Mexico in the late nineteenth and early twentieth centuries. The completion of the national railway in Oaxaca in 1910, and in particular the construction of a station in Tlacolula, in Oaxaca's central valley, connected mezcal producers with markets in Mexico City, Puebla, and Veracruz.[136] Historically, most of the agave that was used to make mezcal had been *silvestre*, or "wild." Agave collectors would make trips into the highlands, harvesting the wild agave and bringing it back to their villages by donkey. But as production of mezcal increased, the supply of wild agave could not keep up, leading to periods of shortage. Agave cultivation intensified after 1935, as farmers in the district of Yautepec (and in other communities in central Oaxaca) began cultivating *Agave espadín*, a variety of agave known for its similarity to tequila's blue agave. The farmers then sold their harvested agave to the mezcal distilleries, known as *palenques*, in Oaxaca.[137]

After 1940, production of mezcal began to ramp up in Oaxaca. In the 1940s, the tequila companies, facing a shortage of blue agave and increased demand for tequila, began buying mezcal from Oaxaca. The tequileros would reduce the alcohol content and then mix the mezcal with tequila before selling it simply as "tequila."[138] As the market for mezcal grew, the mezcaleros in Oaxaca invested in "improved" distilleries. They began using wooden fermentation vats instead of pits carved into the ground, and they replaced their clay pot stills with copper pot stills.[139] The tequileros' demand for mezcal also led to the introduction of wooden barrels for aging in Oaxaca.[140] Overall, the industry's founding families, which also included distributors, were relatively well off; many were the first families in their villages to buy cars.[141] Most of the mezcal produced was sold in bulk, in the local communities and in stores and bars in Oaxaca City and beyond.[142] For example, Pedro Mercade Pons, the founder of what would become Mezcal Monte Albán, traveled "from the Yucatán to Ensenada in his old Ford," peddling mezcal and other spirits.[143]

Over time, the mezcal industry began to shift beyond the family and the village and toward more formal (and more distant) markets. Some distributors started branding and bottling their mezcal instead of selling it in bulk to bars and restaurants. Pedro Mercado Pons began selling his mezcal in 1945 under a number of brands. Gusano Rojo ("Red Worm" in English), another major brand, was registered in 1950 by a liquor-store-employee-turned-mezcal-bottler who got the idea to add a worm to each bottle of his mezcal as a distinctive touch.[144] The number of palenques in Oaxaca increased; by 1950, there were more than fifty palenques in the town of Santiago Matatlán—the "world capital of mezcal"—alone.[145] Increased regulation of mezcal production and sales during the 1950s gave elites in Oaxaca the opportunity to consolidate their power.[146] Local bosses, colluding with government officials, developed regional monopolies. Their ties to government inspectors, combined with their monopolies over resources like distillation equipment and wood, allowed them to block others from stealing their business.[147] Production of mezcal continued to increase. By the mid-1970s, Oaxaca had twelve hundred palenques in operation.[148] However, the market for Oaxacan mezcal remained small compared to the market for tequila.

The 1970s was a profitable period for the mezcal industry. High demand supported an extensive network of small distilleries and contributed to the growth of spin-off industries, including those operated by people who made equipment like fermentation vats and stills.[149] Large mezcal producers and retailers expanded their markets. Bottlers began selling mezcal in Mexico City, Puebla, and Guerrero; one study estimated that three hundred *expendios*, or small mezcal stores, were established during the 1970s, many in Oaxaca City and in other states.[150] By 1980, 80 percent of registered mezcal was being produced in the district of Tlacolula, with neighboring Yautepec emerging as the center of agave cultivation.[151] Three powerful groups had emerged to dominate the industry: Oaxaca's elite Chagoya family, and Mexico City–based bottlers Gusano Rojo and Mezcal Monte Albán. (The latter was the first company to export mezcal, starting in 1975.)[152]

Yet even as a handful of big firms based in Oaxaca and Mexico City intensified their production, most of the distilleries in Oaxaca, Guerrero, Michoacán, and other parts of western Mexico remained small and oriented toward local markets. In Oaxaca, Zapotec peasants would gather the agaves and firewood, using another person's palenque to roast and mash the agave piñas and then ferment and distill the juices to make mezcal; in exchange, the owner of the palenque would receive one-fifth of the final product.[153] In Guerrero, indigenous Nahuatl communities developed associations that worked together to harvest the wild agave and share the work of making mezcal.[154] Agave collectors and mezcaleros led precarious lives: many did not have running water or electricity, and most distilleries had dirt floors. In many highland communities, mezcal represented the only—albeit a marginal—source of income for most of the population.[155] Even when small producers were able to sell their mezcal on the formal market, the bottlers and distributors captured the majority of the profits.[156]

CRISIS AND CROSSROADS

By the 1980s, supplies of wild agave had been depleted, although small producers continued to use it. The larger distilleries in Oaxaca were relying almost exclusively on *Agave espadín*, cultivated in the flat terrain of the central valley.[157] Starting in 1985, a severe shortage of blue agave in Jalisco drove up prices in Oaxaca, and tequila producers began illegally buying Oaxacan agave; the price of agave in Oaxaca increased twentyfold over a six-month period in 1985.[158] Landowners in Oaxaca began planting agave in response to the shortage, but it takes years for agave to mature. Over a thousand palenques in Oaxaca went out of business as a result of the high agave prices, shortage of labor, and economic problems in Mexico more generally.[159] Many of the remaining palenques began adding low-quality cane alcohol to their mezcal to cut costs.[160] This led to unfair competition between traditional mezcaleros and those who were mixing in cane alcohol, because it cost about five times more to produce mezcal than cane alcohol.[161]

By the early 1990s, the industry was in crisis—and at a crossroads. A surplus of agave, the result of the expansion of agave cultivation during the mid-1980s, sent prices plummeting. In 1994, after forty people in a small town in Morelos died after allegedly drinking methane-tainted mezcal at a local festival, government agencies launched public health campaigns about the dangers of mezcal, and consumers started boycotting mezcal.[162] According to William Foote, by this point everyone—"from the poorest palenque to the poshest bottling plant"—realized that change was necessary.[163]

There was less consensus on the direction that the industry should take. An influential group of local elites argued that mezcal producers needed to modernize, industrialize, and cut costs in order to compete with the tequila distilleries and access lucrative foreign markets. Industry leader Porfirio Chagoya argued that Oaxaca's small palenques were "just a phase," and that the quality, volume, and price demanded by the global market required things "that the outmoded [palenques] simply [could] not deliver."[164] To the contrary, some governmental representatives and mezcal producers advocated developing and highlighting the traditional production methods that distinguished Oaxaca. In a landmark research project, funded by the state of Oaxaca during the 1980s, Alberto Sánchez López surprised many when he did not recommend modernizing the industry (as he himself had expected to). He concluded that following the path adopted by the tequila distilleries would jeopardize the quality and taste of mezcal; instead, he emphasized the need to support the thousands of families involved in the production of mezcal, stating that development strategies needed to go "beyond technical and financial solutions and consider social and ecological variables."[165] It was in this context—with the mezcal industry in crisis and amid heated debates about how to fix it— that the DO for mezcal was established.

DEFINING MEZCAL

The DO for mezcal, established in 1994, restricted the production of mezcal to five states: Durango, Guerrero, Oaxaca, San Luis Potosí, and Zacatecas. In subsequent years, municipalities from three states—Guanajuato, Tamaulipas, and Michoacán—were added, in 2001, 2003, and 2012, respectively.[166] The accompanying quality standard, modeled after the standard that regulated the tequila industry, specified strict parameters for certified mezcals—including the alcohol content, acidity, and maximum levels of methanol and higher alcohols—but provided few guidelines about the production process itself. The Mexican Regulatory Council for the Quality of Mezcal, a private, nonprofit organization similar to tequila's CRT, was created in 1997 to verify and certify compliance with the DO and the quality standard. (Because the organization was eventually renamed the Mezcal Regulatory Council, or CRM, I refer to it as the CRM throughout this book.)[167]

The DO, the quality standard, and the CRM were all framed as part of an effort to improve the quality and image of mezcal and contribute to economic development in Oaxaca and other places that produced mezcal. But as I show in this book, although some of the people behind their creation had good intentions, these protective institutions are better understood as part of an effort to consolidate the power of political and economic elites within the industry and enable better access to global markets.

TEQUILA TODAY

Though the trajectories of tequila and mezcal have diverged radically from their shared beginnings, their stories are linked—by the growing global demand for Mexican spirits and by the institutions that protect and define them.

Today, the tequila industry works hard to promote its image as a traditional product that is rooted in an authentic Mexican heritage. For example, advertisements for Cuervo's Mundo Cuervo (literally, "Cuervo World"), the multiacre estate that served as my introduction to tequila tourism, pro-

Figure 4. Stainless steel pot stills in a tequila distillery, Jalisco. Photo by David Suro.

claim, "We cannot speak of the history of Mexico itself without considering the history of José Cuervo."[168] Marie Sarita Gaytán argues that the tequila companies rely on images of "hacienda fantasy heritage" to promote and preserve their reputations as "simultaneously reverent of Mexico's past and present." [169] "Hacienda fantasy heritage" refers to a specific form of commercialized nationalism that memorializes tequila as "indelible to the idea of Mexican heritage itself, one rooted in a romantic, innocent, and above all invented past."[170] In reality, of course, the way tequila is made today is very different from what this traditional rhetoric implies, and the industry is vastly different from the way it looked a century ago.

Of the 150 companies that are registered to produce tequila, 119 are small firms or microbusinesses. These, however, represent a very small volume of production: less than 6 percent of the tequila produced in 2012.[171] The number of small distilleries and microdistilleries surged with the tequila boom that started in the mid-1990s, as agave farmers, unable to find buyers for their agave during periods of surplus, started their own tequila companies.[172] Many of these distilleries are self-sufficient in their

Figure 5. Roller mill and steel fermentation vats in a tequila distillery, Jalisco. Photo by Sarah Bowen.

supply of agave, and most small distilleries produce 100 percent agave tequila.[173] This category includes some firms that produce superpremium brands, as well as many companies that operate on the margins of the industry. Although some small distilleries have expanded over time, many lack a viable market niche and are vulnerable to failure whenever the market floods or the demand for tequila contracts.

Another thirteen companies are classified as medium-sized.[174] Distilleries in this category produce mixto tequila and 100 percent blue agave tequila in roughly equal proportions.[175] Some were established by large agave growers during periods of surplus, when it became difficult for them to sell their agave. Compared to the largest tequila companies, these distilleries are more likely to source their agaves from smaller regions—for example, from farmers in the vicinity of their distillery—instead of from across the entire DO region, as the largest companies do.

It can be difficult to distinguish between the micro, small, and medium tequila companies. Distilleries in these categories produce tequila for both national and export markets. They selectively adopt a combination of industrial and more traditional methods, depending on their market niche. For example, at one of the distilleries I visited, the owners used autoclaves to cook their agave, but had decided to bottle all their tequila on site, including the mixto tequila,[176] in order to have more control over quality. Many small- and medium-sized firms function as maquiladoras, firms that produce tequila for foreign distributors and bottlers. The owner of one small distillery said that "their salvation . . . [was] the *maquila*." He continued: "We produce what we know how to do, and someone else sells [our tequila]; it's a gringo, the owner of the brand, from the United States."[177] But although foreign firms bring expertise and market opportunities that these distilleries wouldn't have access to otherwise, they also retain most of the profits and can easily switch distilleries if the terms of the contract become unfavorable.

A growing number of small and medium-sized distilleries also make craft and superpremium tequilas, primarily oriented toward wealthy foreign consumers. These companies are adept at marketing the unique characteristics of their tequila: for example, their use of traditional practices, or the way their tequila reflects the terroir of the estate where their agave is grown. Tequila Fortaleza is one example of how to market tradition. Guillermo Sauza, the great-great-grandson of Cenobio Sauza, launched Tequila Fortaleza in 2005, when he renovated an old distillery on the family hacienda. Although the Sauza family had sold Tequila Sauza to Pedro Domecq in 1976, Guillermo makes Tequila Fortaleza "in the same way it was made over 100 years ago," with a small masonry oven, tahona, wooden fermentation tanks, and the two original copper pot stills from one of his family's haciendas.[178] Other niche brands rely on more modern methods but find other ways to differentiate their tequilas. For example, Casa Dragones makes its 100 percent agave "sipping tequila" with column stills and an "ultra-modern filtration system," and then packages it in handcrafted bottles. By emphasizing their small-batch production and highlighting the way their innovative process produces a tequila that is uniquely modern and "exceptionally smooth," the company aims to walk the fine line between what they call the "centuries-old art of tequila making" and modern (and cost-effective) methods.[179]

What remains are the thirteen largest companies, which produce 79 percent of all tequila.[180] These firms make a range of tequilas, from

Herradura's Selección Suprema (Supreme Choice)—which is aged for four years and, at more than three hundred U.S. dollars a bottle, marketed to "true connoisseurs"—to cheap, mass-produced mixtos, exported in bulk and bottled in the United States. In general, the biggest firms focus on using advanced technologies to maximize efficiency and achieve enormous economies of scale, in combination with splashy and well-financed marketing campaigns. Perhaps the most absurd example of one of these campaigns was Cuervo's 1996 purchase of an eight-acre Caribbean island, "CuervoNation," that guaranteed its citizens the right to "life, liberty, and the pursuit of a good time."[181] An NPR segment on CuervoNation called it "a bold experiment in advertising via nation building"[182]—one which, ultimately, did not pan out.

Of the thirteen largest companies, Cuervo, which dates to 1758,[183] and Sauza, founded in 1873, have long dominated the industry in terms of both market share and influence. Both produce large quantities of mixtos and have continually adopted technological innovations in order to maximize. In the nineteenth century, they were among the first companies to begin using column stills and masonry ovens. Today, both use diffusers. Diffusers, one of the most controversial technologies in the tequila industry, are machines that wash fermentable sugars out of shredded agave piñas. One distillery representative described them as a "giant power washer for agave."[184] Diffusers can be used in two ways. The first way is as a final step, after roasting the agave in a masonry oven or an autoclave, to extract the remaining sugars. The more controversial method entails using the diffuser without cooking the agave. In this system, the raw agave piñas are finely shredded and then mixed with hot water (and sometimes sulfuric acid). This process extracts 99 percent of the sugars from the agave, yielding a liquid that can then be cooked in an autoclave.[185] Cuervo uses a diffuser at its modern Camichines plant, which is not open for tours.[186] Sauza has fully embraced the industrial model and uses diffusers to make all of its tequila; they call the result of this process "fresh pressed agave."[187] Tequila companies that use diffusers do it in order to more efficiently extract the fermentable juices from the agave. However, the companies are essentially flipping the production process on its head, by extracting the juice and *then* cooking it. This strips the tequila of its cooked-agave flavor.

Diffusers are not the only innovation being adopted in the tequila industry. At its Camichines plant, Cuervo automated the entire fermentation process; the result is that fermentation takes only fifteen hours, as opposed to the sixty hours that is common at other plants.[188] During the agave shortage at the start of the twenty-first century, Sauza and Herradura began reproducing their agave plants via micropropagation.[189]

Although most of the big companies produce large volumes of mixto tequilas, they generally produce a line of premium tequilas as well. This allows them to continue emphasizing their commitment to traditional methods. For example, although Cuervo produces most of its tequila at its main industrial distillery, the company proudly showcases the masonry ovens and copper pot stills at its La Rojeña distillery. These are used in the production of some of Cuervo's high-end tequilas. Herradura, maker of El Jimador, Mexico's best-selling 100 percent blue agave tequila, has historically produced mostly 100 percent blue agave tequilas and marketed itself as a more traditional tequila company.[190] On tours of its distillery, guides emphasize the brick ovens and the fact that the company uses only wild, airborne yeasts to ferment its tequila.

Patrón is the most notable example of a company that is both large and high-end. Established in 1989 by John Paul Dejoria, founder of the Paul Mitchell line of hair care products, and California architect Martin Crowley, Patrón now accounts for over 70 percent of the ultrapremium tequila market.[191] Patrón is the second-best-selling brand in the United States, coming in behind Cuervo.[192] According to Patrón's website, the company is also the world's biggest exporter of 100 percent agave tequila.[193] Some aficionados credit Patrón with having created the ultrapremium category, through its innovative marketing campaigns, its owners' ties to Hollywood stars, and touches like its distinctive handblown bottle. The Hacienda del Patrón, the home of Patrón's showcase distillery, is a sight to behold. When I visited it in 2014, they walked us past row after row of masonry ovens, wooden fermentation tanks, and copper stills. They showed us their motorized tahonas, inviting us to compare the taste of a tequila made with a tahona with that of a tequila made with a roller mill.[194] It was impressive to see artisanal methods being employed at such a large scale; one of the people on the tour mused that the distillery must have been built by a "mad genius." At the same time, it was also somewhat unsettling. The hacienda looks like a grand colonial estate, but it was built in the last decade—the epitome of "hacienda fantasy heritage." And although we asked to visit Patrón's other distillery, located in another part of town, they wouldn't let us. They claimed it was "too dangerous," but some people on the tour wondered if they were hiding something. Started by two Americans, Patrón is not a Mexican company by any stretch of the imagination. Patrón remains controversial: for some, a status symbol; for others, a producer of a high-quality artisanal spirit; and for still others, just another example of foreigners appropriating Mexican traditions.[195]

STANDARDIZATION AND GLOBALIZATION

The distinctions between tequila companies are important, but the seeming diversity of tequila conceals the dominance of a model focused on standardization and homogenization.[196] Despite the growth of the market for superpremium tequila in recent years, the mass market remains significant. In 2014, mixto tequila represented 57 percent of all tequila.[197] Even within high-end markets, distilleries often choose methods that allow them to frame their products as exclusive while pursuing an industrial model. Although many distilleries have abandoned traditional methods in favor of innovations like autoclaves and diffusers, they conceal these shifts. The industrial facilities are rarely open to tour groups; and instead of being precise in how they describe all of their practices, many tequila companies focus on certain aspects, like the barrels they use for aging—whether they are French oak or American oak, new or used. Recently, some companies have also begun triple-distilling their tequila, instead of just distilling it twice, as required by the standard. They argue that this makes for a smoother and purer tequila. However, critics argue that tequila companies are increasingly trying to produce something that is closer to cognac or, more outrageously, vodka. "Pure is good," wrote one brand owner. "Except that [in the case of triple distillation] purity comes at the expense of flavor and complexity."[198] For many aficionados, trends like triple distillation, the use of diffusers, and the focus on aging degrade "the real essence of tequila" and mask the spicy, distinct agave flavor at the heart of a good tequila.[199]

It is virtually impossible for a company to access foreign markets without being linked to a multinational firm, and most successful tequila companies are affiliated with or directly owned by multinational liquor companies. Sauza, first partially and then fully held by Pedro Domecq,[200] was purchased by Fortune Brands/Beam Global (now Beam Suntory) in 2006. After relying on a series of distribution contracts with multinational firms (starting in the 1970s with Heublein and then shifting to Grand Metropolitan, which merged with Guinness in 1997 to become Diageo), the Beckmann family, descendants of the Cuervos, reacquired the company in 2002.[201] Tequila brands across the spectrum are owned and distributed by multinational firms: Cazadores, a large, mass-market brand, is owned by Bacardi; Don Julio, a high-end brand, is owned by Diageo;[202] Avión, a new superpremium brand, is distributed by Pernod Ricard; and Bacardi has a "significant" minority interest in Patrón. And of course, this doesn't include the Hollywood celebrities who have started their own tequila companies. The trend started with Patrón and Sammy Hagar's Cabo Wabo (now owned by Gruppo Campari) and has continued with brands like George Clooney's and Rande Gerber's Casamigos and Justin Timberlake's 901 Tequila (now co-owned by Sauza and called Sauza 901).

Foreign consumers, too, play an important role in the tequila industry. Tequila companies started exporting in the nineteenth century, but exports increased substantially in the 1980s.[203] As exports have grown, the industry's leaders have adopted an increasingly global orientation, which in turn has influenced the strategies that they employ in their distilleries.[204] Rogelio Luna Zamora argues that the globalization of the tequila industry ushered in a new generation of tequila entrepreneurs, trained in elite universities and linked to international markets. The new generation focuses on developing export markets and increasing technological efficiency while continuing to promote tequila's ties to Mexican history and heritage.[205]

For a long time, Herradura represented an important exception to the industry's global orientation. Herradura had a reputation for being a more traditional and more "Mexican" tequila company. In the 1960s, Herradura was one of the few tequila companies to speak out against the proposal to allow up to 30 percent (and eventually 49 percent) generic sweeteners.[206] As other tequila companies were being bought out by multinational firms,

Herradura remained family-owned.[207] A 1996 *New York Times* article characterizes Guillermo Romo de la Peña, the head of Herradura, as a traditionalist, describing his passionate crusades against mixto tequilas and the exportation of bulk tequila. Romo is portrayed as staunchly opposed to the industrial model employed by Cuervo and Sauza. "For us the product is first," he states, staking out his position. "Marketing has always been secondary."[208] However, in 2006, Herradura was purchased by Brown-Forman, one of the largest American spirits companies. Since then, critics have accused Herradura of selling out, altering its methods, and compromising its principles for the sake of profitability. Lindsay Ruhland, an American bartender and spirits professional, told me, "The purchase of Herradura by Brown-Forman was one of the saddest days of my life . . . because it was the little engine that could. It was a family-owned tequila that tasted so good, that was holding its own against the big multinational companies. So it was still that traditional fare. The cultural identity was still truly there; and when that sale went into place, it was one of the saddest days ever. And just watching as that product has gone into the toilet—it's just so disappointing."[209]

Despite critiques like Ruhland's, Mexican companies do not necessarily adopt more traditional methods, just as foreigners do not inevitably push for more industrial methods. In fact, although many aficionados emphasized the differences in Herradura's tequila before and after its purchase by Brown-Forman, the distillery reportedly began producing mixtos and using a diffuser several years before the sale.[210] Furthermore, the shift toward premium tequilas has been largely driven by retailers and consumers from the United States. What is undeniable is that Mexican tequila producers and agave farmers have less and less of a say in how tequila should be defined, protected, and marketed.

DIVERSITY AND DIFFERENTIATION OF MEZCAL

While the mezcal industry has expanded in scale and scope in the last twenty years, there are still thousands of mezcaleros operating small distilleries in the highlands and rural regions of Mexico, particularly western Mexico. It would be impossible to define a characteristic taste of mezcal, although many people argue that the smoky flavor that comes from roasting the agave in the ground is one of mezcal's defining features. Beyond that, to say that there is one kind of mezcal would be like saying that there is one type of French cheese or one kind of barbecue. The agave used may be wild or cultivated, and production practices range from labor-intensive to high-tech. The diversity of mezcal is its most essential characteristic.

Mezcal is made from many different agave species. In some regions, producers rely primarily on one particular species, such as *Agave cupreata*, a type of agave that grows in the highlands of the Río Balsas watershed in Guerrero and Michoacán.[211] Some species, like *Agave potatorum*, described as "growing naturally only in the highest altitude canyons in the shade of trees, like truffles,"[212] are highly valued for the unique flavors that they impart. In some regions, mezcaleros mix many varieties of agave into their mezcal. Carmela Robles, a fourth-generation producer from Oaxaca, told me that her family bought their agave, much of it wild, from farmers and collectors in five nearby villages, and that one batch of mezcal might contain twenty-five or thirty varieties of agave.[213] Javier Salcido, a mezcalero in southern Jalisco, cultivated at least twelve different varieties of agave on his family's small parcel of land, intercropping the agave plants with corn, beans, and other crops. "We say they are cultivated, but 'cultivated' in quote marks," he said, "because we don't add any herbicides or pesticides; we just leave them to grow. All that we do is protect the agave from animals [that would eat it]."[214]

Agave cultivation practices are also rooted in the cultures and histories of particular places. For example, Carmela Robles said that the people in her village had never grown their own agave, but instead had long-standing relationships, stretching across generations, with the communities where they bought their agave. She explained, "There was a system of markets that revolved around mezcal here until 1940 or 1950. Once a week there would be an agave market. The producers from around here would harvest their agave, bring it in their wagons . . . and come to sell their agave. And the *palenqueros* [mezcal producers] would come here to buy it and take it to their palenques."[215] Paulina Reyes, a researcher with a Mexico City–based nongovernmental organization, explained that in Guerrero, indigenous communities collectively decided when, where, and how much agave would be harvested, in order to preserve the sustainability of the system. In some cases, agave was a common resource, divided

Figure 6. Field of *Agave cupreata*, Guerrero. Photo by Sarah Bowen.

Figure 7. Field with diverse varieties of agave, Jalisco. Photo by Sarah Bowen.

among community members, while in others it was held by community leaders and dispensed to the *mayordomos* (fiesta organizers) for the fiestas of the village.[216]

As wild agave has gotten scarcer and the scale of mezcal production has increased, some communities have started planting agave in order to ensure that the supply is maintained. An association of mezcal producers in Guerrero agrees on rules about how much agave each person is allowed to harvest, and its members work together to replant agave each year. In southern Jalisco, researchers are working with small mezcal producers to encourage them to grow diverse varieties of agave from seed, which increases the genetic variability of the agave. However, in response to the threat of shortage, the dominant response in the industry has been to shift to an industrial model: one based on the cultivation of high-yielding agave varieties in monoculture with the aid of a regimen of chemical inputs. State and federal government agencies have actively promoted this shift by conducting research, establishing agave nurseries, and giving financial incentives to encourage planting. In most cases, the new fields are planted with *Agave angustifolia* (also known as *Agave espadín*, or just espadín), a species that is similar to tequila's *Agave tequilana* Weber. Driving down the highway that runs through the "mezcal region" in Oaxaca's central valley, one sees uniformly planted fields of espadín that are strikingly reminiscent of the blue agave fields. Espadín dominates because it fits easily into an industrial model that values efficiency and profitability, but the implications of exchanging a diverse, small-scale system for one based on intensive cultivation of genetically uniform plants remain to be seen.

The production practices used to make mezcal vary considerably, too. The smallest distilleries produce less than ten thousand liters of mezcal annually, operating only during part of the year.[217] In comparison, Cuervo sells an average of eight times this amount of tequila every day, just in the United States.[218] Most small producers roast the agave piñas in pits in the ground; the pits are lined with stone and covered with layers of dirt, stone, and fiber mats. This process takes several days and gives mezcal its characteristic smoky flavor. Practices of fermentation and distillation vary by region and even by village within regions. Some mezcaleros chop or pound the piñas by hand, in hollowed-out logs or on wooden pallets; others use

Figure 8. Small mezcal distillery, Guerrero. Photo by Sarah Bowen.

a stone tahona pulled by an animal or powered by an engine. Some ferment their mezcal in pits dug directly into the ground, while others use
wooden, plastic, or cement vats or even animal hides. Even though adding
yeasts or other fermenting agents would speed up the process, most do not
add anything during fermentation; they told me that this made their mezcal "natural."[219] The length of fermentation varies according to the type of
agave, the altitude of the distillery, the microclimate in the region, and the
time of the year; depending on the conditions, fermentation can take a
month. Most small producers use wood-burning clay or copper pot stills;
some use a version of the Filipino still that many archaeologists believe
was used by the very first mezcaleros.

Amid the stubborn continuity of the small mezcaleros, a growing group
of industrial distilleries has begun mass-producing mezcal. These producers, primarily based in Oaxaca and Zacatecas, explicitly aim to follow the
tequila model. Their production and marketing strategies are similar to

those employed by the largest tequila companies.[220] Instead of roasting the agave in the ground, they cook it in masronry ovens or autoclaves, and at least one of these distilleries uses a diffuser. They add yeasts during fermentation and use column stills for distillation. Many also add artificial ingredients to adjust the color or flavor of the final product. These distilleries operate at a huge scale; the largest, Casa Armando Guillermo Prieto, has a production capacity of 4.5 million liters per year.[221]

THE MARKET FOR MEZCAL

The prices and markets for mezcal fluctuate widely. The cheapest mezcals, made by small, uncertified distilleries, are sold in bulk to individuals, local bars and retailers, and bottlers. The bottlers mix mezcal from many small distilleries together and then sell it under their own label. A survey of producers in Oaxaca found that this type of mezcal typically sold for between 10 and 40 pesos, or less than 3 U.S. dollars per liter.[222] In addition, some small producers bottle their own mezcal, still uncertified, relying on informal regional networks to establish their reputations. Prices generally range between 50 and 150 pesos, or between about 4 and 11 U.S. dollars, per liter.[223]

The CRM began certifying mezcal producers in 2005. Certified producers are a small but growing (and privileged) group, representing between 10 and 20 percent of all mezcal producers.[224] Bottled, certified mezcal commands the highest price, with most producers getting between 100 and 300 pesos, or up to about 23 U.S. dollars, per liter.[225] This category includes mass-produced mezcals, as well as high-end traditional and artisanal mezcals. Some artisanal mezcals are highly sought after by devoted aficionados in the United States and major Mexican cities; they go for a retail price of up to 200 U.S. dollars per bottle. But because small mezcaleros often lack the financial and organizational resources to become certified on their own, they almost always work with intermediaries. The intermediaries help them navigate the process but also capture much of the profit.[226]

More specifically, many of the producers who manage to export their mezcal rely on foreign elites or multinational corporations. Just as with tequila, the larger mezcal companies are increasingly owned by or affiliated with multinational corporations. Casa Armando Guillermo Prieto is owned by a huge firm that also bottles Coca Cola in Mexico. In 2013, Bacardi signed an agreement that gave it the right to distribute Casa Armando Guillermo Prieto's mezcals in Mexico, making Bacardi Mexico's leading mezcal distributor. Celebrities have also taken an interest in mezcal; in 2011, country star Toby Keith introduced Wild Shot mezcal with the slogan "Blame it on the worm." He admitted that he never visited the distillery that makes his mezcal. "They just sent me the bottles," he said, and he guessed that the distillery was "in the eastern part of Guadalajara," in Jalisco, when it is actually in another state, San Luis Potosí.[227] Toby Keith is an easy (and deserving) target, but he is far from alone. As the market for traditional mezcal grows, foreign celebrities and retailers are increasingly "discovering" small mezcaleros—the more rustic and isolated, the better. Consumers increasingly fetishize the local, the obscure, the handcrafted—precisely those characteristics that are threatened by the pressures of globalization.

THE SPIRIT OF MEXICO

Tequila and mezcal share common origins. The first mezcals were produced in western Mexico more than four hundred years ago, and some scholars hypothesize that indigenous populations may have started distilling before the arrival of colonial settlers. Distillation of agave spirits spread throughout western Mexico, including to the town of Tequila. Especially over the last century, however, the paths of tequila, which is produced mainly in Jalisco, and mezcal, produced throughout rural Mexico, have diverged. Tequila is now largely made in modern, high-tech factories by multinational liquor companies. In contrast, most mezcal distilleries are nestled in remote rural areas and produce small batches for local markets. At the same time, some industrial mezcal distilleries have begun copying the tequila model, adopting capital-intensive innovations and relying on multinational liquor companies to facilitate access to global markets.

Tequila and mezcal are both protected by DOs and quality standards. These institutions restrict production to certain regions and ensure the safety and authenticity of tequila and mezcal. They have contributed to the expansion of the markets for these spirits in the last twenty years, but they also rely on a narrow and technical vision of quality that, in turn, reflects the power dynamics that underlie these industries. In the following chapters, I examine the effects of this process on the people who make tequila and mezcal and the places where they live and work.

3 Whose Rules Rule?

CREATING AND DEFINING TEQUILA QUALITY

In March 2006, I accompanied a group of American and Canadian tequila aficionados on the first of their annual organized tours of Jalisco's "tequila promised land." The group included tequila distributors, people who had started tequila-tasting businesses, and a bunch of "weekend warriors"—people who sat in cubicles during the week but dedicated their weekends to tasting and discussing tequila. We were united by our shared obsession with tequila. For three days, we tromped through distillery after distillery, with lots of time to buy and taste tequila. My fellow travelers waxed poetic about the handful of distilleries that still used tahonas to crush the agave piñas, and debated whether American or French oak barrels were better for aging. We were invited to private tastings of rare tequilas that weren't available to the public. At one distillery, we tasted a limited edition tequila that had been aged for five years in French oak barrels, pouring it directly from the barrel into our cups. At another stop, I snapped a picture of myself trying Tres, Cuatro, y Cinco, which at four hundred U.S. dollars a bottle was then rumored to be one of the world's most expensive tequilas.

Tequila has made the leap "from hangover to high-brow."[1] On distillery tours and in interviews, people consistently emphasized tequila's evolution into a "quality product," a distilled spirit that could compete with the best whiskeys and cognacs. They told me stories about how tequila had made its way to Europe (where French tasters had reportedly confused it with cognac); how celebrities, from famous Mexican singers to the king of Spain, had their favorite tequilas; and how tequila had become so smooth that—dare to think!—even women were drinking it. As an indication of how seriously some people took their tequila, Riedel, an Austrian glass manufacturer, designed a dedicated tequila tasting glass. ("What I would have done for a nice tequila glass; where is my Riedel?" reflected one of the people on the tour, recalling a particularly memorable stop.)

Tequila's metamorphosis didn't just happen. Over the last twenty years, public and private organizations have engaged in a concerted effort to redefine and rebrand tequila. For example, the Mexican Tequila Academy, established in 2000, began demonstrating how to properly taste and rate tequilas, as part of a broader effort aimed at orienting consumers to the quality of tequila. Members of the academy taste and then rate tequilas on a twenty-point scale, with points given for its visual, aromatic, and taste properties. Afterward, officials compile the scores and publicize the results. The Distinctive T program, a joint effort of the Tequila Regulatory Council (CRT, according to its Spanish acronym) and the National Chamber of the Tequila Industry (CNIT, according to its Spanish acronym), is another example. Established in 2003, the program recognizes bars and restaurants that meet certain requirements, including employing a tequila specialist, providing tequila-based training for personnel, offering a designated tequila glass, and buying and disposing of tequila according to proper procedures. Individual companies have also worked to redefine tequila through their marketing campaigns. A 1996 *New York Times* article discussed Herradura's effort to convince consumers that their liquor was "pure and sophisticated, the Mexican equivalent of cognac,"[2] and Patrón's long-running "simply perfect" campaign has painted a convincing picture of Patrón drinkers as sophisticated, interesting, and discerning.

Despite the contributions of organizations and companies like those mentioned above, most people, when asked what had caused the "tequila boom," focused on three institutions: the denomination of origin (DO), the quality standard, and the CRT, which together define and guarantee the quality and authenticity of tequila.

DOs confer on a place the right to produce a certain food or drink, when the place's "natural and human" factors give that product its unique taste or characteristics. Mexico's definition of DO is modeled after the French definition of controlled appellations of origin. DO is defined as "the name of a geographical region of a country that serves to designate a product originating therein, the quality and characteristics of which *are due exclusively to the geographical environment, including natural or human factors.*"[3] It is significant that Mexico's law recognizes not only natural or environmental factors but also human or cultural factors. Since geographical conditions and production practices evolve together over time, it makes sense to protect them under the same institution. For example, in France, each DO not only outlines the territory in which goods can be produced but also includes a set of specifications that define the production practices that make that good unique. The Mexican system also recognizes both natural and cultural factors, but regulates them under separate legislation. In Mexico, the DO defines only the geographical boundaries, while a quality standard outlines the conditions of production.

As part of a broader series of neoliberal reforms, the Mexican government revamped its regulatory system in the early 1990s. Within the tequila industry specifically, the quality standard was revised in 1994 and the CRT created in the same year, to verify compliance with the standard and the DO. After this point, the DO for tequila defined *where* tequila could be produced, the quality standard outlined *how* to produce tequila, and the CRT ensured that everyone was following the rules.

The revision of the standard and the creation of the CRT coincided with the start of what became known as the "tequila boom." In just a four-year period, between 1995 and 1999, annual tequila production nearly doubled.[4] Production had tripled by 2008. Many people attribute tequila's success in the global marketplace to the protection of the DO, the revamped quality standard, and the efforts of the CRT. But this interpretation ignores how the DO and the quality standard have adopted a narrow and technical definition of quality. They have failed to protect tequila's tie to a specific place or any particular practices. Over time, tequila has become less and less recognizable as a distinctive Mexican product, even as tequila companies continue to engage in marketing efforts that fetishize tradition.[5]

DEFINING TEQUILA QUALITY

The standard that regulates tequila production defines quality in very specific ways. As many scholars have noted, the creation and enforcement of quality standards is highly politicized, in that various people and institutions strategically interpret, negotiate, and represent competing notions of quality.[6] At the broadest level, definitions of quality articulate not only what makes foods (and drinks) good in different ways (pure, natural, or appetizing) but also the kinds of "knowledge, labor, and social relations [that] can and should assure food's goodness."[7] Although ideas about quality are often taken for granted,[8] struggles over definitions of quality shape market access and the distribution of profits, privileging certain groups while excluding others. Tequila is no different. Negotiations over, and changes made to, tequila's regulatory institutions over the last sixty years are tied to broader conflicts and underlying inequalities.

The first quality standard for tequila, established in 1949, resulted from concerns about the increasing adulteration of tequila. It defined tequila's chemical parameters and standardized the alcohol content (between 45 percent and 50 percent) and acidity levels. It also required distilleries to sell their tequila in bottles instead of barrels.[9] Most consequentially, the standard stated that tequila had to be made from 100 percent *Agave tequilana* Weber, or "other species of the same genus, cultivated in the state of Jalisco, in soils and climatic conditions that are characteristic."[10]

Agave tequilana Weber, or blue agave, was named after Franz Weber, the German botanist who classified it.[11] According to agronomist Ana Valenzuela Zapata, blue agave became the dominant cultivar only in the late nineteenth century. Before that, several varieties of agave had been cultivated and used to make *mezcal de Tequila*.[12] Toward the end of the nineteenth century, large plantation owners began selecting the blue agave cultivar, because it had a shorter maturation cycle and higher sugar content than other varieties, and because it was more compatible with the industrialized processing methods being adopted by the largest distilleries at the time.[13] Over time, other varieties and family heirloom selections gradually disappeared. The 1949 standard canonized blue agave as one of tequila's defining features.

Compared to later versions, the first standard doesn't provide a lot of details; it takes up barely more than a page. The 1949 standard aimed to ensure that tequila met certain quality and safety requirements, while at the same time protecting the characteristics that distinguished tequila from other products. As the standard has evolved over the last sixty years, it has continued to focus on maintaining the safety of tequila and preventing defects, but it pays less and less attention to the characteristics that make tequila unique.

It wasn't long before the tequila companies began lobbying for less stringent rules. During shortages of agave, the tequila companies successfully pressured the government to reduce the minimum required percentage of blue agave sugars, to 70 percent in 1964 and then to 51 percent in 1970. In addition, in 1968, the standard was revised to permit the cultivation of blue agave outside the state of Jalisco and allow flavorings and colorings to be added to tequila.[14]

At the same time, the tequileros appealed to the government to better protect them from distilleries outside Mexico that were making their own "tequila." DOs provided one avenue for doing this. Mexico became a party to the Lisbon Agreement, the international treaty on DOs, in 1964; and in 1973, Mexico instituted an official protocol for establishing DOs.[15] In 1973, the Regional Chamber of the Tequila Industry (now the National Chamber of the Tequila Industry, or CNIT) and Herradura submitted an official request to the Mexican government to recognize tequila as a DO. In late 1974, tequila became the first product outside of Europe to be protected by a DO. The territory defined by the DO included the entire state of Jalisco and parts of three bordering states: Guanajuato, Michoacán, and Nayarit.[16] The ink had barely dried on the DO when a distillery from Tamaulipas (a state on the other side of Mexico) submitted a petition to add several municipalities from Tamaulipas to the DO territory.[17] As I will discuss further, a heated debate ensued; and in a controversial decision in 1977, eleven municipalities from the state of Tamaulipas were added to the DO.[18]

The 1980s was a period of upheaval in the tequila industry and throughout Mexico. The combination of the economic crisis and a severe agave shortage caused many distilleries to go out of business. Starting in the late 1980s, neoliberal reforms in Mexico focused on deregulating various sectors of the economy, privatizing state-owned enterprises, eliminating subsidies, and promoting foreign direct investment.[19] With the establishment of the 1992 Federal Law on Metrology and Standards, the government aimed to increase transparency and accountability throughout the Mexican regulatory system.[20] The revision of the quality standard and the creation of the CRT in 1994 were part of this shift.

In many ways, the 1994 standard was similar to earlier versions.[21] Like those, it specified the chemical parameters of the final product. It required a minimum of 51 percent agave sugars and provided precise definitions for the categories of tequila (blanco, reposado, and añejo). But the new standard diverged from previous renditions in important ways. Most significantly, it outlined an extensive set of steps for demonstrating compliance. The standard also mandated the creation of an independent certifying organization to verify adherence to the rules; this resulted in the establishment of the CRT. The process for demonstrating compliance became significantly more complicated. A CRT inspector was assigned to each distillery, and the paperwork that each distillery was required to file increased considerably.

As I discuss later in this chapter, several changes—some small, and others more controversial—have been made to the standard over the last twenty years. However, the year 1994, with a major revision to the standard and the creation of the CRT, represented a sea change in the tequila industry. That was also just before the beginning of the tequila boom, and for many people these two shifts are inextricably linked.

CONTROLLING TEQUILA QUALITY

Tequila's regulatory infrastructure sounds like something we should believe in, and indeed, most of the people I interviewed—at least those at the upper echelons of the industry—did believe in it. On paper, the dizzying set of rules with which tequila producers must comply is comprehensive. Every agave plant must be registered with the CRT, which records the year it was planted and its precise location, including the GPS coordinates of the field. Records are kept for every step of the process. Distilleries must conduct chemical analyses of their tequila at various stages of production. Every barrel of tequila is sealed by a CRT official; the seal can be removed only by a CRT representative, to guarantee the legitimacy of the aging process. Humberto Vargas, a high-level CRT employee, explained how the process had become more efficient and more rigorous. "Before, when the Mexican government verified compliance with the standards, the industry never produced more than 80 million liters," he said. "Two inspectors were responsible for verifying compliance. The paperwork to become certified to export tequila could take a month [to process]. Today, we have ninety-four inspectors working in the distilleries and the agave plantations, and ten additional people who are trained to do the certification process. The certification to be able to export tequila takes twenty-four hours."[22]

Again and again, industry leaders expressed their faith in the DO and the quality standard. For them, the DO and the standard protected Mexico's (and Jalisco's) ownership of the word *tequila* and ensured the consistency of their product. They emphasized that the DO gave them a market advantage, by preventing producers in places like South Africa or Spain from selling fake tequila. The DO also guaranteed consumers that they were drinking authentic tequila. Many people argued that the added rigor of the standards and the efforts of the CRT had led to a notable decrease in defects and in sanitation or safety threats. Oscar Orozco, a well-known artisanal tequila producer, told me that, for him, the advantage of the DO was the "strict control—which the CRT [was] in charge of—of the production of tequila." Oscar appreciated having "clear rules to produce a determined product," which gave "certainty to the consumer that what he or she was consuming [fell] within a certain range of quality."[23] Jesús Martínez, the director of a medium-sized distillery, explained that, previously, "the tequila industry had no direction," but that with the creation of the CRT, there had been "a momentous change in terms of the professionalization of the industry."[24] Miguel Zamora, the plant manager for another medium-sized company, similarly recalled an overall lack of quality control in the past, but said that, today, tequila was made "according to high quality standards" that allowed it "to compete with high-quality drinks like cognacs or whiskeys, at this level, in bars anywhere in the world."[25] Many people referred to the stricter standards when comparing certified tequila, which they said was safe to drink and free of harmful chemicals and by-products, to the pseudo-tequilas sold by the side of the road, which came with no guarantees. While the pseudo-tequilas could give you a headache or worse, more than one person told me that the quality standards for certified tequila were so strict that you could drink an entire bottle and wake up the next morning without a hangover. (I did not test this proposition.)

When explaining what they meant by tequila quality, the tequileros emphasized controlling the production process, exercising care at each step along the way, and producing tequilas of standard and uniform quality. For example, Gerardo Silva, a high-level executive at one of the biggest tequila companies, told me that the key was being "congruent and consistent" in quality, so that consumers knew what they were getting. Jesús Martínez said that maintaining "a controlled production process," down to the water that was used to make the tequila, was fundamental.[26]

Perspectives like these represent the culture of quality that has been developed and institutionalized in the tequila industry over the last two decades, one that emphasizes traceability, consistency, and enforceability. By guaranteeing compliance with the quality standard, the CRT ensures that tequila is safe for consumers. This is an essential function, especially given recent food-safety scares and escalating consumer fears about the origins of their foods and drinks.[27] Furthermore, by linking production of tequila to a particular region, the DO helps legitimate tequila as the "legacy of all Mexicans," as the CRT president proclaimed in 2005.[28] The problem is not that the regulatory institutions focus on guaranteeing the safety of tequila and Mexico's right to produce it, but that they do so almost exclusively. The CRT and the Mexican government have developed tunnel vision. They have ignored the characteristics that differentiate tequila from other spirits, including its link to a particular place and the essential practices that are representative of that place.

TEQUILA'S TERRITORY

The 1949 standard defined both a place (Jalisco) and a specific type of agave (*Agave tequilana* Weber) as intrinsic to tequila quality. It was ironic—given that the first standard was motivated by concerns about adulteration—that the large tequila companies soon began lobbying the government to lower the required percentage of agave sugars, engaging in what critics called the "legal adulteration" of tequila.[29] During an agave shortage in the early 1960s, the tequila companies persuaded the federal government to allow them to introduce other sweeteners into their tequila. In 1964, the minimum percentage of agave sugars was lowered to 70 percent; the other 30 percent could come from any generic sweetener.[30] But despite the modification, the supply of agave could not meet the demand for tequila. In 1968, only forty-three out of fifty-six tequila distilleries were in operation, owing mostly to a shortage of agave.[31] In 1968, the standard was revised again to permit the use of flavorings and colorings and to allow for the cultivation of agave in regions outside the state of Jalisco.[32] This was still not enough, and in 1970 the largest distilleries persuaded the government to again lower the minimum percentage of agave sugars, this time to 51 percent. According to tequila historian Salvador Gutiérrez González, as a result of the revisions made to the standard between 1964 and 1970, "an irreconcilable antagonism" developed between two factions within the industry. One group, led by Herradura, argued that the term *tequila* should be reserved for spirits made exclusively with blue agave. But the purists were outnumbered and outmaneuvered by Cuervo, Sauza, and other industrial producers. The group maintained that they should be able to produce a distillate that included 49 percent "sweeteners of unknown origin" and still call it tequila.[33]

The decision to allow tequila to be made with generic sweeteners represented a fundamental break with the premise that tequila's unique characteristics were worth protecting. According to Gutiérrez González, by allowing for the legal adulteration of tequila, the revisions "degraded the status of tequila from something comparable to cognac to something comparable to rum." In fact, the sugars most commonly added to tequila—cane and corn—are the same as those used to make rum, a drink that is famous for "not dominating, but [instead] combining," precisely because of its *lack* of organoleptic characteristics.[34]

With each new revision, the agave, the "raw material that binds tequila to Mexico," became less important.[35] Yet in the 1970s, the same tequila companies that had pushed for the revisions began petitioning the Mexican government to establish a piece of landmark legislation that would tie tequila production to a particular place. The DO for tequila, established in 1974, gave Jalisco and parts of three adjacent states (Guanajuato, Michoacán, and Nayarit) the exclusive right to produce tequila.[36] However, the DO did not prohibit the use of generic sweeteners or even require that they come from the DO region.

The process of defining the DO territory was contentious from the beginning. The original requests for the DO, which were submitted by the Regional Chamber of the Tequila Industry and Herradura, had included only municipalities in Jalisco and Nayarit. It did not take long for representatives of other states to begin arguing that the boundaries should be expanded. Most petitions were for the inclusion of regions in states that were adjacent to Jalisco, but several groups requested that parts of Tamaulipas be added.[37] Tamaulipas, a state that borders the United States, is far away from tequila's region of origin; the distillery that submitted the petition is almost five hundred miles from the town of Tequila. In the conflict that ensued, the tequileros from Jalisco faced off against one of Tamaulipas's elite families, with the Mexican government in between.

The origins of this story date back to the 1960s. In 1966, agave in Jalisco was in short supply, and Guillermo González, one of Tamaulipas's wealthy landowners, planted large quantities of blue agave, reportedly at the request of one of the large tequila distilleries.[38] Other farmers in the region did the same. However, according to González, when the agave matured several years later, the distillery stated that it would not buy the agave. It no longer needed it; by this point, tequila could be made with up to 49 percent generic sweeteners, and demand for agave had fallen. The agave from Tamaulipas was now useless. But González, the great-grandson of former Mexican president General Manuel González, was no ordinary farmer. He established his own distillery, La Gonzaleña, and, according to company history, "became a warrior in his own right, fighting for the inclusion of Tamaulipas in the DO territory."[39]

In response to the original 1973 application for the DO for tequila, La Gonzaleña and several other groups from Tamaulipas appealed to the federal government to allow tequila to be made in Tamaulipas. However, after "studying all of the pertinent evidence," the Secretary of Industry and Commerce, the organization in charge of DOs at the time, rejected the requests to include Tamaulipas. The Secretary concluded that the requests were based "simply on the basis of the existence of *Agave tequilana* Weber plants," and not "on the industrial production of the liquor referred to as tequila."[40] But González did not give up. In 1976, La Gonzaleña submitted an official petition to add several municipalities from Tamaulipas to the DO territory.[41]

Not surprisingly, some of the tequileros from Jalisco objected. However, after again reviewing the evidence on both sides of the issue, the federal government concluded that the objections were not sufficient to prevent Tamaulipas from being added to the DO region. The official decision cited the fact that some of the tequila companies had promoted agave cultivation in Tamaulipas, also noting that the investment in the region had been considerable. It further concluded that agave grown in Tamaulipas met the quality requirements set by the standard, and that the expansion of the market for tequila demanded larger volumes of agave.[42] By 1977, González's victory was complete; the DO was revised to include eleven municipalities in Tamaulipas.[43]

Almost thirty years after the decision was made, the people I interviewed were still talking about it. Many of the tequileros in Jalisco emphasized the politics and money involved. Tequila distiller Oscar Orozco told me that what had happened in Tamaulipas "was a political arrangement." He continued: "The [great-grandfather] of the founder of the factory had been president of Mexico at one time. And based on these political influences, they succeeded at getting this region included in the DO region, supported by the two biggest tequila companies. I am not going to say their names, but everyone knows who they are: they are the biggest tequila companies in the country, who wanted to produce tequila close to the border, to reduce their costs of transportation to the United States."[44]

The precise role that the largest tequila companies played in the negotiations is difficult to discern, especially after so much time has passed. According to Rogelio Luna Zamora's history of the tequila industry, Cuervo and Sauza began mobilizing to establish their own distilleries and plantations of agave in Tamaulipas as soon as the DO was revised in 1977.[45] However, the agave grown in Tamaulipas reportedly did not have the same flavor or sugar content as the agave grown in Jalisco, and the liquor derived from this agave did not have the characteristics typical of tequila. The distilleries in Tamaulipas also suffered from shortages of both water and qualified workers. Luna Zamora reports that Sauza and Cuervo began moving their equipment back to Jalisco in 1982.[46] For Luna

Zamora, the attempt to create a new tequila region in Tamaulipas represents "one of the great failures in the history of the tequila industry," exemplifying the irreducibility of nature, in that even the big tequila companies concluded that the environmental (and social) conditions in Tamaulipas weren't appropriate for making tequila.[47]

As Cuervo and Sauza were pulling out of Tamaulipas, however, La Gonzaleña was making its move into the United States. In 1983, a two-person company introduced La Gonzaleña's tequila, sold under the brand name Chinaco, to the United States.[48] This was the first high-end tequila available in the United States, and it quickly attracted a cult following among Americans who were tired of the cheap swill that passed as tequila. Curt Miller, a well-connected American bar owner, told me what happened the first time he tried Chinaco. He recounted, "In June of 1983, I was working at a bar and did a lot of the buying in Southern California and somewhere else, and I was a whisky drinker at the time. A guy came in and he goes, 'They have a new product, I want you to taste it, I think you'll like it. . . . It's tequila.' I almost shooed him right out the door. . . . He goes, 'No, really, take a minute.' . . . He opened up a bottle of Chinaco, and I took one case of it. I [said], 'Wow, this is really different. This is really awesome.' . . . I bought three cases of it on the spot, of the three different expressions: blanco, reposado, and añejo."[49]

When the tequila industry collapsed in the mid-1980s, La Gonzaleña, like many other distilleries, went out of business. Guillermo González's sons were able to buy it back in the 1990s, and it remains the only tequila distillery in Tamaulipas. It lacks the fame and fortune of the biggest tequila companies, but many still credit La Gonzaleña, and Chinaco, with introducing premium tequila to the United States. *Wine & Spirits Magazine* called it one of the ten brands that had most shaped the American spirits market over the last twenty-five years. Of the 1983 Chinaco añejo, they wrote, "The packaging and the price matched the high quality of this first super-premium tequila. . . . In 1983, this heady, perfectly balanced tequila was a revelation."[50]

The story of La Gonzaleña and Tamaulipas is complicated—a success story for some, a tale of deceit and failure for others. Thirty years after it happened, it is hard to know exactly what played out behind the scenes. What is clear is that the fight over the boundaries of the DO ultimately boiled down to economic criteria. In making its decision about whether to include Tamaulipas, the Mexican government considered factors like the previous investments that had been made, the jobs that would be affected, and the increasing demand for tequila. Notably, the government did not consider the legal definition of the DO—the idea that DOs are reserved for products whose "natural and human factors" are determined by the place where they are grown or made. Tamaulipas has neither a geography that is consistent with that of Jalisco nor a history of tequila production. La Gonzaleña itself claims that the high elevation, proximity to the sea, and soils of the fields where their agave is grown make their tequila different from others. Perhaps Tamaulipas deserves its own DO, but it is difficult to argue that the environmental or cultural conditions of the state have anything in common with tequila's region of origin. By including Tamaulipas within the DO boundaries, the Mexican government egregiously violated its own legal definition of DO, since the law explicitly requires that "the delimitation of the territory of origin" be based on "geographical characteristics and divisions," and not political motivations.[51]

WHAT THE STANDARD LEAVES OUT

The changes made to the standard in 1994 represented a significant shift in the regulation of tequila quality. The standard has been revised several times since then, but still retains the essential characteristics of the 1994 version. The standard primarily focuses on two things: first, defining the range of physical and chemical parameters for tequila; and second, outlining the procedure for verifying tequila quality and authenticity.

Surprisingly, the standard offers almost no guidelines about the production process itself. There are a few exceptions. For example, the standard states that tequila must be aged in oak barrels, and it gives minimum time periods for each aging category.[52] However, the vast majority of decisions about production are left to each individual distiller: whether to cook the agave in a masonry oven or an autoclave, crush the agave with a tahona or a mechanical roller mill, use copper serpentine stills or stainless-steel column stills, or age the tequila in new or used barrels.

Arguably, it is all of these little decisions, made by each producer, that over time imbue tequila with the qualities that make it distinct from other spirits. The DO and the standard ostensibly define the practices that are fundamental to the quality and taste of tequila. But because the DO and the standard are virtually devoid of guidelines about how tequila is made, distilleries have shifted away from traditional practices and toward industrial techniques that maximize profitability but strip tequila of its flavor.

Conflicts over how the agave is cooked provide one example of how distilleries increasingly make decisions that prioritize economic efficiency over the quality or taste of tequila. Masonry ovens, introduced in Jalisco in the late nineteenth century, are one of the hallmarks of a traditional tequila distillery. Ernesto Zepeda, one of the founders of the Mexican Tequila Academy, argued that "when they roast the agave in a [masonry] oven, the flavor is fuller and more profound, and exhibits more of the characteristics of the agave."[53] However, it takes at least forty-eight hours to roast agave in a masonry oven. So, starting in the 1960s, many distilleries began shifting to autoclaves, which could cook the agave in about twelve hours.[54]

The tequileros who use autoclaves insist that the autoclaves don't negatively affect the taste of their tequila. Plant manager Miguel Zamora told me that he didn't believe that the autoclaves gave his tequila a different flavor. "There are people who say that cooking in an autoclave gives a lower-quality tequila than cooking in an oven," he said. "Or that it gives a different flavor. And that isn't true." He compared it to different ways of cooking beans, explaining, "In Mexico we eat a lot of beans, and we say that beans that are made in clay pots [*frijoles de olla*] are much tastier than the ones that are made in a pressure cooker [*olla express*]. And that is not true, because everything depends on the cook. There are times when you eat beans that are so good that you ask if these beans are from a clay pot. . . . No, it is that my mama cooked them in a way that is delicious. And here it is the same." Zamora argued that because he paid attention to quality, the autoclave did not affect the taste of his tequila. Yet in his next breath, he contradicted himself, arguing that the autoclave actually imparted good flavors to his tequila. "In the ovens, there is a lot of evaporation; the ovens do not seal everything perfectly, so the vapors escape and you lose important aromas," he said. "And here [with the autoclave], we take care of all of that." Zamora concluded, "I am convinced that

Figure 9. Masonry oven in a tequila distillery, Jalisco. Photo by David Suro.

everything depends on the cook. If the agave is cooked well, the tequila is going to come out delicious, because when it is well-cooked, the flavor of the agave is exquisite."[55]

But although many tequileros insisted that tequila made with an autoclave was just as good, most people believed there was a relationship between the cooking method and the taste of tequila. Many high-end dis-

Figure 10. Workers loading an autoclave in a tequila distillery, Jalisco. Photo by David Suro.

tilleries continue to use masonry ovens, despite their inefficiency; the tequileros at these distilleries are adamant that the flavor of the roasted agave comes through in the tequila. Even some of the big companies (like Tequila Cuervo) roast a certain proportion of their agave in masonry ovens, reserving this agave for their priciest lines. Ernesto Zepeda argued that autoclaves imparted "a more citric or green flavor" to the tequila, as if the agave "had not been cooked long enough."[56] What Zepeda called a "green flavor," some companies market as "smooth." On its website, Tequila Partida, an upscale brand, states that while most distilleries cook their agave "the old-fashioned way, in stone ovens that are rarely cleaned," their distillery uses only "state-of-the-art stainless steel ovens to bake [their] agave, creating a smoother, cleaner, agave taste."[57] But when pressed, most people acknowledged that autoclaves did not contribute the same sweet flavor of roasted agave. Gerardo Silva, an executive for one of the biggest tequila companies, said that masonry ovens "gave a flavor profile with the taste of the caramelized agave, while the autoclaves contributed less of this flavor." Like most innovations adopted in the tequila industry in the last century, autoclaves not only are more efficient but also produce a tequila that is more neutral, with "less of the agave soul," as one high-end distiller put it.[58] This makes sense for companies that are trying to develop a product that can compete with vodka, but not from the perspective of people who are committed to preserving the unique taste of Mexico's famous spirit.

In the absence of any guidelines defining the practices or tastes that distinguish tequila from other spirits, the production process has continued to evolve. During the agave shortage that began in the late 1990s, the tequila distilleries needed to come up with a way to extract even more sugars from their agaves. As I explained in chapter 2, diffusers, machines that wash fermentable sugars out of shredded agave piñas, provided one answer. Diffusers can be used to extract additional sugars from piñas that have already been cooked. However, more controversially, some tequila companies, including Cuervo and Sauza, began using diffusers *before* cooking the agave. After finely shredding the raw agave piñas, they mix them with hot water (and sometimes sulfuric acid), employing a process that extracts the sugars from the agave and produces a liquid that can then be cooked in an autoclave.[59] Diffusers are extremely efficient, extracting 99 percent of the sugars from the agave, compared to a reported 85 percent from agave processed with a mechanical roller mill, and 70 percent from agave that has been pressed with a tahona.[60] Gerardo Silva's company exclusively used diffusers. When I asked him why, his answer was all about efficiency. "It gives a better yield, better extraction of the agave. Because [otherwise] you lose too much of the sugar," he said.

At the same time, there is a stigma associated with diffusers. Many companies are intentionally vague about whether they use diffusers, or claim that they use them only for their low-end mixtos and not for their premium tequilas. (Conveniently, it is almost impossible to verify this). Diffusers are controversial because, while they are efficient, they also represent a shift even farther away from tequila's origins. For centuries, agave piñas were cooked, mashed, and then fermented. By allowing companies to extract the juice from raw piñas and then cook it, diffusers flip the process on its head. A kerfuffle that played out on Twitter illustrates just how contentious diffusers have become. One tequila aficionado asked which

Figure 11. Diffuser in a tequila distillery, Jalisco. Photo by David Suro.

distilleries used them. "Most distilleries would prefer NOT to tell you that they are. Herradura has been known to use them," someone responded. Herradura responded almost immediately, tweeting, "Herradura does not use [the] diffuser method. Our tequila has been crafted using [the] same methods since 1870s." The tequila enthusiasts pounced, noting that an executive at Herradura had admitted that the company started using diffusers during the agave shortage that occurred between 1999 and 2003, in order to extract an additional 3 percent of juices and sugars from the cooked agave fibers.[61] "Talk about a kid getting caught with hand in the cookie jar. Big companies will always deny," one person tweeted.[62]

Many purists argue that tequila made with a diffuser is not really tequila. Matt Clark, an American bartender, told me that diffusers produce tequila that "is not going to taste like tequila, because it's not baked in agave." When one aficionado had the chance to taste the extracted sugars from the diffuser, he described the taste as "very bitter . . . with hardly any sweetness."[63] In contrast, oven-roasted agave has a very sweet taste. Distilleries that use diffusers have to add artificial flavors during the finishing process, in order to make their tequila taste like tequila. Before

2005, the standard had allowed distilleries to incorporate caramel coloring, wood extracts, glycerin, and sugar-based syrups into their tequila.[64] A 2005 revision expanded the list to allow for "sweeteners, coloring, flavoring, or aromas permitted by the Secretary of Health . . . in order to provide or intensify [tequila's] color, aroma, or flavor."[65] The largest distilleries pushed for the change in order to help them compete with flavored vodkas. But people also speculated that the revision was made to allow distilleries that were using diffusers, which stripped tequila of its agave flavor, to artificially put the taste of agave into their products.

THE TASTE OF TRADITION

The main premise behind any DO is that certain practices (and certain places) are worth protecting, because they are reflected in the unique taste of a food or drink. In my research on Comté cheese, France's best-selling DO cheese, I learned how the cheesemakers and farmers used the rules of the DO to protect the practices they deemed fundamental to authentic Comté cheese. For example, they required that the milk be heated in copper vats and the cheese aged on pine shelves. The people who made Comté cheese believed that these practices, passed down from their grandparents, were expressed in the flavors present in the milk and the cheese. The president of the CIGC, the organization that regulates the DO for Comté cheese—the equivalent of the CRT—told me that establishing the rules had been controversial because some people argued that using plastic shelves and stainless steel vats would be more sanitary. He explained that they tried making Comté in stainless steel vats for a brief period, but that it changed the taste of the cheese, making it "inedible." In the end, their decision was based on maintaining the qualities that made Comté distinct. The CIGC's president explained, "We realized that the copper had a positive effect on Comté. . . . These aspects—the wooden shelves, the copper vats—contribute to the quality of the product, and modern materials go against the quality of the product; they kill the typicity of the product."[66] In the Comté case, besides helping preserve what cheesemakers called the "typicity" of the product, the rules also helped small producers maintain their foothold in the market, by making it harder for big dairy companies to achieve economies of scale in the production of Comté cheese. Protecting the practices that made Comté cheese unique thus contributing to the preservation of both the cultural traditions of the Comté region and the livelihoods of the people and families there.

The Comté case is a good example of how protecting and institutionalizing certain aspects of quality can create spaces for maintaining rural communities and cultures.[67] Coming back to the tequila case, the people I interviewed were proud of tequila's heritage and the characteristics that made it unique, including the type of agave, the regions where it was grown, and certain production practices. Santiago Delgado, the director of a high-end tequila company, explained that what was important about the DO was that it wasn't just created out of thin air. Instead, it grew and developed over time, in a particular place. He explained, "The DO brings together a series of conditions and characteristics—a specific topography, climate, and tradition. . . . We believe in the DO. It protects our heritage. . . . This is something unique, like Champagne, Ribera del Duero, Roquefort, and Guatemalan coffee." Moreover, many distillery owners and master distillers—particularly those who were making high-end tequilas—emphasized how traditional practices contributed to the distinct quality and taste of *their* tequilas—whether it was their use of masonry ovens, tahonas, wooden fermentation vats, natural yeasts, or copper stills. Diego Soto, the owner of another high-end company, said that his company used traditional methods at every step of the process, including masonry ovens, a tahona, and copper stills. For Soto, these practices contributed to the "unique characteristics, flavors, and aromas" of his tequila. Oscar Orozco used similar methods at this distillery, and said they produced a tequila that was "much more intense," with a stronger agave flavor.

At the same time, even tequileros who chose to adopt traditional practices were reluctant to identify any specific practices as essential to maintaining tequila quality. Instead, most people believed that each company should have the freedom to respond to the demands of the market. For example, Julieta Carrillo, the owner of a distillery in Los Altos, said that her company used only masonry ovens, because this gave them the flavor profile that they wanted. However, she didn't criticize other companies' decisions to use autoclaves. She concluded, "As long as we respect the standard, it is completely valid [to make different choices] corresponding with the tastes of the consumer and the type of brand that they prefer. [Different tequilas] have different flavors, different aromas."[68] Martin Porras, the owner of a high-end brand, agreed, despite his conviction that traditional methods were superior. For Porras, making a good tequila started with "slow and even cooking . . . using good quality water, fermenting in a natural way, . . . not accelerating it." He also felt that it was important to use pot stills, because he believed that column stills and diffusers removed "the memory of the raw material."[69] And yet when I asked Porras whether the DO or the standard should prohibit diffusers or define certain practices as essential, he said, "I don't say that using column stills or diffusers is necessarily wrong within the category. In some ways, making tequilas in different ways gives a broader variety. . . . I feel like the more industrialized and commercial methods—let's call it 'cutting corners'— that different brands use, make a hole in the market for people who do respect [traditional methods] and want to make the highest quality products they can."[70]

The tequileros' refusal to specify particular practices is reflective of their appreciation for innovation and creativity, qualities valued in the global market. When I asked Julieta Carrillo about the challenges that she faced as a distillery owner, she answered, "We have to be more creative. And our [relatively small] size allows us to be more flexible, to move more rapidly. But the competition is very strong. . . . We are always thinking about what the market needs, to be able to offer it." The tequileros knew that the market was fickle, and they did not want to support regulations that would limit their ability to innovate in response to changing market conditions. But in the absence of guidelines concerning how it is produced, tequila has become increasingly untethered from its origins, almost indistinguishable from other industrial spirits. Thomas Evans, a wine and spirits consultant, explained that there were still "brilliant tequilas out there," tequilas with a "rustic earthy quality to them that would make you think of earth and dirt."[71] However, tequilas like these were getting harder and harder to find, and he worried about the direction the industry was taking. "What's happened in Jalisco is a really scary thing," he told me: "the fact that we are using diffusers, and that what used to take weeks, now can take hours."[72]

Figure 12. Copper pot stills in a tequila distillery, Jalisco. Photo by Sarah Bowen.

AGAVE HEARTS AND TEQUILA TERROIR

The standard fails to protect not only the practices that make tequila unique but also the ingredient at its heart, the agave. Mexico is the center of origin for agave and is known for its agave spirits. The agave farmers believed that the soil, climate, and their own practices (for example, intercropping or pruning to control weeds) influenced the quality of the agave they grew. Fernando Quevedo, a farmer and agricultural day-laborer who had been cultivating agave for thirty-five years, explained that, for him, the taste of tequila was inseparable from the quality of the agave. He told me that agave plants grown "in red soil, which is the good soil," are "very sweet, very flavorful," and that this in turn produces the best tequila. Quevedo also warned against using agave that is *tierno* ("tender," used to refer to agave that has not fully matured), which he said yields a tequila that is "neither flavorful nor fragrant."[73]

The owners and managers of the tequila companies also emphasized the importance of the agave, even discussing how the taste of their tequila was influenced by the regions where the agave was grown. Ernesto Zepeda, of the Mexican Tequila Academy, argued that a tequila produced in Los Altos does not have the same flavor as a tequila produced near Tequila, because the qualities and the flavors depend "on the altitude, the soil, the climate, the time of harvest, and the agave cultivation techniques." As the notion of terroir has gained traction in Mexico and the United States, companies have begun actively promoting the places where their agave is grown, with some even advertising their tequilas as "estate-grown." For example, Tequila Partida says that every ounce of their tequila "begins with a carefully cultivated supply of blue agave . . . grown near a dormant volcano in the Tequila Valley."[74] Tequila Ocho, a "single estate" tequila launched in 2012, takes it a step further. Every bottle of Tequila Ocho designates "the precise field from which the family grown agaves were sourced."

The emerging cachet of estate-grown agave in the tequila industry is undeniable. F. Paul Pacult, one of the foremost spirits experts in the United States, recently declared that the best tequilas came from estate-grown agave.[75] Yet, as I discuss in the next chapter, the rise of estate-grown agave is not just the result of the tequila companies' new appreciation for terroir. It is also a strategy for guaranteeing a more stable supply of agave in the face of ongoing cycles of surplus and shortage. Furthermore, despite the tequileros' rhetoric about the importance of the agave, the DO and the standard almost completely ignore the way the agave is grown. The industry's regulatory institutions do little beyond delineating the boundaries of production and the species of agave that can be used to make tequila. The DO region is huge, and it includes many places without a history of agave production. Companies can choose to tell consumers where their agave comes from, but they don't have to, and many companies are deliberately vague about the source of their agave. The standard does not include any requirements concerning the quality or maturity of the agave or particular cultivation practices.

In 2005, the standard was revised to eliminate the only minimal reference to agave quality. Previously, the standard required that tequila be made from "the mature heads [*cabezas*, also known as piñas] of agave." Now even that stipulation was removed. The agave farmers told me that the big tequila companies had pushed for the change, so that they could use their own immature agave instead of being forced to buy mature agave from independent farmers.[76] Gustavo Contreras, a high-level official at Jalisco's Secretary of Agriculture, explained that they had considered several methods for determining whether the agave was mature: by age (at least six years old), weight (at least twenty-five kilograms) or sugar content (at least 16 percent sugar). The farmers proposed that the standard require that the agave meet at least two of these criteria before it was harvested. But the tequila companies rejected their suggestion. Contreras recounted, "Because the industry rejected the proposal . . . there are no rules for defining the maturity [of the agave]. The farmers wanted a standard definition of maturity, so that they would be able to prevent the tequila companies from using [their own] three- or four-year-old agave, and so that the farmers would be able to sell their agave. But the tequila companies won the vote."[77] It is likely that only a few large tequila companies pushed for the change, which negatively affects both the agave farmers and the quality of tequila. It is in keeping with a regulatory system oriented toward maximizing the flexibility of the largest producers.

GLOBAL AMBITIONS

Most regulatory decisions over the last sixty years have been pushed by a handful of large tequila companies, the majority of which are owned by or affiliated with multinational firms. A few examples of recent conflicts over the standards illustrate how a small cadre of elites has shaped the direction of the industry, in order to continually industrialize the production process and increase access to foreign markets.

First, many people have suggested over the years that all tequila should be bottled in Mexico. All 100 percent blue agave tequila must be bottled in the DO region, but the cheaper mixto version can be sold in bulk and bottled outside of Mexico. In the late 1990s, close to 90 percent of tequila exports were being shipped in bulk from Mexico and bottled abroad, mostly in the United States.[78] Herradura and other tequila traditionalists argued that requiring that all tequila be bottled in Mexico would improve tequila's quality and reputation. But Cuervo and Sauza, who together accounted for more than half of all tequila exports, opposed making a new rule.[79] They shipped their tequila across the border in tanker trucks and then bottled it under their own labels in the United States. The two companies argued that bottling in Mexico would slow production and drive up prices. The director of Sauza declared, "We believe in going where free trade leads us."[80]

Tensions flared. In 1997, Jesús López Román, the owner of Tequila San Matias, was shot down outside his factory in a still-unsolved killing. According to one person I interviewed, Román "had been one of the strongest supporters" of requiring that all tequila be bottled in Mexico, and he had created enemies within the industry because of it.[81] Despite the controversy, local and state governmental officials, the CRT, and some tequileros came together in support of an official proposal, introduced in 2003, that would require that all tequila be bottled in Mexico. As Ernesto Zepeda recalled, "The CRT doesn't have enough people to be able to monitor [everything in the United States]. So they proposed that all tequila be bottled here, so that they could have absolute control, and so the quality wouldn't change."[82] But despite being backed by the Mexican government (including then-president Vicente Fox himself, people told me), the proposal got nowhere. In January 2006, the United States and Mexico signed an agreement in which Mexico dropped the proposed ban on bulk tequila exports, in exchange for "increased transparency" of the quality-control process in the United States.[83]

In interviews conducted just a few months after the proposal was dropped, many people described the opposition as coming mostly from the United States. Indeed, the proposal was fought by the Distilled Spirits Council of the United States and by individual bottlers and distributors.

They argued that it would raise costs for consumers and violate the principles of free trade. But powerful tequila companies like Cuervo and Sauza
also organized against the proposal. Gabriel Ávila, the owner of a medium-
sized tequila company, stated that he believed there had been almost "no
chance" of the rule passing. "The big companies got together, and they had
very particular interests; they took charge of the situation," he said. "Their
interests are foreign interests. I'm not saying this is good or bad, just that
they are not concerned with the quality of tequila, or with the interests of
the region that produces tequila," he explained.[84] The global orientation of
the largest companies triumphed over local concerns.

Recent debates over flavored tequila provide another example of the
direction in which the industry is going. As I noted earlier, a 2005 revision
of the standard allowed tequila to be supplemented with artificial sweeteners, coloring, and flavors. The largest tequila companies argued that the
change was necessary in order to allow them to attract a new segment of
young consumers. Cuervo was the first major company to release flavored
tequilas, launching three (lime, orange, and tropical) just a few months
after the new rule went into effect.

Almost ten years after the revision was made, the verdict on flavored
tequilas is not clear. A report on the spirits industry in the United States
noted that sales of flavored spirits were growing ten times faster than
those of total spirits. Although vodka and whiskey represent the majority
of the flavored spirits market, sales of flavored tequilas are rising.[85] The
spirits brand that grew fastest between 2010 and 2011 produced, among
other things, peach- and grapefruit-flavored tequilas.[86] Even some superpremium tequila brands have introduced flavored spirits; for example,
Patrón's XO Café is a coffee liqueur made from Patrón Silver tequila and
the "pure, natural essence of fine coffee."[87] At the same time, as companies
experiment with increasingly creative flavor combinations, like Cuervo's
Cinge (cinnamon-infused tequila), tequila looks (and tastes) less and less
like the traditional spirit upon which the industry's reputation is based.
Jorge Cruz, the owner of a high-end tequila brand, worried that the introduction of flavored tequilas was setting the industry back fifty years. He
argued, "After all that we have obtained, after we have positioned ourselves in the world of liquors and spirits. In the last ten years, we [the
tequila industry] have succeeded at obtaining a certain recognition of

quality and complexity, but we are going back, and we are losing our credibility. I can't believe that one day I am going to see a single-malt cognac with 'tutti-frutti' flavor."[88]

THE ROLE OF THE STATE

Why would the Mexican government and the CRT allow the standards to become so watered down that tequila, which the CRT president called a "symbol of Mexico and legacy of all Mexicans," is increasingly indistinguishable from industrial liquors that are produced all over the world?[89] Although an influential group of industry elites has pushed for most of the changes made to tequila's regulatory infrastructure over the years, the role of the Mexican state is critical. Increasingly focused on promoting foreign investment and making Mexico "safe" for capital, the Mexican state has set up regulatory institutions that leave no space in which to consider broader dimensions of quality or ensure the representation of everyone involved in the production of tequila.

The General Directorate of Standards (DGN), part of the federal government, oversees for the process of writing, revising, and getting public feedback about all Mexican quality standards.[90] A number of provisions ensure representation of the different sectors and the public during the process of creating and modifying the standards.[91] Many of the people whom I interviewed, both from within and outside the government, were proud of the rigor of the system and the standards it had produced. However, the system itself is biased toward a technical understanding of quality, and this has contributed to a loosening of standards and the systematic exclusion of certain groups and issues.

These biases manifest in two ways. First, members of the committee that advises the DGN are heavily drawn from two groups: the biggest industry players, and government agencies charged with protecting consumer safety.[92] There is little opportunity for farmers, small producers, environmental groups, or community organizations to get involved. Moreover, because the standards are published in the *Diario Oficial* with little notice, many people might not even know about a proposed revision until it is too late.

Second, the procedure for creating, revising, and negotiating the standards rests on the provision of technical evidence and cost-benefit analyses. Fernanda Gutiérrez, a high-level official at the DGN, explained how the process worked. She said that if someone proposed to lower the maximum level of methanol in tequila, he or she would need to make a scientific argument about the potential impact on consumer safety. Further, the person proposing the modification would have to do a cost-benefit analysis, weighing the benefits of protection (primarily for consumers) against the costs of regulation. What Gutiérrez implied, but did not state explicitly, was the fact that other kinds of benefits—for example, for farmers, communities, or the environment—are rarely considered. She explained that the DGN does consider "authenticity" as a criteria for products protected by a DO. However, it is inherently difficult to prove, using scientific evidence, why a particular cultural practice is essential to a product's taste or key attributes. So, according to Gutiérrez, the DGN focuses on preserving only "the *minimum* characteristics that served to justify the DO."[93]

The Mexican regulatory system leaves little space in which to consider broader cultural or environmental dimensions of quality, even though Mexican law defines DOs as protecting "the natural and human factors" that make a product unique. In this context, it's almost inevitable that the standards and DOs will be watered down over time. The system privileges expanding market access and minimizing costs. This means that arguments about the importance of protecting cultural traditions—whether this entails particular agave cultivation practices or the use of pot stills or masonry ovens—won't hold up.

In 2012, in response to a proposed revision to the tequila standard, 372 people—tequila producers, academics, bartenders, and consumers—submitted a petition to the DGN. The petition suggested that the name "tequila" be reserved for spirits made with 100 percent agave, and that mixto tequilas, if permitted, be required to list the percentage of generic sugars on their labels. But the suggestions made no headway. In the official response, the DGN committee wrote that it had decided to reject the suggestions "because there was already an existing infrastructure" for producing mixto tequila.[94] Jorge Cruz, one of the people who organized the petition, told me that he felt that the DGN had used the signatories to increase the perceived legitimacy of the process. "We made a list of points," he said, "and they didn't take anything into account. But because we had made suggestions, they incorporated our names [into the documentation] to justify themselves, and there [in the standard] are our names."

It's tempting to believe that arguments based on technical evidence produce objective, value-neutral conclusions. But our faith in science can lead us to ignore dimensions—cultural, social, and ethical—that are not easily reduced to scientific analyses or calculations of risk.[95] In her analysis of disputes between French scientists and producers over issues of terroir, Geneviève Teil found that, for scientists who are unable to reduce it to "a stable list of determining factors," terroir is a "self-referential construction without any 'objective' referent," but that, for producers, terroir is a real object.[96] In Mexico, the entire regulatory system is focused on "objective" economic and technical criteria (to facilitate market access, guarantee consumer safety, and ensure product consistency), at the expense of the cultural and environmental systems in which these products are embedded. Moreover, the mechanisms by which standards are evaluated privilege elites with college degrees, and not farmers and workers.[97] The system provides no effective mechanism for keeping the power of the Mexican tequila companies and multinational liquor companies in check. And because of this profound imbalance of power, those who have maintained the legacy of tequila over generations are in danger of being eliminated altogether.

4 The Heart of the Agave

FARMING IN TEQUILA COUNTRY

The world of tequila is defined by stark contrasts, and while I was living in Guadalajara in 2006, I was reminded of these stunning contrasts on a daily basis. In the mornings, I interviewed the owners and managers of the distilleries, some in their glitzy corporate offices in Guadalajara's fanciest neighborhoods, others while touring their distilleries in Tequila or Los Altos. I waited in sleek lobbies, sipping coffee and admiring the secretaries' impossibly high heels, until eventually, after some minimum waiting period (the more important the person, the longer the wait), I would be ushered past the secretary's desk. The men (and handful of women) in charge were all exceedingly nice, and very proud of their tequila. Nearly all of them emphasized how far tequila had come. For them, tequila's story was one of success: for their own distilleries, for the industry as a whole, and for Mexico itself. Tequila had evolved from a cheap, working-class drink to the pride of Mexico,[1] and many people in the industry had gotten rich along the way.

In the afternoons, I took the one-hour local bus to the small town of Amatitán, where I was interviewing agave farmers. The buses were filled with mothers and children (sometimes packed three to a seat), candy and trinket vendors, traveling musicians, and factory workers returning

Figure 13. Agave fields in the Amatitán-Tequila valley, Jalisco. Photo by David Suro.

home from their jobs in Guadalajara. Nestled between the foothills of the Tequila Volcano and the valley of the Río Grande de Santiago, the Amatitán-Tequila valley is where the first tequila distilleries originated.[2] During the dry season, the sun is hot and almost unbearably bright, and it seems like the sky is always a vivid blue. The highway that connects Guadalajara to Amatitán (and then Tequila) is surrounded by agave: rows and rows of spiky blue agave plants, with the red soil scrubbed clean in between. Each afternoon, the bus would let me out by the side of the highway, on the outskirts of Amatitán, around four in the afternoon. By this time, families had generally finished their main meal of the day and were most likely to be home. I walked through the streets, trying to find the agave farmers on my list.

The people I interviewed were all registered with the CRT as having some land planted with agave. Some of them—those with relatively large agave plantations or good off-farm jobs—were doing okay, but most were struggling. Many had planted agave as an investment in their future but now doubted they'd be able to sell it when it matured. Others had rented out their land to another farmer or to one of the tequila companies, and worried that the pesticides that they were using would harm it.

In 2006, when I interviewed the agave farmers, the industry was enjoying record production volumes. But for the farmers in Amatitán, tequila's success had not trickled down. A surplus of agave had flooded the market, and the price had fallen below the cost of production. Many tequila companies weren't buying any agave from independent farmers.

The *agaveros*, or agave farmers, were worried and angry, even as they spoke with pride about the industry that gave their region its identity. They blamed both the tequila companies and the Mexican government for fostering an untenable situation. As farmer Ernesto Castillo told me as we sat outside his house, in a small village in the hills above Amatitán: "It's not fair that people are selling tequila for three hundred pesos per bottle, and then buying agave from the poor people for one peso [per kilogram]. If I could, this is what I would do—change the laws in favor of the *campesinos* [the farmers, or peasants]." Castillo continued: "It is not fair, if I invest over a period of seven years to bring the mezcal [agave] to maturity,[3] to get it ready for harvest, and then I go to the factories and they say, 'No! Go away!' The mezcal is going to rot in the fields. But the government doesn't care about us. If we are going to be able to grow mezcal here, we need a government that is also for us, for the poor."[4]

Tequila sales have more than doubled in the last twenty years, and tequila is sold in the nicest bars and restaurants in Guadalajara, Los Angeles, and New York. But as Castillo noted, the process by which the globalization of the tequila industry was achieved has marginalized the agave farmers and workers. New ways of organizing production, enacted by the largest tequila companies, are the key driving forces. The most vulnerable people in the supply chain are increasingly being excluded from the production process altogether. And the Mexican state, the legal owner of the denomination of origin (DO), plays a role.

THE LIVES OF THE FARMERS

By interviewing farmers, I hoped to understand the impact of changes taking place in the tequila industry on the communities where tequila is produced. After my many visits to the CRT, one of my contacts there finally gave me a list of all of the registered agave growers in Amatitán.[5] I randomly selected a group of names from the list, and then began traveling to Amatitán every day. I walked through the hot, dusty streets, knocking on doors and inquiring among neighbors and shopkeepers to try to find the people on my list. (This was harder than I had expected; although I had people's addresses, very few of the streets in Amatitán were labeled.)

I interviewed a total of twenty-seven farmers in Amatitán. Amatitán is the fourth-ranking municipality in the DO region in terms of the number of agave plants grown.[6] The Amatitán-Tequila valley is also recognized as tequila's birthplace. Solidifying the region's importance, in 2006, UNESCO awarded World Heritage status to nearly eighty-six thousand acres of the "agave landscape" in the Amatitán-Tequila valley.[7] The World Heritage designation has both symbolic and material consequences. Marie Sarita Gaytán notes that it "bolsters local tourism at the same time that it legitimizes the tequila industry as . . . intrinsic to Mexican national identity."[8]

Tequila is central not only to the identity of people in the valley but also to its economy. The region has few alternative industries, and the arid climate and largely unirrigated land make it unsuitable for most crops besides agave. As Rigoberto Navarro, a farmer who had been cultivating agave for forty years, told me, "Here . . . in all of the villages, we survive on nothing but agave."[9] About three-quarters of the people I interviewed depended on the tequila industry as their family's primary source of income. They worked on their own land as agave farmers, or they worked on other people's land as agricultural day laborers or *jimadores,* the workers who harvest the agave piñas. One person worked for a family who owned one of the tequila companies, but I did not interview anyone who actually worked in the distilleries, although the distilleries are also a source of employment in the region. The others farmed part-time. They held a variety of jobs—some were bricklayers or construction workers, for example, while another held a position in the local government—and generally cultivated a small parcel of agave as an investment or form of savings.

The amount of land planted with agave varied between farmers, from around two acres to almost four hundred, with a median of about twenty acres. Many people had started cultivating agave when they were very young. Ernesto Castillo, one of the first people to plant agave in his village, said he had a forty-five-year-old scar that came from the *penca*, or spine, of an agave plant.[10] A few farmers had planted their first fields of agave just a few years earlier, during the shortage that lasted from 1999 to 2003, when agave prices had reached record highs. And many farmers had gradually transitioned into becoming agaveros; they had started out growing corn, but as corn prices stagnated and the cost of fertilizers increased, they had shifted to planting more and more agave.

Farmers in Amatitán told two kinds of stories about the tequila industry. The first was the success story, the collective dream held by people who had grown up in the area. They were proud of their region's association with a product as famous as tequila, and they assured me that the best agave came from their valley. Santiago Morales, a thirty-six-year-old farmer who said he had been cultivating agave "all of his life," told me, "This is the region that produces the best agave for tequila. . . . There are other places where they also grow agave, but it isn't as sweet." Many farmers saw agave as an investment, a hope of building something bigger for themselves and their families, seven-year cycle by seven-year cycle. A few people's lives exemplified this "tequila dream." Over time, their hard work had paid off, allowing them to support their families and build a stable income. A couple of families had even financed an addition to their home or bought a car with the money from a successful agave harvest.

The story of Jaime Medina, a sixty-three-year-old farmer, was a classic example of what many people strived for. At age fourteen, Medina had started growing corn on his ten acres of *ejidal* land (the land distributed as part of the postrevolution land reform).[11] For a while, this was enough for his family to survive on; but when corn stopped being profitable, he and his wife moved to the United States. They lived in California for ten years, and they saved up to buy twenty-five additional acres of land. They cobbled together enough money to plant agave on their land; and when the agave matured, Medina took the money and planted more. Now, he had 156 acres planted with agave, significantly more than most farmers in Amatitán. But he still worried, because prices had fallen and he didn't think he could continue to support his family with his agave.

Although Medina had concerns about his future, his farm was now one of the largest in town, even though he had started out poor and had gone to school only through the third grade. Other stories like this circulated in

Amatitán: about farmers who had started with just a few acres of land and gradually expanded, staggering the ages of their agave plants to reduce their vulnerability to the cycles of surplus and shortage. These were the stories that kept people planting agave, even just a few acres, with the hope of a brighter future.

Some tales of success were even more dramatic, although harder to verify. For example, José Guadalupe Ortega, a forty-year-old farmer, told me about a person he knew who had made it big. "He was not very well-off. He was broke; he was not rich," he said. "Sometimes he wouldn't be able to drive because he didn't have [money to buy] gas, and this is how I know he was not rich." When the price of agave skyrocketed during a period of shortage, the man's fortune changed. Ortega recounted, "This man had a lot of agave, and he made millions of dollars—he went from having nothing to being a millionaire. He got rich. Some people had great fortune. There is a residential neighborhood in Guadalajara with very expensive houses, very nice houses, and he bought a house there. He goes back and forth between here and Guadalajara . . . and his kids are in private schools."[12] Indeed, for people who happened to have a lot of agave that matured during shortages like the one that occurred between 1999 and 2003, when agave prices reached sixteen pesos per kilogram,[13] the windfall could be huge. But in most years, the reality was much less spectacular.

A second kind of story was more representative of the lives of most small farmers: one of persistent poverty, uncertainty, and the transfer of wealth into the hands of a few. Another one of the farmers I met was Ignacio Guzmán, a fifty-six-year-old bricklayer with less than four acres of land, inherited from his father. Guzmán had tried to cultivate agave on his land, but he was forced to rent his land to his cousin when his wife got sick and they needed money. He explained that the tequila companies had refused to rent his land, because his parcel was too small and steep. His cousin had paid him about ten thousand pesos (close to one thousand U.S. dollars) for his land, and then took over all the work of maintaining the agave. His cousin would also get all of the money when the agave was harvested. It wasn't the deal that Guzmán had hoped for, but he didn't have many other options.

Guzmán explained that he had grown corn in the past, but that doing so no longer made sense. "You bring cheap corn from over there," he explained,

referring to the United States, "and the price here doesn't go up. A kilogram of tortillas costs seven or eight pesos, while a kilogram of corn costs
less than two pesos. . . . Before, everyone around here grew corn . . . but
now the chemicals [the fertilizers] that we use have gotten very expensive."[14] Guzmán hoped that after his contract with his cousin ended in a
few years, he might be able to plant his own agave. "It's better to plant your
own," he explained. "It's better for a person to care for his or her own land.
I made the contract out of necessity, because my wife was sick. Hopefully I
will be able to. You have to save up a little something." He seemed doubtful
that it would work out, though. "I pray that the agave plants won't be too
expensive," he said, referring to the price of the *hijuelos*, the infant plants
that represent the main start-up cost for an agave farmer. He wondered
what condition his land would be in when the contract ended, since he
didn't have any say in how it was being managed.

I also interviewed Avellino López Rubio, a sixty-year-old agricultural
day laborer who worked six days a week in the tequila companies' agave
fields. On Sundays, his day off, he took care of his own agave, which he
grew on little plots of land, "scattered here and there," over a total of about
five acres. Because he didn't have his own land, he rented it from other
landowners. The arrangement for all of his parcels was the same. The
landowner provided the land, and Rubio provided the hijuelos and took
care of the agave until it matured: fertilizing it, pruning and weeding it,
and applying pesticides as necessary to prevent infestations. At the end,
when they harvested and sold the agave, the landowner would keep 40
percent, while Rubio would get 60 percent. But he wasn't sure what price
they would get or if they'd even be able to find a buyer. When I asked
Rubio if he thought he would be able to sell his agave to one of the tequila
companies, he replied, "That is my hope, but there's no guarantee."

Rubio proudly showed me his tools—a long-handled spade called a *coa*,
which he used to prune the agave, and a machete that he used to cut back
the weeds. He told me that he was glad that I was interviewing a laborer,
someone who really worked in the fields, instead of someone who just
paid people like him to do their work. But Rubio was frustrated, because
he had time to work in his own fields only on Sundays. During the rest of
the week, he followed the instructions of the field manager who directed
the laborers. Rubio worried that as the tequila companies increasingly

grew their own agave, they were destroying one of the region's main sources of employment. "They have planted millions of agave plants," he said, "with their tractors and their herbicides, and it just goes on and on. What could be employing a hundred souls, they are able to do much faster. They are taking away job opportunities. The engineers are not mezcaleros."[15]

Stories like Guzmán's and Rubio's were not uncommon, and they epitomize bigger shifts taking place in the industry. In the past, farmers in the Amatitán-Tequila valley grew not only agave but also corn and other crops. But as corn prices fell—one study estimated a 66 percent decline in real producer prices between the early 1990s and 2005—farmers shifted to agave almost exclusively, especially given the lack of irrigation in the region.[16] People remembered times, like the period of shortage between 1999 and 2003, when agave farmers had "gotten rich overnight." But by 2006, when I did these interviews, the tequila industry was again experiencing a surplus of agave. The price had dropped below the cost of production, and almost 20 percent of the farmers in my study reported a net household income of less than zero for the previous year. Many farmers doubted that they would be able to sell their agave when it matured. They told me that the tequila companies weren't buying from small farmers like them, if they were buying at all. Some farmers had formed associations in order to better negotiate with the tequila companies; the associations staged massive protests from time to time, blocking the entrances to the distilleries until the tequila companies agreed to buy from them. But, as in the past,[17] they hadn't been very successful in pushing for any meaningful changes, and the government wasn't doing much to help.

People were desperate. If they couldn't find a buyer for their agave, they would be forced to let it dry up in the fields, and the time and money that they had invested would be wasted. Some of them begged me, an ostensibly powerful outsider, to do something, to communicate how bad it was for the farmers. Others seemed to have given up. Rigoberto Navarro, who had eight acres planted with agave and had made no money during the previous year, told me, "The tequila companies won't buy agave from us . . . and there is no money. We can't sell our agave, and the people are completely ruined. There is very little commerce here, and it hurts all of us. It hurts us, the farmers, and it hurts the storeowners, because if we don't have money, the businesses are not going to be able to survive."[18] As Navarro noted, the effects of the cycles are compounded by the Amatitán-Tequila valley's dependence on the tequila industry. Sergio Calderón, a regional governmental official in Tequila, argued that the DO for tequila had led to a "monoculture of blue agave in this region." He continued: "If there is a virus in the agave here, we die of hunger. The problem with the DO is that people become so specialized that they forget about everything else. . . . This makes the region very vulnerable."[19]

PRODUCING CYCLES OF SURPLUS AND SHORTAGE

Growing agave is inherently complicated. Few crops require such a long time—between six and eight years—between planting and harvest, and the blue agave plant is vulnerable to insect and disease infestation. The long growing cycle makes it difficult to coordinate supply and demand; this has only become more complicated as the production has increased. But the cycles that have long plagued the industry are neither natural nor unavoidable. They are fundamentally linked to decisions made by people—agave farmers, tequila distillers, and people in the regulatory organizations—over multiple generations.

During periods of shortage, rising prices encourage farmers and land-owners to plant more agave. When the price of agave is high, the price of the hijuelos also increases, which multiplies the economic risk involved. This makes it even more devastating six years later, when prices fall, as all the agave planted during the last shortage matures. During periods of surplus, farmers often stop fertilizing their crops or being vigilant about preventing infestations of insect pests and disease. This increases the vulnerability of their plants. Others, unable to find a buyer, allow their agave to dry up in the fields. Farmers who can't sell their agave don't have the capital to plant new agave, and the low prices discourage others from planting. This leads to another shortage several years later, starting the cycle over again.

Many people assumed that the cycles of surplus and shortage were inevitable. A tequila importer explained, "When there is plenty of agave and the price for mature plants is quite low, [the farmers] don't replant because it looks like a losing proposition. They plant other things. . . . So what happens when that maturation cycle goes full course? Obviously, they are short of plants."[20] A *New York Times* article attributed the cycles to "cycles of nature, the laws of supply and demand, the thirst for margaritas."[21] But what these explanations miss is the complicity of the tequila companies, the regulatory organizations, and the government in creating the cycles.

1999–2003: AGAVE SHORTAGE

The shortage that took place between 1999 and 2003 was the worst that anyone could remember. The mid-1990s had been a period of surplus, and farmers abandoned their fields when the distilleries stopped buying agave. Fidencio Mercado, a forty-seven-year-old farmer who had cultivated agave his whole life, told me, "The agave dried up; it reached maturity, and no one would buy it. . . . There was a lot of land, entire fields, where the agave just dried up." In addition, an unusually cold winter in 1997 killed many of the younger plants.[22] Next, a series of insect and disease infestations struck the agave fields. A weevil, a fungus, and several different bacteria spread quickly throughout the region.[23] The weevil bored the edges of the agave leaves and stalks and also acted as a vector for the bacteria, which caused the piñas to rot.[24] The fungus moved quickly, attacking the base of the agave plant, causing the leaves to dry up and rotting the heart of the plant. It could wipe out an entire field in just a few months. By 1998, insects and diseases had afflicted up to 25 percent of the plants in Jalisco.[25] The farmers were scared, especially of the fungus, which they called *el SIDA*, or the AIDS of agave. Alfonso Domínguez, a sixty-four-year-old farmer who had been cultivating agave since he was a teenager, stated, "They call it 'el SIDA' because there is no cure for it. It is like a cancer."[26]

The agave plants in Jalisco suffered an incredible decline, with the inventory falling by 50 percent between 1997 and 1999.[27] The shortage was exacerbated by the increased demand for tequila that began in the mid-1990s. The average price of agave skyrocketed, with the real price of agave (expressed in 2014 pesos) shooting from around two pesos per kilogram in 1998 to twenty-eight pesos per kilogram in 2000, eventually reaching twenty-nine pesos per kilogram in 2002.[28] Many small tequila distilleries, unable to pay the exorbitant prices, went bankrupt.[29] Thirty percent of the tequila distilleries in Mexico were forced to shut down during the shortage.[30] The smallest distilleries were the worst off, but no one was completely insulated from the effects of the shortage; even the largest firms were forced to cut production volumes. Between 2000 and 2003, tequila production decreased by almost 20 percent.[31] Tequila prices increased by 20 percent or more; talk of a "tequila crisis" swirled around bars from Manhattan to Los Angeles.[32] One New York bartender even invented a margarita substitute called the "rum-a-rita."[33]

THE TEQUILEROS RESPOND

The agave shortage revealed how unstable the industry's foundation, the supply of agave, really was. In response, the CRT, in cooperation with research centers in Jalisco and other states, began investigating potential solutions. One study, on weevil infestations, recommended destroying plants with too many weevils so they wouldn't spread.[34] Other studies focused on identifying the most effective insecticides and fungicides.[35] Some of the big tequila companies hired their own scientists to do sophisticated research into plant breeding and production techniques.[36]

The tequila companies and the CRT aimed to develop technical solutions to their problems. But as Fidencio Mercado, one of the agaveros, told me, "No one, not even the engineers, could control it." What the tequila industry and the CRT failed to acknowledge was how the organization of the industry itself had led to the shortage. In their 2003 book on sustainability and the tequila industry, Ana Valenzuela Zapata and Gary Paul Nabhan argued that the epidemic was caused by the fact that the agave was cultivated in monoculture and further aggravated by the even age of the transplanted clonal offshoots of the agave plants, a direct result of the cycles of surplus and shortage. They concluded that the main problem was one of demographic vulnerability: two-thirds of the 200 million agaves in Jalisco had been planted within a few years of one another, and all were derived from the same clone.[37]

For scientists like Valenzuela Zapata and Nabhan, the crisis was a wake-up call to start paying attention to the way that dominant farming practices had increased the industry's vulnerability. "We told them this was going to happen," said Nabhan. "But they wouldn't listen to us."[38] To reduce genetic uniformity, they recommended intercropping (interspersing rows of beans or peanuts between rows of agave), allowing some of the agave plants to flower and cross-pollinate, and even considering allowing other varieties of agave to be used in tequila production.[39] Other people, like some of the farmers I interviewed, focused on the need for government intervention, in order to establish a floor price for the agave, stabilize the supply, or just help the farmers navigate the process of finding a buyer. In other countries and other contexts, there are many examples of governments or collective organizations intervening to prevent overproduction and stabilize prices, and this is especially true for collectively managed products like DOs.[40] This strategy would seem particularly appropriate in the case of tequila, given the challenges posed by agave's long growing cycle. As one newspaper article put it, agave farmers not only "have the typical farmer's worries of rainfall, blight, frost, and pests," but they also have "an economic forecasting burden that would faze Alan Greenspan."[41]

However, the organizations that manage the tequila industry did not try to collectively address the unstable social or environmental conditions that had contributed to the crisis. Instead, the CRT and the Secretary of Agriculture continued to fund research on technical solutions to the industry's phytosanitary problems, and the CRT took an inventory of all of the agave plants in the DO region. Meanwhile, the largest tequila companies focused on insulating themselves from future shortages by becoming more self-sufficient in their supply of agave. The result was an intensification of the system that sociologist Rogelio Luna Zamora calls a *neolatifundio financiero*, which roughly translates as a new financial estate, a reference to the colonial hacienda system. The new system allows the tequila companies to maintain their control over the supply of agave without holding legal title to the land (as they did before the revolution).[42]

The postrevolution land reform, which took place in the Amatitán-Tequila valley between 1927 and 1942, had shifted responsibility for the production of agave from the tequila companies and elite landowners to small farmers.[43] After this point, whether they sold their agave on the open market or had a contract with one of the distilleries, the farmers themselves grew the agave; they (and their families) provided the labor, and they made the decisions.[44] At the same time, the tequila companies exerted tremendous control over the price of agave, which did not rise above one peso per kilogram for decades.[45] Starting in the late 1990s, the largest tequila companies began buying up land or renting it from farmers. A contracting company, often affiliated with or directly owned by the tequila companies, took over the entire production process, bringing in the capital, machinery, labor, and other inputs needed to grow the agave. When they rented land from farmers, they paid an annual rent and/or gave them a percentage of the final harvest, but did not allow the farmers to make any decisions about how to manage the land.

As responsibility for agave production shifted from small farmers to the engineers employed by the tequila companies, traditional practices were replaced by an increasingly mechanized and chemical-intensive cultivation system. Practices like intercropping the agave with corn or beans or pruning the pencas of the agave plant to control pests have become less and less common.[46] The owners and managers of the tequila companies value the expertise of trained engineers over the recommendations of experienced but uneducated agave farmers. Gerardo Silva, who managed the supply of agave for one of the biggest tequila companies, told me how he had to "break" the farmers of their habits. "Unfortunately, the people in this area [Amatitán] are very particular," he explained. "They say, for example, 'We have to apply fertilizers, why? We have the soil, and the climate, and this is enough.' These are the kinds of ideas that they have. So, we are trying to break these idiosyncrasies, these customs."[47]

In assuming that the farmers' decisions resulted from their "particularities" or "idiosyncrasies," Silva failed to understand how farming practices are affected by the cycles of surplus and shortage. Although farmers do sometimes apply insufficient fertilizers or fail to maintain their crops, this is often because they can't afford to do otherwise when the prices are low. Furthermore, the tequila companies' sole objective is to grow agave as efficiently as possible—to produce big plants with a high sugar content in the shortest possible time frame. Farmers may have other priorities. To Silva, the farmers' skepticism about intensive cultivation practices reflected their "idiosyncrasies," while in reality it may represent their consideration of other factors. Farmer Ernesto Castillo described his view of the changes that had taken place in the industry. He said, "I have been

Figure 14. Blue agave (*Agave tequilana* Weber) plants, Amatitán-Tequila valley, Jalisco. Photo by Sarah Bowen.

cultivating agave since I was very little. Before, we had to prune the agave by hand. Now—not anymore, now they just spray a bunch of chemicals. It is easier. And before, the agave would take ten years to mature. Now it takes six or seven years, because they apply a lot of vitamins [fertilizers]." However, for Castillo, the increase in efficiency had come with costs. "Before, the agave was natural—it would take ten years, but the piñas were much bigger," he explained.[48] Avellino López Rubio, a farmer and day laborer, worried that the tequila companies were "destroying themselves" by letting the engineers, rather than small farmers like him, make all the decisions. Rubio told me, "The engineers don't know—they just read about it in books. They don't have the experience, and they don't know the agave plant." Rubio explained that the "old way" had involved using a coa to cut back weeds, but that now the companies just hired people to spray herbicides. He had tried herbicides, but said that he wouldn't use them again. "If I don't feel like pruning with the coa, I can spray today and tomorrow the soil is going to be clean, but this leads to soil erosion, while the coa doesn't do that," he said.

By 2006, the largest tequila companies were growing almost all of their agave themselves. However, in order to find sufficient quantities of land

and more complicit farmers, they had to move into new areas, places that were inside the boundaries of the DO but had no history of growing agave. The farmers in these areas were more likely to accept the terms of the contracts, whereas many farmers in the Amatitán-Tequila valley were adamant that they continue to grow their own agave, despite the risks. Some farmers seemed to see farming as a subversive act. For instance, Rigoberto Navarro explained that he had decided to continue cultivating agave, instead of renting out his land to the tequila companies, because the tequila companies wanted "to take all of the land, to become self-sufficient . . . in order to control everything." "That is what they want," he stated, "to be self-sufficient and to push us to the side. If we do that, what are we going to do? We need to work as well."[49] He emphasized that if all the farmers rented out their land, the tequila companies would eventually eliminate them.

The tequila companies' search for new land has altered the geography of tequila production. Until the agave shortage that lasted from 1999 to 2003, almost all of the agave used to make tequila was grown in and around Tequila and Los Altos.[50] But while Jalisco accounted for 97 percent of all the agave cultivated in the DO region in 2000, this had fallen to 81 percent by 2005 and just 71 percent in 2010.[51] Even within Jalisco, the tequila companies have moved into new areas. Agave grown in southern Jalisco, for example, represented just 2 percent of the total in the state in 1999 but 19 percent in 2010.[52] Luis García, the director of agricultural operations for one of the largest tequila companies, told me that his company grew only 16 percent of its agave in the Amatitán-Tequila valley (where the company had originated), compared to 25 percent in Los Altos, 35 percent in southern Jalisco, and 24 percent in the neighboring state of Nayarit.[53]

I interviewed farmers in southern Jalisco in 2004. Before 1995, there had been almost no agave planted in the region, but by 2004 there were more than five thousand acres of agave fields just in the municipality where I did my interviews.[54] Much of the land that was put into agave cultivation had been previously used to grow staple crops like corn. When one of the tequila companies arrived in the area in the mid-1990s, they offered farmers the equivalent of the value of one ton of maize (at the time, thirteen hundred pesos per hectare, or about four hundred U.S. dollars per acre), in addition to a small percentage of the final harvest, if they would rent out their land for agave cultivation.[55] This wasn't a lot of money; but given the low corn prices at the time,[56] unpredictable rainfall, and uncertain yields, it seemed like a good option. When I asked Rodrigo Nuñez, an ejidatario with five acres of land, why he had rented out his land, he told me, "[Before,] you would put a lot into the land [to grow corn] and the yields you would get would be low, and then sometimes the bank would have to loan you money and you would be left in debt." Many farmers in Nuñez's town had rented their land to the tequila companies, and most hoped to save enough money to eventually plant some agave of their own. Most, like Nuñez, lacked the resources to do this, but they couldn't forget how high agave prices had been just a year or two before. But in 2004, when I interviewed Nuñez and the other farmers in his town, the supply of agave had already started to recover. Agave prices were dropping, and it seemed clear that another surplus was on the horizon.

Ultimately, the tequila companies' increased self-sufficiency and their entry into new regions are strategies that, not surprisingly, benefit the tequila companies but offer few possibilities for farmers and rural communities. Marco González, a geographer, argued that because the contracts exclude the small farmers from the production process, they have failed to significantly improve farmer incomes and/or stimulate agricultural productivity.[57] Ecologist Daniel Zizumbo-Villarreal and colleagues found that as the tequila companies have moved into parts of southern Jalisco, they have undermined traditional agricultural systems like the *milpa* system, in which farmers combine cultivation of diverse varieties of agave and crops like corn, beans, and squash with the production of mezcal for local consumption.[58] Finally, some research suggests that the rental agreements allow the tequila companies to transfer the environmental costs of production (for example, those resulting from the overapplication of fertilizers and pesticides) to the farmers and then move to another area after exhausting all the resources.[59] In 2003, one of the municipal governments in southern Jalisco filed an official complaint with the office of the Secretary of the Environment and Natural Resources, accusing the tequila companies of overapplying agrochemicals, contributing to "deforestation, desertification, and erosion" and killing thousands of *guamúchil* trees planted close to the agave fields.[60]

FARMERS IN CRISIS

The tequila companies' strategy may not have been environmentally sustainable, but it worked, at least in the short term: the number of acres of agave planted each year grew, and tequila production rebounded. As the supply of agave increased, the price began to drop, from almost 29 pesos per kilogram in 2002 to around 20 pesos per kilogram in 2003, and then down to under 6 pesos per kilogram in 2004 (prices expressed in 2014 pesos). By 2006, when I interviewed the farmers in Amatitán, the real price of agave had fallen to between 2 and 3 pesos per kilogram.[61] It had become very difficult for small farmers to sell their agave. If they did succeed in finding a buyer, the price was at or below the cost of production (estimated by the CRT to be 3.78 pesos per kilogram as expressed in 2014 pesos).[62] My interviews reflected the farmers' desperation at that time. Alfonso Domínguez told me, "Agave is our life. If we did not have agave, we would be in ruins." Domínguez explained that with such low prices, the farmers in Amatitán were "very hard up, to be able to pay for the inputs." "It demoralizes us, because the costs are very high," he lamented. "If you can't sell your agave, [then] instead of earning money, you lose money."[63]

Again and again, farmers told me that the biggest threats to the industry were the cycles of surplus and shortage and the lack of a stable market for agave. I spoke with Santiago Morales, a thirty-six-year-old farmer who had planted about sixty acres of agave, all on rented land. Morales had always sold his agave on the open market, but this was getting harder and harder to do. He explained, "If you go directly to the factories, they won't listen to you. Right now—it is too much work; they aren't buying any agave from the producers. You can knock on door after door after door, and nothing."[64] Like most of the farmers I interviewed in Amatitán, Morales did not have an advance contract for his agave. Since the tequila companies had largely stopped buying directly from small farmers, he would have to accept whatever price he could get by selling his agave to an intermediary known as a coyote. By buying and selling huge volumes of agave, the coyotes maintain control over prices. They "buy it all, large quantities of agave," Morales said, disapprovingly. "They pay a certain price, and they sell it to the tequila companies for another one. And the producers sell their agave to them, even though the price is so low, because it is better than just letting the agave rot in the field."[65]

Many farmers called on the government to intervene. "I want the government to come here, to see the situation that we are living in," said Rigoberto Navarro.[66] Santiago Morales agreed. He stated, "The government should support the producer, too. Because a few years ago, they gave subsidies to the factories, and now, we can't sell our agave, and the government doesn't do anything. And the price is very low. And now, nothing. This is what we want—some support from the government. Because when the price got so high, the government helped the tequila companies out a lot. And now that the price is very low, they should support the countryside a little, don't you think?"[67] Ernesto Castillo, another small farmer, argued, "If I were part of the government, then I would make new laws, to change the laws in favor of the poor people, so that we could also cultivate agave. . . . I would not allow [the tequila companies] to buy or rent all of the land, to cultivate all of the agave. I would tell them, 'You can't plant all of the land with agave; you have to buy a part of your agave from the farmers, at a fair price.'"[68]

During previous shortages, the government had intervened on behalf of the tequila companies, most notably by reducing the minimum percentage of agave sugars. During a shortage in the early 1990s, the government even permitted tequila to be made with only 30 percent agave sugars for a brief period of time.[69] Yet neither the government nor the CRT seriously considered any large-scale, collective strategies to stabilize the price of agave or otherwise help struggling farmers. Instead, everyone stressed the need for organization among the farmers. For example, Manuel Romero, a top official at the CRT, explained, "We are starting an informational campaign, in which we are going to say, 'Farmer, my friend, plant in a responsible way, establish an arrangement with one of the tequila companies, plant with a contract arrangement, because if you don't, well, you are out of luck.'"[70] By focusing on how farmers needed to make more responsible decisions, Romero's perspective was not unlike those offered by the tequila companies, who also blamed the farmers. Luis García, an executive at one of the biggest tequila companies, stated that the cycles were caused by "a lack of order" among the farmers. "You can't prohibit people from planting what they want," he explained. "Sometimes the agave is worth a lot, and they earn a lot of money. In those times, everyone plants agave, without any order. So I plant, and I don't know who I am going to sell my agave to; I do not have a contract with a company. A lot of people do this."[71] When I asked him how to solve the problem, he answered, "We have to make a requirement, that if someone plants agave that they have to have a contract with one of the tequila companies."[72] A representative of the CNIT also emphasized the need for contracts, advocating the establishment of "a more direct relationship between the tequila producers and the agave producers, meaning that the agave producers would cultivate only as much agave as the tequila producers requested."[73]

The problem with all these perspectives is that they ignore how the tequila companies have contributed to the cycles. Furthermore, they do nothing to address the unequal power relations between the agave farmers and the tequila companies, or the fact that the tequila companies are increasingly unwilling to establish contracts with the agave farmers, particularly contracts that would provide the farmers with some degree of autonomy. In almost the same breath in which he explained that the industry needed to require contracts between the farmers and the tequila companies, Luis García told me that *his* company didn't do that anymore. "For almost all of our contracts, we do all of the work," he said. "We have almost no contracts in which we just buy the agave. We used to. In 2001, we bought 20 percent of our agave [from independent farmers]. Two years later, we had stopped."[74] Like many of the large tequila companies, García's company had become fully self-sufficient in its supply of agave.[75] Because the CRT and the federal government refuse to consider any collective strategies or regulations to regulate the supply or price of agave, they are allowing the tequila companies to push the agave farmers out of the supply chain altogether.

HARD TIMES COME AGAIN

The agave surplus continued to get worse. The price of agave dropped from between 2 and 3 pesos per kilogram in 2007, to 1.85 pesos in 2008, to 1.30 in 2009, where it stayed for the next two years (prices expressed in 2014 pesos).[76] With prices so low, many farmers abandoned their crops. It

became harder to find work as a laborer.[77] In my interviews with the agaveros in Amatitán, I asked whether some people were better farmers than
others. I expected them to tell me about certain practices or forms of
knowledge, but most people explained that good farmers were the ones
who had money to invest in their crops. Alfonso Domínguez laughed when
I asked the question, as if he couldn't believe I had to ask. The best farmers are the ones with money, he said. "The farmers are very poor, and to be
able to eat and maintain the agave—we don't have the resources. How can
you compare a rich person with a poor person? A poor person who wants
to be able to eat."[78] Many farmers said that, given the low prices and pervasive sense of uncertainty, they had stopped fertilizing their fields or had
become less vigilant about preventing insect and disease infestation. Lucio
Vega, a forty-eight-year-old farmer who had about five acres of agave
planted on rented land, explained, "What happened is that the [inputs]
that we apply to the agave, are too expensive. And afterward, the prices for
agave are very low. And sometimes it is not affordable [to maintain
them]."[79]

Because farmers are often unable or unwilling to invest in their crops
when prices fall below the cost of production, the economic and ecological
processes that drive the cycles are mutually reinforcing. The diseases and
pests that had afflicted 25 percent of the agave in Jalisco in the late 1990s
resulted, in part, from farmers abandoning their fields during the previous surplus. Almost ten years later, in 2006, Ana Valenzuela Zapata drove
me through agave-growing regions in the Amatitán-Tequila valley and
Los Altos, pointing out whole fields that had been abandoned. She predicted a severe outbreak of insects and disease. She was right; according
to an inventory conducted by the National Health, Safety, and Agro-
Alimentary Quality Service between 2009 and 2011, 40 million plants
were afflicted by insects or disease, and another 90 million were at risk.[80]
There were about 253 million agave plants in the DO region in 2010;[81]
this means that about half the plants in the region were afflicted or at risk.

As many had predicted, but few seemed to have adequately anticipated,
the combination of the low prices and the pest and disease outbreaks
led to another shortage. According to the president of the Chamber of
Blue Agave Farmers for the State of Jalisco, 30 million fewer plants had
been planted annually than were required in order to keep up with the

demand for tequila between 2009 and 2012.[82] Insect and disease infestations continued to spread. Agave became increasingly scarce, and prices began to rise again. The price of agave increased to four pesos per kilogram in 2013 and 2014 (prices expressed in 2014 pesos).[83] In 2014, the CRT announced that the total supply of agave had fallen from the previous year's levels.[84] To cut costs, the tequila distilleries began producing more mixto tequila and less of the 100 percent agave tequila. Whereas 100 percent agave tequila represented 60 percent of the market in 2011, this had dropped to 43 percent in 2013.[85] Total production volumes fell by 13 percent over the same period.[86] A 2014 article published in *Revista Quo*, a science magazine, warned that "tequila was in danger of extinction."[87] The article cited Rodrigo Medellín, a researcher at the Institute of Ecology at the National Autonomous University of Mexico, Mexico's largest university. Medellín warned that without a major change in the industry's agave cultivation methods, tequila could disappear within the next ten to fifteen years. According to the article, between 35 and 45 percent of the agave plants in Jalisco in 2014 were already afflicted by insects or diseases, and more were at risk.

The shortage meant that farmers with agave ready for harvest earned more than they had in years, but many had already lost their crops to infestation or stopped planting. The president of the Chamber of Blue Agave Farmers for the State of Jalisco called the agaveros "a species in danger of extinction," owing to the extremely low prices paid by the tequila industry between 2004 and 2012.[88] And many small tequila companies will likely close as a result of the shortage. Jorge Cruz, the owner of a high-end tequila company, predicted in 2013 that "very difficult times [were] coming, like we saw in 1999–2002, when [the small tequila companies] vanished." He explained, "These are very dangerous cycles, and they are coming. They are knocking on the door, they are here. I think that if the price continues to go up at the pace that it has been, . . . we are going to have many companies out of business."[89]

The deleterious effects of the cycles have spread beyond Jalisco, to other parts of Mexico. In 2013 and 2014, people reported seeing trucks from Jalisco traveling to Oaxaca to buy agave, even though the DO for tequila prohibits the use of agave from Oaxaca or anywhere outside the DO region. A mezcal retailer told me, "I don't know what's going to happen. . . . The resources have been tapped and there's not a lot of agave around anymore [in Oaxaca, where he worked], because these people from Jalisco are coming down and getting it."[90] In March 2014, the price of agave in Oaxaca increased tenfold in just a few weeks, and a newspaper article reported that the mezcal industry there was "on the verge of a crisis."[91] In the same article, the president of the Mezcal Regulatory Council predicted that the price of agave in Oaxaca would double by 2016. In October 2014, a group of producers in Oaxaca staged a protest of what they called "the lack of support of the government."[92] Under signs reading "Without agave, there is no mezcal," and "Tequileros, *espadín* [the species most commonly grown in Oaxaca] is not your mezcal," the mezcaleros dumped two hundred liters of mezcal in the streets.[93]

INVISIBLE WORKERS AND LABOR HIERARCHIES

Even more vulnerable and less visible than the agaveros are the people who work in the agave fields. (And in fact, as the tequila distilleries have become more self-sufficient in their supplies of agave, independent farmers are being converted into wage laborers who work for the tequila companies or for large agricultural contractors.) Very little of the work associated with the cultivation of agave is mechanized, and workers are needed to harvest (and then replant) the hijuelos (baby agave plants), prepare and fertilize the soil, maintain the plants (by pruning and/or applying pesticides), remove the *quiote* (the flower stalk produced by the plant),[94] and harvest the mature piñas. In 2005, the CNIT estimated that 12,000 farmers and 11,200 day laborers were involved with the cultivation of agave, in addition to 3,793 field employees, people who worked for the tequila companies and helped supervise the day laborers.[95]

Within the tequila industry, the *jimador*—the person who harvests the agave piñas—retains a particular symbolic significance. At most of the distilleries I visited as a tourist (as opposed to the visits that I did as part of an interview), our tour began with a demonstration by a jimador. The jimador, usually dressed in a pristine white uniform and sandals, would silently begin chopping away the pencas of the agave plant, until the agave piña was revealed. As tourists snapped photos, a guide narrated the proc-

Figure 15. Demonstration by a jimador during a tequila distillery tour, Jalisco. Photo by Sarah Bowen.

ess, emphasizing the jimador's expertise and his ability to select only the best piñas. As Marie Sarita Gaytán notes, the "combination of the jimador's silence, coupled with his quaint regalia, . . . reinforced the impression of the [tequila] company's venerable qualities, respect for tradition, and connection to a noble past."[96]

These romantic images conceal the low wages, deplorable working conditions, and chronic health problems from which jimadores suffer. In 2014, several colleagues and I met with a group of jimadores in Los Altos. They agreed to come only when we assured them that their supervisors would not find out about our meeting. The jimadores explained that they were part of a *cuadrilla*, a team of between ten and fifteen men who work together to harvest the agave, load it onto a truck, and then unload it in the factory. On a typical day, they get together around 5:30 in the morning, then travel in the back of a pickup truck to the field where they will be working. The trip can take up to an hour and a half. Often their day ends

Figure 16. Working jimador, Jalisco. Photo by David Suro.

after about eight hours of work, but if there is a lot of agave to be harvested, they may work twelve or more hours in a day, coming home after dark.

The cuadrilla receives 0.15 pesos for every kilogram of harvested agave. On average, the team harvests the equivalent of about three tons per person per day.[97] In total, on a good day, one jimador could make 450 pesos, or about 32 U.S. dollars. Incredibly, the jimadores told us that their pay had not increased in the last twelve years; even when the price of agave skyrocketed in 2002 and 2003, their pay remained the same. This was partly because they did not work directly for the tequila companies; instead, they were hired by an intermediary, a coyote. As noted earlier, coyotes buy and sell large quantities of agave; they also hire cuadrillas. The coyote negotiated a price with the person or company who owned the agave, then paid the leader of the cuadrilla, who divided the payment among the group after deducting the cost of gasoline for the truck. The jimadores told us that they were generally able to find work only two or three days a week. This meant that their total weekly wages were frequently less than 100 U.S. dollars, making it hard for their families to get by. "I have four children in school," said Hector Herrera, one of the jimadores. "There are a lot of costs, and I am getting 800, 1,000, 1,200 [pesos, or between 60 and 90 U.S. dollars] a week. And because there are so many bills to pay, it's not enough. We don't even have enough to eat."[98]

The jimadores suffer from more than low pay. They have no guarantee of work, and sometimes go long periods without it. The jimadores that I met with had finished up a job the day before, but said that now they would be without work for at least another month. "This is a slow month," explained Felipe Aceves, another jimador. "If they said, 'Look, I am going to have to stop, but I'll give you a little help—not much, but a little, so that you can eat,' . . . that would help us. . . . But they don't do that. They are focused only on themselves."[99] Their working conditions have gotten worse over time. They explained that a few years ago, the company or person who hired them would pay a separate group of workers to load and unload the piñas and split them in half or in quarters. Now, they are required to do all of that work themselves, but their pay has not increased. "[Before], we were getting 0.15 [pesos per kilogram], but we only had to harvest. So you would get home early and with good money [con su buena lana]," said Luciano Fuentes, another jimador. "Now we put in five extra hours [of work] that before we didn't have," added Herrera.

The jimadores also endured significant health problems, and none of them had health insurance. Because jimadores are paid by the piña, they must work quickly, and it is easy for jimadores to cut themselves with the coa, the sharp tool that is used to chop away the pencas. "If you cut yourself, you can go up to two weeks without being able to work," Fuentes told us. The jimadores also suffered from chronic health issues, including back problems associated with lifting the heavy piñas, which weigh more than a hundred pounds each on average.[100] The men we met were in their twenties and thirties but looked (and said they felt) much older. "What is bad," explained Fuentes, "is that this is a job that leaves you all bent over, with rheumatism. . . . Everything is starting to hurt, and we aren't going to be able to defend ourselves in old age. . . . We have nothing, they give us nothing [for the future]. . . . We are all going to end up screwed [*jodidos*]."

I asked the group whether they had seen pictures of the white-clad jimadores at the distilleries. "Yes," they replied, laughing. They explained, more seriously, that sometimes they were asked to dress in the white costumes and demonstrate the process of harvesting the agave for busloads of tourists. Sometimes the distilleries did not even compensate them for their time. "At times they call us to do that kind of work, but we end up losing money," said José Luis Camacho, another jimador. "They don't pay us."

Despite the deplorable working conditions they face, the jimadores are not the most vulnerable workers in the tequila industry. Workers are also hired as planters, fumigators, and loaders, with many people rotating between different types of jobs.[101] With a few exceptions,[102] other jobs in the agave fields pay less than what the jimadores make. The jimadores that we talked to in 2014 did other jobs when they couldn't get work as jimadores, and they said they were paid 200 or 220 pesos (between 14 and 16 U.S. dollars) per day to plant agave, apply chemicals, and cut back weeds.[103] Agricultural work is difficult and dangerous; workers regularly came into contact with harsh pesticides, and few precautions were taken (in terms of training or protective clothing, for example) to prevent pesticide exposure. Luciano Fuentes said that he had suffered from pesticide poisoning. "We didn't know that it was dangerous or anything," he said. "I started feeling dizzy, and I started to lie down. They took me to the health clinic, and they put me on a drip [an IV] and I drank a lot of milk. . . . Everything began to look fuzzy. I couldn't see very well."

As soon as he was able, Fuentes was back in the fields. Workers do not demand better working conditions or higher pay, because they are afraid that they will lose the little work they can get. There is currently a surplus of workers in the region, in part because the tequila companies started bringing in indigenous workers from Chiapas, Mexico's poorest state, about ten years ago.[104] Today, an estimated twelve hundred laborers from Chiapas live and work in Los Altos.[105] Native Jaliscans have retained the more specialized and slightly better-paying jobs (for example, working as jimadores), while the "Chiapanecos" are slotted into the most physically demanding and lowest-paying jobs. According to another study, a laborer from Chiapas noted, "There is almost no work. . . . The companies have started to pay very little, and you can't say anything or ask for anything else, because they know that there are a lot of people looking for work."[106] In addition to being exploited in the workplace, the laborers from Chiapas face discrimination and social exclusion.[107] For example, one researcher told me that housing for workers was divided between indigenous and nonindigenous, with the nicer rooms reserved for the nonindigenous laborers.[108] Employers rely on stereotypes based on ethnicity to justify the exploitation of the indigenous workers. One employer argued, "There are many differences between a worker from Chiapas and a worker from [Los Altos]. You have to tell them ten times in order for them to do what you want them to do. . . . They are like donkeys [*burritos de trabajo*]."[109] Racism is used as an instrument of exploitation and exclusion.[110]

In his ethnography of the lives and working conditions of migrant farmworkers in the United States, medical anthropologist Seth Holmes showed that class, race, and citizenship intersect to create hierarchies of structural vulnerability and suffering on the farm. Similarly, in the case of the jimadores and other farmworkers in the tequila industry, race and class form the primary fault lines of power.[111] As was the case of the berry farms that Holmes studied, the lower someone is located in the hierarchy—whether he or she is an independent farmer, a jimador, a farmworker from Jalisco, or a farmworker from Chiapas—the more structurally vulnerable and less visible that person is.

THE BREAKDOWN OF THE SOCIAL AGRARIAN PACT

The cycles of surplus and shortage reflect a system that is inherently unstable, exploitative, and unsustainable. In order to minimize their risk from the cycles that produce agave shortages, the large tequila companies have shifted production to new areas and begun growing their own agave, cutting the independent farmers out of the supply chain and increasingly relying on underpaid workers. The state is complicit in this process.

The land reform that took place nearly a century ago represented the creation of a social contract between the Mexican government and the formerly landless peasants whose marginalization had led (in part) to the revolution. According to Jorge Llamas, the land reform signified "the start of a slow process of construction of citizenship" among the campesinos, the peasant farmers.[112] Gabriel Torres describes it as a "social agrarian pact" between the state and farmers. The creation of the ejidos was a response to peasant farmers' demand for land, one of the most pressing demands of the revolution. It also fostered the assimilation of rural civil society into the new regime.[113] Within the tequila industry specifically, the land reform meant that the tequila distilleries became reliant on small farmers for their supply of agave. This led to various contract arrangements between the distilleries and the farmers. In addition, in the 1960s, the state began giving agave farmers loans to invest in their crops; and in 1975, the state financed a cooperative tequila distillery.[114]

Although the land reform and provision of credit were important developments—both within the tequila industry specifically and within rural Mexico more generally—it is important to put these events in context. As sociologist Philip McMichael and others have noted, the "development project" enacted in Mexico (and throughout the Global South) in the 1950s and 1960s focused on modernizing the production of staple crops like corn and wheat through green revolution technologies (for example, improved seeds, intensive irrigation, and chemical fertilizers) in order to feed the growing population of workers in urban industrial centers.[115] Between 1940 and 1970, a period of high population growth and increasing urbanization in Mexico, public investments were channeled to urban planning, road and airport construction, domestic industries, tourism, and the provision of basic services for urban residents.[116] Rural Mexico was largely ignored by the state, and agriculture began contributing less and less to the GDP each year—its share dropped from 18 percent in 1940 to 11 percent in 1970.[117] Nevertheless, some sense of a social contract was palpable, as the government pursued a development strategy focused on making Mexico self-sufficient.

The neoliberal reforms that followed the Mexican debt crisis of the 1980s have almost completely severed any social contract that rural people once had with the state.[118] In the last twenty years, the state has opened up the agricultural sector to foreign capital and trade, invested heavily in agro-exports (particularly "nontraditional" crops like fresh fruits and vegetables, as well as beef), and ended most guaranteed prices for agricultural crops.[119] Between 1990 and 2008, agriculture's share of Mexico's jobs fell from 23 percent to 13 percent.

Mexico's neoliberal turn is reflected in the evolution of the institutions that regulate the tequila industry. The revision of the quality standard, the establishment of the CRT, and new certification procedures all exemplify neoliberal priorities. These shifts are the tequila-specific manifestations of larger national priorities: opening up the market, privatizing state-owned institutions, and increasing transparency and accountability throughout the Mexican regulatory system in order to create a more favorable business climate for foreign investors.[120] These changes have had important effects on the agave farmers and rural communities in the DO region. If, before the 1980s, the state provided some modicum of support for rural areas—albeit uneven and unequal support—now these areas and the people who live in them appear to be on their own.

The standards that regulate tequila production say almost nothing about the quality of the agave and, in fact, have become more lax over time; this gives the tequila companies more flexibility in their sourcing arrangements and helps insulate them from agave shortages. Similarly, neither the state nor the CRT have taken significant steps to reduce the farmers' vulnerability to the cycles that produce surplus and shortage. Governmental officials and members of the CRT blamed the farmers for planting too much agave and talked about helping them plan their plantations more rationally. In reality, they have done very little to help develop and strengthen the organizational capacity of the agave farmers, and their focus on the farmers' lack of organization absolves the tequila companies of blame for their role in creating the cycles.

In 2012, a revision in the quality standard further shifted responsibility to the farmers. Farmers are now required to establish a contract with a buyer before they can register their agave. The standard also increases the reporting requirements for registered producers. According to CRT officials, these measures will help stabilize the supply of agave.[121] However, many of the tequila companies have stopped making contracts with small farmers, and the new rules do not include any provisions to help farmers access the market.

All of the official responses to the cycles of surplus and shortage share a common problem: they do not address the unequal power relations between the agave farmers and the tequila companies, and they fail to recognize the farmers' fundamental contributions to the quality and taste of tequila. Many of the farmers I interviewed pleaded for the government to help them by establishing a floor price for agave or changing the laws to require that the distilleries buy some of their agave from small farmers. Mexican law defines DOs as protecting "the natural *and human* factors" that give products their unique qualities and characteristics; the government thus has an opportunity—and, I argue, an obligation—to step in on behalf of the farmers. But in reality, the Mexican state's policies largely ignore the public good in favor of protecting private industry. Because of the lack of rules related to the distribution of power and profit within the chain, and the state's refusal to intervene on behalf of the agave farmers or agricultural workers, the largest tequila companies have become more and more powerful over time and have used the quality standards to further consolidate their power. The tequila industry looks increasingly like it did at the turn of the twentieth century, when the concentration of land and capital enjoyed by the big tequileros existed in stark contrast with what Rogelio Luna Zamora calls the "increased pauperization of the living conditions of the working class."[122] The agave farmers are being pushed out of the supply chain altogether, and the jimadores and agricultural workers who are so vital to the production of agave are rendered almost completely invisible, ignored, and exploited.

5 Making Mezcal in the Shadow of the Denomination of Origin

Eduardo Gallegos is one of many small mezcaleros in the highlands of northern Michoacán.[1] I met him in March 2010, when an acquaintance from the local university took me to visit his *viñata* (the word used to refer to "mezcal distilleries" in Michoacán). As we followed the winding road that led to Gallegos's property, the air began to feel noticeably cooler. He stood on the dirt path outside his house, which was barely noticeable in the dense thicket of pine trees that covered his land. Whereas most mezcaleros had seemed happy to talk with me, Gallegos treated me with suspicion. He almost immediately launched into a series of questions, to assure himself that I wasn't going to turn him in to the government for making uncertified mezcal. I answered his questions about my job and my background as honestly as I could, and after a few minutes he seemed satisfied. He led us, on foot, several hundred yards up a steep hill, to a small brick viñata in the forest clearing. I struggled to catch my breath as we chatted about his operation. Because Gallegos's mezcal is uncertified, his distillery is illegal. He told me that he mostly sold his mezcal to friends and neighbors, but that he also sold some in a town that was about two hours away by car.

Gallegos has been making mezcal for forty years. He believes that the key to good mezcal is the agave. Gallegos mainly uses *maguey bruto*

(*Agave inaequidens*), which historically grew wild in the region where he lives. He buys his agave from small farmers, paying them, as he always has, with mezcal: two liters of mezcal per load of agave. Gallegos explained that maguey bruto was more expensive than the blue agave used to make tequila, because it grows more slowly, usually taking between twelve and fourteen years to mature. As maguey bruto became harder to find, Gallegos, like most of the mezcaleros in the region, started adding small quantities of blue agave to his mezcal. However, he can't add too much or people will reject it, because then it would taste like tequila instead of mezcal. "We're used to the good stuff," he explained.

Gallegos showed me where he roasts the agave piñas: in a large dirt pit lined with stone. He then showed me his fermentation vats, which he had dug straight into the ground and lined with tile. The most interesting part of his viñata was how he distills his mezcal, using a method that has not changed much over the last four hundred years. Gallegos extracts the fermented mash from the fermentation vats. He pours it into a copper pan, which sits atop a brick-lined oven and below a pear-shaped clay pot, open at top and bottom. Once the mash is in the pan, Gallegos places a second copper pan, one with a rounded bottom, into the opening at the top of the clay pot, sealing it off. He then opens a spigot that brings cool water, transported through a hollowed-out log, into the upper pan. He maintains a wood-burning fire in the oven throughout the distillation process. The wood fire heats the mash; this produces steam that condenses on the underside of the upper pan because of the cool water in the pan. The condensation drips down into a simple funnel made from an agave penca (spine), which is set in the middle of the clay pot. The penca directs the mezcal into a bamboo tube. The tube sticks out of the middle of the pot and directs the mezcal to a smaller clay pot that sits outside the larger one. "Mezcal distilled in clay pots has a better flavor than mezcal distilled in copper stills," Gallegos told me proudly. Gallegos's system is distinct from the clay pot stills used by mezcaleros in parts of Oaxaca, where two clay pots are frequently stacked on top of each other. In general, however, many aficionados agree with his assessment. "If most mezcal is a kind of slow food," wrote one journalist, "then clay-pot mezcal is especially, and deliciously, unhurried."[2]

After our tour of the viñata, Gallegos invited us to taste his mezcal. He held a jicarra, a dried-gourd cup, under the bamboo tube, filling it with

Figure 17. Clay pot stills in a small mezcal viñata (distillery),
Michoacán. Photo by Sarah Bowen.

mezcal. He swirled the clear liquid around, showing me the bubbles it
produced. "This one is strong," he told me. "Around 50 percent." Gallegos
was using an technique passed down from earlier generations of mezcaleros. By looking at the size and quantity of the *perlas,* the bubbles that form
on the surface of the mezcal, and by seeing how long they last, a master
mezcalero can precisely determine the alcohol content of a sample of mezcal. For many people, this is an important aspect of traditional knowledge.
A historical account of mezcal production in Oaxaca argued that this

method was "the heritage of all of the mezcaleros." The author wrote, "For this reason, it bothers us when the chemical engineers or the retailers tell us that the perlas don't mean anything to them. . . . For the [mezcalero], the perlas represent the beads of sweat of our sons and of ourselves; they are our pride and a sign that we are artisanal mezcaleros."[3]

After he had assessed the mezcal coming out of the still, Gallegos went to a corner of the viñata and retrieved a bottle of mezcal, a sample that was, ironically, stored in an old tequila bottle. "This one is smoother," he explained, pouring it into jicarras.[4] I inhaled deeply and took a sip, even though it was before noon and I hadn't had much to eat for breakfast. It was smoky and spicy, one of the best I had tasted. Later, I gratefully accepted Gallegos's offer to give me some of his mezcal to take home with me. Since he had run out of the empty tequila bottles in which he usually stored his mezcal, he put it in an old plastic Coke bottle. He walked us back to the truck, and we began our descent down the hill. When I flew back to the United States a few days later, a guard at Guadalajara airport seized the bottle immediately. He seemed almost apologetic, but said that they couldn't let me get on the plane with uncertified mezcal.

Gallegos lives in a part of Michoacán that is included in the denomination of origin (DO) for tequila. If he had wanted to, he could have legally produced tequila. He also could have sought certification for his mezcal as an "agave distillate," either on his own or with an association.[5] But certification wasn't worth it, he explained, because he would have to pay for the bottles and the labels, and then pay taxes on top of that. After all of that, he didn't think he would get a substantially higher price for his mezcal. Our acquaintance commented that the certification process was like "throwing lambs to the lions." In this analogy, small producers like Gallegos were the lambs, while the government and banks represented the lions. Gallegos laughed in agreement. "I make good mezcal, and it doesn't make sense for me [to start the process of certification]," he said.[6]

There are thousands of mezcaleros who, like Gallegos, are unwilling or unable to join the formal market for mezcal. Some are outside the boundaries of the DO for mezcal. Others are within the designated territory but do not want to get certified, because it would require them to alter their production practices, or the costs are too high, or they do not trust the regulatory organizations. These producers exist in a liminal space: outside the legal realm, never captured in industry statistics and governmental records, yet a vital part of local communities across Mexico.

So far in this book, I have focused mainly on the tequila industry and on tequila's evolution into a standardized product managed by multinational liquor companies and shipped all over the world. But there are mezcaleros all over Mexico who are still making mezcal the way previous generations did: by harvesting wild agave from the hillsides or cultivating it in small plots, roasting the piñas in the ground, and distilling the fermented juice in wood-fired pot stills. Mezcal has retained the local specificity that tequila has lost; the type of agave and the practices used to make mezcal still vary from region to region. Every decision—the variety of agave, way the agave is cooked, method of mashing the agave, ingredients that are added (or not added) during fermentation, type of still, and water source—influences the taste of mezcal, producing mezcals that are both complex and diverse. Yet, in the early 1990s, the Mexican government took unprecedented steps to standardize where and how mezcal could be produced, to bring mezcal—and the thousands of small producers that make it—under its control.

The DO for mezcal delineates the region in which mezcal can legally be made, while the quality standard defines the parameters of the final product.[7] The Mezcal Regulatory Council (CRM) verifies that producers are complying with the DO and the standard.[8] The DO, the standard, and the CRM were all modeled directly after the parallel institutions that regulate the tequila industry. Advocates argue that they help ensure the quality and safety of mezcal and help mezcal producers compete with global spirits producers. But the institutions that regulate mezcal ultimately protect the interests of a small group of powerful elites more than anyone else. They threaten to make mezcal look more and more like tequila and to eliminate small mezcaleros from the supply chain altogether.

MAKING MEZCAL OFFICIAL

As I discussed in chapter 2, mezcal has a long history of clandestine production, largely in response to periods of prohibition and taxation, which have varied widely between states. In the 1940s, a handful of larger producers and bottlers began expanding their markets, at first mostly selling their mezcal in Oaxaca City and Mexico City.[9] In 1975, mezcal was first exported to the United States.[10] However, even as the size and scope of the market for mezcal expanded, most mezcaleros remained small, producing mezcal for their families and local markets. In a 1977 study of the industry, State Department attaché Mylie Walton wrote that, except for the commercial distilleries near the Pan-American Highway that ran through central Oaxaca, mezcal-making "was a small-scale operation carried on mostly by Indians who gathered wild agaves or cultivated them on village lands." According to Walton, when demand for mezcal was high, "any small river course back in the mountains [could] serve as the site for several makeshift palenques."[11]

In the 1980s, a shortage of agave drove more than one thousand small distilleries out of business. Many of the producers who were left began mixing their mezcal with cane alcohol. As described by writer William Foote, the "little mezcal [that] was still being produced had plunged to the category of rotgut at best, poison at worst."[12] Worried consumers started boycotting mezcal. By the early 1990s, the industry was in desperate need of change. The debates that ensued were linked to larger debates over the regulation and protection of local food systems. One group focused on preserving the traditional methods that distinguished small mezcaleros from Jalisco's industrial tequila distilleries. This perspective reflected the growing global interest in protecting traditional foods and drinks from the "sea of mass production" engendered by the global food system.[13] But the perspective that ultimately prevailed was one that emphasized following in tequila's footsteps, promoting the modernization of mezcal production and adopting protective institutions that embodied the Mexican government's embrace of neoliberalism.

In 1994, the National Chamber of Commerce for Mezcal submitted an official petition to register mezcal as a DO. The organization, assembled a few years earlier, was composed of large bottlers and producers, primarily from Oaxaca but also from Durango, Guerrero, San Luis Potosí, and Zacatecas. Pedro Mercade Pons, the first president of the Chamber, had been the first person to export mezcal to the United States, under the label Monte Albán; Jorge Chagoya, a member of one of Oaxaca's elite mezcal-producing families, succeeded him. The Chamber aimed to protect its members' right to produce mezcal and to advocate for regulations that would bring the mezcal distilleries in line with the strict sanitary and quality standards of foreign markets.[14]

Both the DO and the quality standard for mezcal were established in 1994.[15] Like the institutions that regulated the tequila industry, the DO defined *where* mezcal could be produced, while the standard outlined *how* it was to be made. Controversially, only five states (all represented by the National Chamber of Commerce for Mezcal) were included in the DO, even though at least twenty-four of the thirty-one Mexican states and the Federal Distict of Mexico have a documented history of mezcal production.[16] Furthermore, in designing the standard, the Mexican government essentially copied the standard for tequila, despite the fact that mezcal and tequila have very different histories and cultures of production. There are slight discrepancies between the two standards, but their underlying principles and many specific requirements are the same. Like its predecessor, the mezcal standard specifies the allowable ranges for the chemical properties of the final product and outlines the steps that producers must take to demonstrate compliance.[17] It provides precise definitions for the categories of mezcal (joven, reposado, and añejo). In two ways, the standard for mezcal is more restrictive than the standard for tequila: it requires a higher proportion of agave (80 percent instead of 51 percent), and it prohibits the exportation of mezcal in bulk. In addition, unlike the tequila standard, which states that tequila must be made with only one species of agave, the mezcal standard lists five species;[18] it also permits the use of additional varieties of agave provided that they are not used as raw material for other Mexican DOs (such as tequila or bacanora, a distilled agave spirit made in northern Mexico). But despite these differences, the standard for mezcal, like that which regulates tequila, is fundamentally oriented toward an industrial model, one that privileges economies of scale and technical efficiency over the the needs of small producers or the cultural or biological diversity of mezcal.

A standard is only as effective as the institutions that enforce it, and reforms made to the Mexican regulatory system in the early 1990s transferred this responsibility from the federal government to third-party (nongovernmental) organizations. Therefore, the CRM, a private, nonprofit organization, was created in 1997. The structure of the CRM is similar to that of the CRT. In 2003, the federal government accredited the CRM as an official certifying organization, which allowed it to finally began certifying mezcal producers.[19]

In the meantime, producers in several other states had petitioned to join the DO. Revisions were made to add parts of Guanajuato and Tamaulipas, in 2001 and 2003, respectively. In 2006, representatives of Michoacán submitted a petition to be included in the DO. The debate that followed dragged out over six long years; finally, in 2012, 29 municipalities (out of a total of 113) from Michoacán were added.[20] In 2009, the standard was modified so that the minimum amount of methanol permitted would be the same as that allowed for tequila.[21]

The volume of certified mezcal has increased quickly, doubling in a period of two years, from just a little over four hundred thousand liters in 2005 to eight hundred thousand in 2007.[22] Almost 1.5 million liters of certified mezcal were produced in 2014.[23] Mezcal exports, too, have increased. In 2014, 116 mezcal brands were exported to forty-two countries; in total, more than 1 million liters of mezcal were bottled for export.[24] The DO, the quality standard, and the CRM represent important steps in mezcal's transition out of the shadows and into more formal markets. But even more significant than the strides that the CRM has made to bring mezcal producers into the formal sector are the thousands of producers who have been left out. In fact, according to CRM representatives and others I interviewed, between 80 and 90 percent of mezcal producers are still uncertified.[25]

DRAWING MEZCAL'S BOUNDARIES

By definition, all DOs tie production to a particular geographic place. In the case of the DO for mezcal, the boundaries were determined somewhat arbitrarily, and they exclude mezcal-producing regions throughout Mexico. The National Chamber of Commerce for Mezcal, the organization that submitted the petition to register mezcal as a DO, was dominated by large producers and bottlers from a handful of states. Not surprisingly, those were the states included in the DO. People told me that the states that got in were simply the ones with the most powerful advocates. Paulina Reyes, a researcher who had been working for years with small mezcal producers in Guerrero and Oaxaca, explained, "At first it was just going to be Oaxaca. . . . I have talked directly with [the people from Guerrero], and they told me, 'We found out one day before that there was going to be a meeting, and so we went running, we went to the meeting, and Guerrero ended up inside the denomination of origin.' . . . The business owners [*empresarios*] from Oaxaca had friends who owned businesses in Zacatecas, Durango, and San Luis Potosí, and so they invited them."[26] Later, when representatives from other states petitioned to be added to the DO region, they were required to submit evidence of their regions' history of mezcal production. But there is no record that the original five states had to submit any evidence at all.[27] And because the DO region is so large, the territories included have little in common, in terms of either their geography or their mezcal culture. Ignacio Treviño, a biologist at the National Commission for the Knowledge and Use of Biodiversity (CONABIO), denounced the DO boundaries as "fictitious" and described them as "based on political, not environmental, boundaries."[28]

There are many communities where people have been making mezcal for generations—for example, in Puebla and southern Jalisco—that are still outside the DO boundaries.[29] Absurdly, this means that the people in these places cannot use the word *mezcal,* a generic term similar to *wine* or *whiskey,* when selling their spirits. In 2009, I attended a meeting in Mexico City between representatives of the federal government and mezcaleros from all over Mexico. At the meeting, a representative from Puebla, a state that still has not been allowed into the DO, pleaded for the government to "open up space to all producers." "We can't let the industrial producers in the protected states close off the borders," he argued.[30] Spirits consultant Thomas Evans wondered how it was possible that Puebla had been excluded, exclaiming, "They're not even on the docket. They're not even close. . . . They're not going to get in as long as the tequila producers have anything to say about it."[31] Many small mezcaleros believed that decisions about where to draw the boundaries were ultimately driven by Oaxaca's political and economic elites. Carmela Robles, a small mezcalera from Oaxaca, told me, "The state that defines the direction of the industry is Oaxaca. It's not Tamaulipas or Guerrero. It's Oaxaca."[32]

A recent conflict exemplifies the tensions between the mezcaleros who are inside and outside the DO's borders. In 2006, representatives from

Michoacán submitted a petition to add twenty-nine municipalities to the DO. They provided historical evidence of their state's four-hundred-year tradition of mezcal production, noting similarities between the way mezcal is made in Michoacán and in neighboring states like Guerrero. Carlos Toledo, the leader of an association of producers from Michoacán, told me that he felt it was an injustice that they couldn't put "mezcal" on their labels, because mezcal is part of the culture of Michoacán, something that "belongs to everyone."[33] But the mezcaleros from Michoacán faced an uphill battle; almost all were small and had limited resources, especially compared to the huge distilleries in Oaxaca and Jalisco that did not want to cede part of their market share.[34] Powerful institutions like the Secretary of the Economy for the state of Oaxaca and the National Chamber of the Tequila Industry, as well as associations of mezcal producers from Guerrero and Oaxaca, argued that Michoacán should not be allowed in. For six long years, people from Michoacán waited for an answer from the federal government. When I talked to Carlos Toledo in 2010, in the midst of their legal battle, he explained that the delay was for political reasons. "We presented our evidence to the government," he told me, "and we complied [with the rules]." But they still hadn't gotten a response. "We know unofficially that the states of Jalisco and Oaxaca contested—[that they] stopped or prohibited the inclusion of Michoacán—but those are political questions," he said.[35]

In 2012, to the surprise of many people, the mezcaleros from Michoacán learned that their hard work had paid off. The president of Mexico himself announced that the DO had been modified to add the municipalities from Michoacán.[36] A statement from the Mexican Institute of Industrial Property (the institution that regulates DOs in Mexico) highlighted the "mezcal corridor" that now stretched continuously from Oaxaca to Tamaulipas. It seemed like a victory for small mezcaleros everywhere; at last, the integrity of the DO had prevailed over political concerns.

The inclusion of Michoacán is a step in the right direction, but it does not negate critiques that the DO boundaries are both arbitrary and exclusionary. The boundaries are simultaneously too open and too restrictive. According to Mexican and international law, DOs should protect products that are made in a specific place, when both the reputation and the characteristics of the product are tied to that place. But because the DO region for mezcal is enormous, the landscapes, soil types, climates, and native agave species that constitute it are quite heterogeneous. This makes it impossible to argue that the mezcal DO has one characteristic terroir. Just as important, the DO excludes many mezcal-producing regions. By doing so, it prevents the mezcaleros in those places, many of whom have multi-generational histories of mezcal production, from selling their spirits as mezcal.

THE QUALITY OF MEZCAL

The quality standard for mezcal, too, manages to be both too open and too restrictive. Because the standard is so general, it fails to protect the link-ages between specific places and the types of agave that grow there. The five species that are listed appear to have been chosen arbitrarily; the standard excludes species, such as *Agave cupreata*, that have long been used to make mezcal, while the five that are named are not even the most important. There is ample evidence of other species with strong, demon-strable links to mezcal production. For example, in a 2003 debate over the expansion of the DO territory, part of the argument that ultimately pre-vailed referred to "seven or more species, cultivated and wild, used in the production of mezcal."[37] At least twenty species of agave are commonly used to make mezcal, with some studies finding more than forty species associated with the production of distilled spirits.[38] However, as written, the standard fails to acknowledge this diversity of agave.

In addition, because the standard allows for the use of any "other spe-cies, as long as they are not protected by another DO," it allows mezcal to be made with almost any type of agave, whether it was historically used in a particular place or not. Mezcal producers are also not required to list the type of agave on the label. Producers frequently opt to use espadín (*Agave angustifolia*), a species known for its similarity to tequila's blue agave. In 2014, 77 percent of certified mezcal was made with espadín.[39] State gov-ernmental organizations actively promote the intensive cultivation of espadín. Victor Álvarez, the production manager for a high-end distillery, said that the government had campaigned to get people to "cultivate espadín, espadín, espadín," which threatened the diversity of agave grown in central Oaxaca, where his distillery was located.[40] Fernando Rosales, the owner of a midrange mezcal brand and a powerful player within the industry, told me that he exclusively used espadín simply because "at the level of the market, it is very complicated." He explained, "Pragmatically, [these other varieties] would generate very few liters. . . . So I am concentrating on a line of products that I know can function, that is already functioning, and one day I would love to experiment and have a more diverse line [of mezcals made with different types of agave], but this is not the time for me, at least commercially speaking."[41] Producers like Rosales use espadín not because of its historical importance or its flavor profile but because of its commercial viability: it can be cultivated intensively, and it has a high sugar content. However, the mounting environmental and economic problems associated with agave cultivation in Jalisco demonstrate the risks of exchanging a diverse system for one based on intensive monoculture.

Just as the standard says little about the type of agave used to make mezcal, it says almost nothing about particular production practices. Following the model of the industrial tequila distilleries, large mezcal producers are scaling up, incorporating more efficient technologies like autoclaves, diffusers, and column stills. At the same time, small producers have retained many of the traditional practices that have been passed down from generation to generation. Small mezcaleros almost always roast their agave in the ground. In many places, people mash the agave by pounding it with wooden mallets, either on wooden platforms or in hollowed out logs known as *canoas*. In other places, they use stone tahonas, pulled by donkeys or horses. Most producers don't add anything to their vats to speed up fermentation; this means that fermentation can take up to a month, with the time varying according to the type of agave, the way it is cooked, and the altitude, temperature, and natural yeasts in the location where the mezcal is fermented.[42] In some places, producers add a bit of pulque to their mezcal. Mezcaleros use wood-fired clay and copper pot stills, depending on the region, and in some areas they make their stills out of hollow tree trunks. What is incredible about mezcal is that it still has a deep connection to place. "This is terroir taken to the nth degree," writes one journalist.[43] However, the standard does nothing to protect these linkages.

Figure 18. Mashing agave piñas in a wooden canoa (canoe), Michoacán. Photo by Sarah Bowen.

Some groups of mezcaleros, organized under collective labels, have worked together to define common practices for the mezcals produced in their regions. For example, one association of mezcaleros developed a series of guidelines related to environmental, technological, and social practices (for example, storing and aging their mezcal in glass bottles instead of plastic bottles, and deciding how and when wild agave could be harvested). But initiatives like this have taken place outside the official institutions that regulate mezcal. The standard completely ignores mezcal's *gusto histórico*, the idea that traditional mezcals reflect the practices that have developed in particular regions. Carmela Robles, a small mezcalera, said that she dreamed of having separate DOs and guidelines for the mezcals produced in particular regions and villages: for example, one DO for *mezcal minero* (from Santa Catarina Minas, Oaxaca, a village known for its use of clay pot stills), and another DO for *mezcal miahuateco* (from Miahuatlán, Oaxaca). "And there are many more," Robles stated.

"More broadly, my dream is that there would be a legal framework . . . that would allow these regions to compete equally with the industrial zones." Robles explained that under the new standard that she imagined, small mezcaleros "would not be obligated to industrialize." She added, "The criteria for measuring quality would encompass more than just a physico-chemical study; the standard would protect the cultural elements that give meaning to the DO."[44]

DEFINING TRADITION

In the standard, there is no official definition of what constitutes a traditional mezcal, but most of the retailers and producers I interviewed agreed on certain principles that differentiate traditional mezcals from their industrial counterparts. Retailer Eric Weber stated that traditional mezcals, "made by farmers, [were] roasted in the earth over hot rocks, [with] no chemicals added, no chemical accelerators, fermentation completely by natural microbes, distilled in copper pot stills or clay stills with bamboo tubing, [with] no water added at the end of the second distillation. . . . Just pure mezcal."[45] Julio Ruíz, the owner of a mezcal bar in Guadalajara, argued that traditional mezcals should be made only from mature agaves, roasted underground, crushed by hand or with a tahona, fermented naturally, and distilled with pot stills. He also felt it was important that the flavors and aromas of traditional mezcals represented the communities where the mezcal is made.[46] Similarly, a Mexico City–based mezcal-education and -tasting organization defined traditional mezcals as those made exclusively from agave, cooked in earthen pits, fermented without chemical accelerants, and distilled in pot stills. The organization further noted that traditional mezcals should be at least 45 percent alcohol by volume and that they should strictly adhere to the "cultural, technological, and historical process that every region, community, and population has constructed throughout its history."[47]

Most small mezcaleros did not articulate formal definitions like these, but my conversations with them coalesced around many of the same points. For example, many mezcaleros said that they would never lower the alcohol content of their mezcal by adding water. For them, a higher

Figure 19. Demonstrating how to evaluate mezcal by looking at the perlas (bubbles), Michoacán. Photo by David Suro.

proof indicated that the mezcal was pure, that it had not been watered down. Carlos Toledo, a producer from Michoacán, said that he had seen mezcals with an alcohol content that ranged between 36 and 38 percent, but that those were "not really mezcals." "How can the standard allow these products to be sold?" he asked. "They need to revise the standard. . . . The percentage of alcohol should be 45 percent to 55 percent. To conserve and promote a traditional mezcal, it should be within this range."[48] Many purists agree with Toledo; there are many *mezcalerías* (mezcal bars) that refuse to sell mezcals with an alcohol content below 45 percent.[49] Discerning consumers look at the perlas produced by a mezcal—an indicator of its alcohol content—as a marker of its quality and authenticity. But the official standard allows the percentage of alcohol to fall anywhere between 36 percent and 55 percent, mostly in order to appeal to foreign palates.[50]

Most mezcaleros also agreed that the agave should be roasted in the ground, and that mezcal should be fermented naturally and distilled using pot stills. Not only does the standard fail to identify any of these practices as essential, it also makes it difficult for producers who are using traditional methods to comply. Alejandra Esquivel, a chemist working in an artisanal distillery in Oaxaca, told me that she thought the government had just copied the requirements established for tequila, without really thinking about how mezcal works or the fact that it is produced on a much smaller scale.[51] Specifically, Esquivel and others argued that the maximum acidity level permitted by the standard was too low. Esquivel explained that in order to get their acidity levels low enough to meet the standard, many small mezcaleros had to alter their entire production process. Indeed, a study of the chemical composition of artisanal mezcals concluded that slow fermentation, without the addition of anything to accelerate the process, favored the production of more acidic mezcals. The mezcals analyzed, all produced using artisanal methods, had acidity levels that were more than double the level permitted by the standard.[52]

Aficionados and retailers argue that the rule negatively impacts not just small mezcaleros but also the taste and quality of mezcal. Brand owner Eric Weber argued that the acidity levels permitted by the standard should be "higher, because the acids give great flavors." He explained that the effect was like that of "fine wines. What makes you salivate and makes you hungry is the acid in the wine. So it's discouraging, to say the least."[53] Even the leaders of the CRM thought that the acidity levels were too low. Emiliano Castro, a top executive at the CRM, told me that "40 percent of producers [were] outside the standard." He clarified that it wasn't "because they [were] adulterating their product, . . . but just because fermentation takes longer. And because they are artisanal, they can't control the acidity."[54]

Small mezcaleros and retailers had been pushing to revise the standard for years. One retailer told me that he had been on a committee to revise the standard since 1995, but said that they had made absolutely no progress over that time.[55] Many people believed that the standard had essentially been written by a handful of industrial producers, and that they resisted any changes that might threaten their ability to compete in the global marketplace. Only one modification has actually been made to the standard thus far—a revision made in 2009 that lowered the minimum level of methanol permitted, bringing it exactly in line with the standard for tequila—and it was pushed by, and serves the interests of, industrial producers. Methanol is produced during the process of cooking the agave;[56] although high levels of methanol are dangerous, exceptionally low levels are associated with the use of a diffuser, one of the most controversial innovations being adopted in the mezcal and tequila industries. In a 2012 newspaper article, one governmental official claimed that Casa Armando Guillermo Prieto, an industrial distillery that uses a diffuser, had bribed regulatory officials to modify the standard so that its mezcal could pass. The governmental official argued that the new guidelines jeopardized the credibility of the definition of what constituted certified mezcal. "Really, what they are producing is tequila, not mezcal," she said.[57]

By setting requirements that are almost impossible for traditional mezcal producers to meet, the standard encourages industrialization. The result is what critics call the "tequilization" of mezcal. Industrial distilleries use diffusers, autoclaves, and column stills. Small producers are encouraged to change their methods in order to achieve greater economies of scale and a more consistent product. For example, Julio Ruíz, the owner of a mezcalería, said that CRM inspectors frequently advised mezcaleros from Michoacán to start using stainless steel fermentation tanks instead of the wooden, stone, or leather receptacles that they had historically used. "It's not a requirement, but a recommendation," he said. He explained that the inspectors would tell the mezcaleros, "You have to improve your process, because your fermentation [process] is very slow, or you aren't getting enough yield from your distillation." Ruíz denounced the CRM's perspective as being "purely commerical," rather than also being concerned with "the cultural preservation of a tradition."[58]

In this context, many people worried about the fate of the small mez-caleros. "It makes me very angry," stated Ruíz, "that someone from Oaxaca can come to tell the producers in Michoacán how to improve their product, which they know nothing about. . . . It's a bureaucratic issue, and it's very sad."[59] Marco Rivera, who ran a Mexico City mezcal bar, told me that he thought it was incredible "that now they are saying what is mezcal and what is not mezcal." He continued, explaining, "The standard is very narrow and is obviously oriented toward industrializing everything. . . . I do see a bit of intention behind it, the way everything is industrializing, because of the control over hygiene and the quality. But in reality it is killing a possibility—these jewels—[the mezcaleros] who just have dirt floors, who are using horses. One day, they are going to say that they [the mezcaleros] can't do it this way. In reality, I believe that we could lose something."[60]

THE PRICE OF CERTIFICATION

The certification process itself is also exclusionary. Although the quantity of certified mezcal has increased considerably since the CRM was accredited in 2003, the CRM estimates that at least 80 percent of mezcal producers are uncertified.[61] Many people argue that the CRM's "one-size-fits-all" policy is not attuned to the needs of small mezcaleros. To become certified, every producer, whether he or she makes five thousand liters a year or fourteen thousand liters a day (the capacity of the largest distillery), must meet an extensive set of requirements.[62] First, the producer must submit the paperwork required to register with the CRM, providing a plan of work, information about where the mezcal will be sold, and a map showing where the distillery is located. He or she must also register the agave used to make the mezcal, submitting, for every agave field, another form that lists the species, number of plants, and year they were planted. Producers are required to take samples and analyze their mezcal at several points during the process. They must submit samples of their final distillation to a laboratory in Mexico City or Guadalajara to ensure that their mezcal meets all the requirements.[63] If they have met them, they submit another series of forms, first to the Mexican Institute of

Industrial Property, which is in charge of the DO, and then to the CRM. A CRM inspector visits the distillery to verify that the required steps have been completed.

This process is similar to the certification process for tequila. But tequila distilleries are run by technocrats who are used to managing large budgets and staffs, and the scale of production is much greater for a tequila distillery. For many small mezcaleros, just the idea of starting the certification process could seem daunting, if not impossible. Furthermore, in order to comply with the rules, producers are sometimes required to make substantial "improvements" to their distillery: to install a concrete floor, for example, or build a small laboratory to do the analyses. Many people cannot afford to do this. Mezcalera Carmela Robles told me that her family felt overwhelmed when they first learned about the certification process. "No one had warned us, and suddenly we had to do all these things that we weren't prepared for," she recounted. "So we had no money, we had a standard we had to comply with, . . . and we were scared because they told us that after 2004, uncertified producers wouldn't be able to sell their mezcal." Robles's family went to the CRM to ask about the requirements. "They gave us a list that was more difficult than you can imagine, impossible things that we had to do ourselves. The distillery was falling apart, and we didn't have any money," she recalled. "We had to have a warehouse to store our product. The distillery had to have a [concrete] floor, and we didn't have one. . . . But we got a loan, and we built the warehouse, put in some floors, started to go through the process. Everything was going well in terms of the chemical analysis—we were within the standard—but it seemed like [the CRM], instead of wanting to help us, was looking for ways to make us fail. The people working for [the CRM] never helped you, never supported you—instead, the way they treated you was to make you afraid."[64]

Robles thought that, over the years, the CRM inspectors had gotten better at working with small mezcaleros. But Paulina Reyes, who had worked with small producers in Guerrero and Oaxaca, said she thought the CRM inspectors treated the mezcaleros like children, without any respect for their knowledge or their reasons for making particular decisions. The social backgrounds of the CRM inspectors and the mezcaleros are vastly different. Most of the inspectors have college degrees but no

direct experience with mezcal production. On the other hand, most mezcaleros have little formal education but started helping their parents and
grandparents in their distilleries as young children. These differences
both reflect and exacerbate the inequalities in the industry and the way
the regulatory institutions privilege technical evidence and the advice of
trained engineers over the knowledge of "uneducated" mezcaleros.

Producers need to be certified in order to access more lucrative markets,
and especially if they want to export their mezcal. But for many small mezcaleros, the financial costs of integrating themselves with the formal market are prohibitive. Simply to solicit permission to begin producing mezcal,
a producer must pay an upfront cost of at least 8,400 pesos (about 632 U.S.
dollars).[65] Every month, they pay a per-volume tax to the CRM: a minimum of 0.40 pesos per liter of mezcal bottled for export or produced for
sale in bulk. Prices increase with greater volumes of production. The seal
affixed to every bottle, a guarantee of certification, is another 0.60 pesos
per bottle. Producers must also pay to ship a sample from every batch of
mezcal to a laboratory in Guadalajara or Mexico City for analysis of its
physical and chemical properties: this costs around 1,600 pesos (about 120
U.S. dollars), in addition to shipping costs. Producers are also required to
pay the travel costs every time a CRM inspector visits the distillery; because
many distilleries are located in isolated rural areas, far from the CRM
offices in Oaxaca City, the trips can be expensive. If an inspector needs to
do an extra visit because of a change in the production process or a modification made to the facility, the producer must pay 150 pesos per day, in
addition to travel costs. One study estimated that in total, the costs of certification could add up to 400 percent or more of the annual income of an
average small-scale mezcalero.[66] The costs make it impossible for small
mezcaleros to become certified on their own, and even cooperatives of producers cannot afford the costs without government subsidies.

Certified mezcal is also subject to incredibly high taxes. For mezcal sold
within Mexico, the Special Tax on Production and Services is 53 percent for
high-proof alcoholic beverages like mezcal, and the valued-added tax is 16
percent. The taxes paid for exported mezcal vary by destination country. In
the end, although the price that mezcaleros get for certified mezcal might
be double the price of uncertified mezcal, for many, it's not enough to
justify the added requirements and higher costs.[67] In anticipation of the

decision to raise the Special Tax on Production and Services from 50 percent to 53 percent in 2010, the president of the National Chamber of Commerce for Mezcal warned that the effect would be to move more and more mezcal producers into the shadows. "The tax increase . . . will hurt the entire supply chain," he said. "Many producers are going to have to close their distilleries, or worse, move into the informal sector. This means that sales of uncertified mezcal are going to increase, with the result that [these producers] won't be paying any taxes."[68]

While the costs of certification can be constraining for big producers like those represented by the National Chamber of Commerce for Mezcal, the barrier is almost insurmountable for small producers. Even the CRM seemed to recognize this. Discussing the administrative headaches and costs associated with certifying small distilleries, Emiliano Castro, one of the CRM's leaders, remarked, "As we say here [in Mexico], the soup ends up being more expensive than the meatballs. It would be very expensive, the structure of what we would have to do, to regulate all the uncertified mezcal." Castro explained that although they were making progress at getting more producers certified, one major obstacle was that the price premium that small producers got after certifying their mezcal was still relatively small. Even so, he remained curiously optimistic. "[Certification] is a huge job," he said when I interviewed him in 2009, "but who knows what could happen in three or four years?"[69]

A few years later, mounting evidence revealed that the CRM faced even greater challenges. In May 2012, the CRM's president and director were accused of having committed widespread fraud and embezzlement. This included transferring ownership of the CRM's Oaxaca City facilities, purchased with federal funds, to one of the elites in the mezcal industry; neglecting to pay taxes and employee wages; and committing fraud by purchasing laboratory equipment from foreign shell companies at artificially high prices and keeping the difference.[70] A new president took over and quickly distanced himself from his predecessors, condemning them for their actions. But the accusations of corruption and nepotism went far beyond the CRM, to other public and private institutions in Oaxaca. Oaxaca's ex-governor, Ulises Ruiz Ortiz, was denounced for granting 300 million pesos to distilleries owned by a handful of industry elites.[71] An investigation found that funds for agave cultivation allocated by the

Secretary of Agriculture had been transferred fraudulently and unequally, and that eight people had captured more than 50 percent of the almost 30 million pesos granted by the agency between 2010 and 2011. The investigation also found that Victor Chagoya, a member of one of the industry's elite families, had engineered the purchase of thousands of fake agave hijuelos, in order to capture funds from the Secretary of Agriculture.[72] Finally, another article accused the leader of a national mezcal organization of funneling 3 million pesos of the organization's funds to his own bottling plant. For the small mezcaleros and agave farmers, all of these examples represented the inherent injustice within the institutions that regulated the mezcal industry.

STANDARDIZING MEZCAL

The CRM's new president began working to reestablish the CRM's reputation and that of the certification process. In 2013, he called on producers to "get [yourselves] in order . . . because mezcal is in style: it is selling and it is profitable."[73] Two years later, with the release of its 2014 annual report, the CRM celebrated its success. The CRM announced that it had certified almost 1.5 million liters of mezcal in 2014, which represented an increase of almost 50 percent over 2011 levels.[74]

As I discuss in the next chapter, emerging evidence suggests that the CRM is earnestly trying to address some of the persistent inequalities in the industry. They have a long way to go, however. Almost all certified mezcal (94 percent) comes from Oaxaca.[75] In a pilot study in which the CRM randomly sampled 750 bottles of mezcal from fifty bars and stores in Mexico City and Oaxaca City, only 20 percent of the bottles were in full compliance with the standard, the DO, and other federal regulations. Ninety percent of the bottles lacked information that would permit consumers to trace the product down to the batch of agave. And mezcals that met the requirements did not sell for significantly higher prices than those that did not.[76]

There are still thousands of producers who are unable or unwilling to get certified. The institutions that regulate the industry exclude thousands of small mezcaleros, both explicitly (by drawing the boundaries in ways that leave out certain regions) and implicitly (by being associated with requirements and costs that are not viable for many producers). Some people blame the mezcaleros for their lack of motivation. One "mezcal educator" declared, "This idea that the standard hurts small producers is a lie." Instead, he argued, people chose not to get certified in order to avoid taxes or because they wanted to sell bad mezcal. "If there are producers . . . who prefer to die of hunger before integrating into the formal economy," he said, "forget them."[77] Others recognize the lack of democracy within the regulatory institutions, but don't propose to do anything about it. Fernando Rosales, a mezcal producer who had held influential leadership roles in the industry, admitted that the standard had been constructed "without consensus and . . . with a very short-term vision."[78] Even Emiliano Castro, the CRM representative that I interviewed, acknowledged that the standard did not protect traditional producers. He stated, "In fact, it's a copy of the tequila standard, and that is not reality. Mezcal is not tequila."[79]

It's true; mezcal is not tequila. The agave, the people, and the distilleries that produce mezcal and tequila have little in common. Tequila is made from blue agave, cultivated on a massive scale, while mezcal is made from many varieties of agave, both wild and cultivated. Tequila is made by (under)paid workers; mezcal is mostly made with (underpaid) family labor. The tequila distilleries are continually innovating, adopting equipment that allows them to achieve economies of scale, while most mezcaleros still roast their agave underground, chop their agave by hand or with a tahona, and use wood-fired pot stills. In 2014, 71 percent of certified tequila was exported, compared to 56 percent of certified mezcal.[80] More important, many small mezcaleros continue to rely primarily on local, informal markets. Given the vast differences in the cultural and social relations that underlie the production of tequila and mezcal, it is odd that the institutions that protect them are virtually identical. Victor Álvarez, the production manager for an artisanal mezcal brand, said that the problem with the DO and the standard was that the rules had been made "by bottlers, by industry executives, and by someone sitting at a desk in Mexico City who doesn't have the faintest idea what's underneath the production of mezcal. . . . Some of these rules are so bad that they were probably drunk." He explained that the DO and the standard were "supposed to protect the world of mezcal. And the problem is that the standard comes from the world of the bottlers and the technocracy and bureaucracy of Mexico, and they haven't come out to see the real villages where they make mezcal, to see how they make it and how they should protect it in the DO."[81]

For biologist Ignacio Treviño, of CONABIO, by forcing some producers to alter their practices, and by excluding many others altogether, the standard represented "an attack against culture, against identity, . . . a violation of human rights."[82] Indeed, for thousands of small mezcaleros in Mexico, making mezcal is not just a way to earn a living but also a central part of their identity: part of their families and part of their culture. As the market for traditional and artisanal mezcal has grown, this has generated new opportunities and new risks for these mezcaleros and their families.

6 Hipsters, Hope, and the Future of Artisanal Mezcal

I first heard about traditional mezcal ten years ago, when I began studying tequila. I wanted to go see the small mezcal distilleries for myself, and I even started planning a trip to Oaxaca, which never worked out. But I never could have predicted just how big mezcal was about to get. In 2009, an article in the *Los Angeles Times* called mezcal "the next spirits category," praising its "distinctive earthiness, herbaceous undertones, and elegant smoky qualities."[1] In 2010, Tales of the Cocktail—billed as the world's premier cocktail festival—gave its award for "best new cocktail bar" to a mezcal bar in New York's East Village. The following year, at the opening of a Museum of Modern Art exhibition of the work of Mexican muralist Diego Rivera, more than two thousand guests sipped cocktails made with an artisanal mezcal from Oaxaca. In 2013, an article in the *New York Times* noted the rising popularity of mezcal, describing it as "tequila's brash, more rustic cousin" and attributing the mezcal craze to consumers' growing appreciation for mezcal's "smoke and swagger."[2] And in its review of 2013's cocktail trends, *Food and Wine* magazine declared mezcal the "next mainstream spirit."[3]

The craft cocktail movement is fully under way in the United States, with everyone from Brooklyn hipsters to San Francisco techies looking for artfully mixed drinks. Growth in a wide range of alcoholic beverage categories, from bourbon to beer, is being driven by craft brands and microdistilleries.[4] Describing the explosion of craft distilleries and breweries in the last several years, historian Garrett Peck proclaimed that "in human history, there has never been a better time to be a drinker."[5]

In this context, mezcal's star has risen. A representative of ProMéxico, an agency that promotes Mexican exports, predicted that mezcal would become "the next tequila in international markets."[6] To be clear, mezcal represents a minuscule percentage—a fraction of 1 percent—of the spirits consumed in the United States. But the market for mezcal is growing quickly; exports of mezcal to the United States increased 114 percent between 2011 and 2014.[7] And as influential tastemakers extol mezcal's unique qualities, industrial tequila and mezcal distilleries have realized that small mezcal producers may encroach on their positions as the exclusive makers of Mexico's national spirits.

So how have traditional mezcals,[8] which until recently were almost exclusively sold and consumed in rural Mexico, made their way to gala events and hip bars in the United States? Many people partially attribute mezcal's meteoric rise to Del Maguey, the first (and for many years, the only) company to sell traditional mezcals in the United States. Del Maguey, meaning "of the maguey, or agave, plant," was founded by an American artist who first encountered traditional mezcal during trips to Oaxaca in the 1980s. According to him, it became too expensive to keep flying down to Mexico to bring back a few bottles of mezcal, so he started his own company. In 1990, he traveled to Oaxaca, where he searched for the right mezcal to fill a special bottle that he had created. "Every third day for three months, I went around dirt roads, asking Indians, Where is the best [mezcal]? And I brought back twenty-eight different samples from twenty-eight different makers," he told me.[9] He sampled the mezcals and chose the two best; in 1995, Del Maguey's first products hit the market: two single-village mezcals from Oaxaca. (Although many mezcals come from a single village, this was his own term, and he succeeded in trademarking it). Over the years, he added more mezcals to his line, from different villages and made with different varieties of agave. The artist-turned-"mezcal visionary" recounted, "I struggled for eighteen years, converting people one at a time, nose to nose. . . . And I changed the perception of what mezcal is . . . from diesel fuel with a worm to one of the most rare heritage beverages in the world."[10]

In the last few years, mezcal's growing popularity has prompted what *Saveur* magazine calls "a sort of gold rush in the Oaxacan hills, with importers combing the countryside for the best *palenqueros* [mezcal producers]."[11] In media coverage and in narratives employed by the retailers themselves, neocolonial evocations of exploration and discovery are common. An article in *Forbes* magazine reassured mezcal fans: "You don't have to wander the trackless cordilleras to taste the good stuff. A committed cadre of American bush scouts with *afición* in their hearts and a few pesos in their pockets have scoured the backcountry to discover and bottle the most ethereal versions and, in some cases, create their own."[12] Steven Adams, an American living in Mexico, recounted the months he spent traveling through the highlands of Oaxaca, visiting palenques and buying and tasting mezcals. Eventually, he found the one he wanted to sell under his own brand. Some retailers keep the methods and even the name of the *maestro mezcalero* (master mezcalero) secret, while for others, the specific practices and maestro mezcalero are an important part of how they differentiate their mezcal.

Mezcalerías have also popped up in Mexico and the United States. In Mexico, the government has not cracked down on sales of uncertified mezcal in bars, so bars can buy directly from small producers. At one mezcalería that I visited, drinkers could choose from more than forty mezcals, listed by region and type of agave. One of the priciest, at 120 pesos (about 8 U.S. dollars) for a *copita* (small glass), was made from thirty-five-year-old agave from Oaxaca. Laws in the United States make buying directly from small distilleries almost impossible, so bars buy their mezcal from retailers and distributors, who, in turn, work with small producers. Although regulations limit the mezcals available in the United States, the number of brands has increased substantially in recent years. A growing group of American bartenders and bar owners aims to promote traditional and artisanal mezcal. These mezcals are presented in contrast to what one bar called "flavored or flavorless agave spirits"—the industrially produced tequilas and mezcals that are made by multinational corporations and have no tie to Mexico's history or heritage.[13]

The retailers and bartenders who have brought traditional mezcals out of the shadows say that they are not motivated only by the market. Instead, they frame their work as part of a moral crusade to fight for the preservation of traditional mezcal and mezcal culture. They describe tequila as "a mezcal that has lost its complexity,"[14] and they emphasize that they are trying to forge a new path for mezcal, by fostering the development of consumers who recognize the diversity of mezcal and its deep roots in Mexican and indigenous culture. Their aims are noble, and most, I believe, are absolutely sincere. The retailers and bartenders and the small mezcaleros are inextricably linked; without the mezcaleros, there would be no mezcal, and without the retailers, the mezcaleros would not be able to access potentially lucrative extralocal markets. And yet the social and spatial distance between the retailers and the mezcaleros is hard to bridge.

MARKETING AUTHENTICITY

Mezcal's rise is no coincidence. In *Foodies: Democracy and Distinction in the Gourmet Foodscape*, sociologists Josée Johnston and Shyon Baumann explain that consumers increasingly reject haute cuisine—for example, fancy French restaurants with formal table-service—in favor of "real" food. Johnston and Baumann argue that foodie discourse coalesces around two key qualities: authenticity and exoticism. Authentic foods are "geographically specific, 'simple,' personally connected, connected to history, and linked to ethnic producers or consumers."[15] Exotic foods are those that are "socially distant" (from white, upper-middle-class consumers) and "norm-breaking," in that they violate the usual standards of the culinary and cultural mainstream.[16] Traditional mezcals are both authentic and exotic.

Mezcal's popularity is also tied to its status as an artisanal product. As Heather Paxson notes in her study of American artisanal cheesemakers, within industrial societies, the figure of the artisan "is an uneasy one, embodying cultural anxiety about middle-class status and security."[17] Artisanal producers—whether cheesemakers or mezcaleros—represent "what many Americans like to tell themselves about their own work ethic, family values, and community cohesion," but they also generate "unrealistic expectations for moral purity."[18] Both of these tensions underlie the relationships between the mezcaleros in Mexico and retailers and consumers in the United States.

For American retailers and bartenders, mezcal's authenticity is central to their love for it. As they take a risk on a product that is less established and more difficult to sell than Jose Cuervo or Patrón tequila, their ability to tell a compelling story is essential. They almost always paint a similar picture of mezcal: of a poor mezcal producer living in a tiny village that is almost impossible to get to, making mezcal as his father and grandfather did before him, using methods that have barely changed in hundreds of years. For example, Matt Clark, a bartender and owner of a well-known mezcal bar, told me about the revelation he had when he first visited a mezcal distillery in rural Oaxaca. He recounted, "I was outside, under a steel shack—you know, two fermentation tanks, not even tanks, wooden tubs. And I'm [thinking]: this is the truth. . . . This is the truth."[19]

Mezcal's American champions seek to protect what they see as an authentic mezcal culture. Lindsay Ruhland, a bartender-turned-mezcal advocate, said that she was drawn to mezcal's spirituality. She explained, "It's a beverage that's so ingrained in the culture of the people. . . . Hearing about the ritualistic use of those spirits that have gone back so many hundreds of years immediately resonated with me. I was hooked, and that was it. I didn't look back at all after that."[20] When retailer Eric Weber told me the tale of how he discovered one of the mezcaleros that he eventually ended up working with, he framed the experience as practically preordained. "We went from this village on up into an old wooded forest, [and] up to these peaks," he said. "I start going down into a canyon with the most beautiful wild agave growing out of the walls of the canyon. . . . And all of sudden there are eight Indians in front of us with rifles. . . . I go, 'Yeah, hey, have you heard of this guy?' And [one of them] goes, 'That's me.' Then he starts speaking in his native tongue to his buddies, and they pass a water bottle over full of a clear liquid, which he hands me. I always have a little clay cup with me; I pour some, and I drink the most exquisite mezcal you've ever tasted."

There is a saying in the mezcal world: "You don't find mezcal; mezcal finds you." People like Ruhland and Weber spoke of the maestros mezcaleros with reverence and awe, describing them as artists and craftsmen. According to Weber, the reason the mezcal he found in the canyon was amazing was "because of the hand of the maker." "Finally, what it comes down to—and this is another one of those God-given gifts—is . . . the art of distillation, that final flavor . . . that final, final art," he said.[21] Steven Adams, another retailer, told me that his goal was to "give the maestros mezcaleros, who [have] been laboring in obscurity, the credit they deserved."[22] Marco Rivera, who ran a mezcalería in Mexico City, explained that the most important aspect of mezcal was "what [was] beneath it . . . the old men, the people who are beneath it, who make it."[23] He portrayed the mezcal producers and their work as "overwhelming" and "magical." In response to a Facebook post about the future of artisanal mezcal, one American bartender wrote that his primary concern was "these guys who have done this all their lives, and their fathers before them and their fathers before them . . . and hopefully now their sons and grandchildren will do it." He continued, explaining that he cared "because something in the culture affects us, not just the mezcal in a bottle that I sell for $20+ a shot."

The bartenders and retailers I interviewed were earnest in their admiration for small mezcal producers. Although the disparities between the retailers and the mezcaleros are enormous, it's critical to acknowledge that the opportunities provided by retailers can be life-changing. The cachet of traditional mezcal allows—although it does not require—retailers to offer higher prices than local consumers can afford to pay. Many retailers see the ability to help small producers as an important part of their work. Thomas Evans, a wine and spirits consultant, told me that he promoted traditional mezcal because he felt it was his "mission to protect [small producers] and to make sure that they still have a future."[24] He told me a story about returning to the first mezcal village he had ever visited, after many years away. "This woman walked up to me and took me by the hand and walked me into the same room where I had tasted mezcal eleven years before," he said. "Now it had a roof, now it had a concrete floor, now it had a table. Back then it had a dirt floor, and at the altar, which every Mexican family has, you know, . . . was a picture of my buddy [a retailer] and [me]. She told me in absolutely flawless Spanish that on that day, her life began to change."[25] Similarly, Eric Weber described how his relationships with mezcaleros had changed their lives. "When I started," he recounted, "no one had a bathroom. No one had running water. No one had showers. And everyone slept on a dirt floor on a palm mat. And then [because of the money that the mezcal brought in] slowly everybody got beds and bedrooms; their houses are bigger. They don't sleep in one big family heap on one big palm mat. They've got showers; they've got toilets. Their lives have changed."[26]

In the isolated rural towns where most traditional mezcals are made, the effects of expanded market access can reverberate through entire communities. Of the villages in Oaxaca where he had worked, Thomas Evans said, "There's enough mezcal being sold now that there's a reason for them to be there; they have a job, and they can help. They can help their families, and they can be proud of their craft—and they don't have to leave."[27] In 2012, NPR ran a story about a tiny mezcal-producing town in Oaxaca. Half of the town's population had emigrated to the United States; but because of growing international demand for traditional mezcal, people had recently started to return to the village. Fabian, a mezcal producer, had been living in the United States, but one day his family called and said, "Come home. There's work now." He told the journalist: "The hope is that if mezcal's popularity keeps rising, everyone will come home to work."[28]

MONEY AND JUSTICE

It is undeniable that "outsiders"—from the United States, and from major Mexican cities like Guadalajara and Mexico City—have created possibilities for small mezcaleros that did not exist a decade ago. Before the mezcal craze, very few family distilleries were able to export their mezcal. But while some retailers are generous, some don't pay the mezcaleros enough to let them break even, and many retailers are deliberately vague when it comes to talking about how much the mezcaleros are paid.

Although generally forthcoming, most retailers were reluctant to discuss prices with me. Some said they paid "above market price" or that they let the producers decide, while others said they preferred not to give specifics. However, the informal conversations that I have had over the years have convinced me of two things. First, the prices that mezcaleros receive vary widely; second, it's impossible to tell from a brand's label or website how mezcaleros are treated. Over lunch one day, I asked a researcher who had interviewed hundreds of producers to tell me which brands were doing a better job of compensating producers. "That one pays well," she said, referring to a well-known, respected brand. I felt somewhat relieved. But she told me confidentially that another high-end brand paid only 35 pesos per liter, less than what it cost to produce the mezcal. (One report estimated the cost of producing traditional mezcals to be between 40 and 80 pesos per liter.)[29] "Some of the retailers will tell you that they let the producers decide the prices, but in such a depressed market the producer is going to say 35 pesos. The retailers that pay well do not say this," she told me.

Julio Ruíz, the owner of a mezcal bar, agreed. "[There are] producers who are selling mezcal for 200 [U.S.] dollars a bottle, and they are paying [the producers] 30 pesos per liter," he said. "It is completely unjust and absurd. . . . [If they are paying] 35 pesos per liter, or 40, 50, or 100 [pesos], in any case it is way too low. . . . It is stealing from the producer and from the consumer."[30] Ruíz recalled an event in Mexico City that he had helped organize. "There was [a well-known mezcal producer] . . . and she explained it perfectly," he said. "She said that if someone is paying a producer 100 pesos for a liter of mezcal, all that means is that the family is dying of hunger, because for 100 pesos per liter, you are sending [that family] into misery."[31] Ruíz bought mezcal directly from mezcal producers in his state and in neighboring states, and paid at least 250 pesos per bottle, paying higher prices for mezcals made using certain practices. However, he explained, when he asked small mezcaleros how much they wanted, they often asked for between 100 and 150 pesos per liter. According to Ruíz, one of the biggest challenge was getting the producers themselves to value what they were doing—their practices and their knowledge. Most small mezcaleros cannot begin to imagine that their mezcals could be selling for 200 U.S. dollars a bottle in the United States, to consumers who record their tasting notes and obsess over every detail of the production process. In this context, it is difficult for them to understand just how much their mezcal is worth.

Prices are the most critical measure of how a producer is being treated, but there are other factors that matter. Paulina Reyes, an ecologist who had worked with producers in Guerrero and Oaxaca, emphasized that the best arrangements allowed the mezcaleros to maintain their autonomy. Reyes felt that, instead of using contracts that specified everything producers had to do, it was better when retailers and producers worked together to adjust practices as necessary. She was skeptical of exclusive contracts, which require producers to sell all of their mezcal to one buyer. In some regions, mezcaleros have historically shared some of their mezcal for community festivals or other collective uses. If a contract prevents producers from contributing, it could isolate mezcaleros from the rest of the community. Reyes explained that even when producers were fairly compensated, their relationships with retailers could create tensions within communities, fostering competition and mistrust among formerly tight-knit groups.[32]

Unfortunately, while savvy consumers and bartenders are increasingly knowledgeable about the type of agave and the specific practices used to make their mezcal, they know little about how the mezcaleros are compensated. In addition, some aficionados have a tendency to romanticize "true" mezcal producers as those who value quality and not money— as opposed to industrial tequila and mezcal producers, whom they frame as focused only on their economic interests. In the Facebook discussion that I mentioned earlier, a bartender wrote, "When you go into the hills with your average mezcalero and they say a prayer before pulling [an agave] out of the ground, that has nothing to do with 'investment.' [They don't do that] because it's a good shtick or because it's a good investment. [They] do that because that's [their] culture. . . . Their investment is multigenerational, also—but it's not based on a spreadsheet." Stories like this reflect a sincere appreciation for mezcal culture. But at the same time, this kind of story also unconsciously emphasizes the distance between the retailers and consumers and the mezcal producers in terms of ethnicity, social class, and geographical location. If mezcal producers start making more money, and are able to upgrade their houses or send their kids to college, will their mezcal be as valuable? What if they decide to alter their methods to be less labor-intensive—for example, by using a tahona, or even a gas-powered machine, instead of mashing the agave piñas by hand?

This tension—between innovation and authenticity, between respecting traditions and stifling adaptation—underlies almost every discussion about the future of mezcal. When retailers told me that the producers they worked with had gotten running water or electricity, or that the people who had emigrated from the village had started coming back, their pride was clear. They cared about the men and women—and really, entire families—that they were working with. And yet the hope that these rural workers will be able to improve their lives, via the financial intervention of

American consumers, at some point conflicts with the narrative itself. The way these retailers market their mezcal depends, to some degree, on the mezcaleros remaining exotic, different from the wealthy consumers who are buying the mezcal.

THE POWER OF THE UNITED STATES

The mezcal craze had not gone unnoticed by the big tequila and mezcal producers, and they did not appreciate ceding a portion of their market share to a bunch of rural hillbillies. A few years ago, they responded by secretly advocating new laws that would make it even harder for mezcal producers outside the region for the denomination of origin (DO).

In late 2011, two controversial proposals came out within a month of each other. One, submitted by the Mexican Institute of Industrial Property, the organization that regulates DOs in Mexico, aimed to brand the word *agave* for the exclusive use of producers associated with existing DOs, such as tequila, mezcal, and bacanora. (The proposal was as if France had proposed granting exclusive use of the word *grapes* to winemakers in the Bordeaux region.) A proposal for a new quality standard, NOM 186, was published the following month. NOM 186 aimed to regulate agave spirits that were not part of the existing DOs. The new regulation proposed that these spirits be labeled using the word *Agavaceae*, the scientific name for the family of plants that includes the genus *Agave*, instead of the more readily understandable (and accurate) term, *agave*. It also allowed generic sugars to comprise up to 49 percent of the spirits' total sugars. The proposal even prohibited producers from listing the percentage of agave on their labels or marketing materials. This would make it impossible for consumers to distinguish between 100 percent agave spirits and other, less pure spirits.

The effect of the two proposed regulations would be to prohibit agave spirits producers outside the DO regions, who were already prevented from calling what they produced "mezcal," from using the word *agave* on their labels. The laws were pushed by the major players in the tequila and (registered) mezcal industries. As news about the proposals spread, retailers, bartenders, and aficionados on both sides of the border were outraged at what they perceived as a major threat to small mezcal producers outside the

DO region. Jorge Cruz, the owner of a high-end tequila brand and a Mexican restaurant in the United States, helped organize a campaign to protest the laws. He told me that in the private meeting in which he first learned about the proposals, one of the big tequila companies' senior executives casually remarked, "There are always going to be people who are screwed [*jodidos*], dear Jorge—that's just the way it is."[33] Although Cruz had come to expect this kind of behavior from the tequila elites, he was shocked by their blatant disregard for the thousands of families who would be affected. Bartender Matt Clark, who eventually became an informal spokesman for the movement, told me that he was infuriated by the fact that "the people who are making the most disgusting [tequilas]," people who don't "give a shit about any kind of quality," were telling small producers in certain regions that they couldn't put the word *agave* on "their 100 percent agave product that their family has been making since before tequila was even a concept." "It's insane," he added. "It makes me want to break things."[34]

But what could they do? Mexican law requires a sixty-day period for public comment on proposals like these. However, the unexpected release of the proposals, as well as the fact that the Christmas holiday came on the heels of the second proposal, limited the amount of time in which opposition groups had to mobilize. Jorge Cruz and a handful of influential bartenders, retailers, and academics in the United States and Mexico mounted a campaign to "stop NOM 186" and defeat the proposal to brand the word *agave*. Cruz recounted that the group considered hiring a lawyer to fight the proposals on legal grounds, but realized they didn't have enough money. Thus, he explained, they took the only avenue available to them: they publicized what was happening. They held fund-raising events to educate consumers, talked to the Mexican and American press, and circulated an official petition via social media.

In just a few weeks, the group pulled together a petition with almost two thousand signatures, many of them from American consumers and bartenders. An accompanying letter, submitted to Mexico's Federal Commission for Regulatory Improvement in late January 2012, argued that the word *agave* was not distinct to the existing DOs. It noted that at least twenty-four states had a long history of producing mezcals using diverse varieties of agave. The letter further asserted that NOM 186 "violated consumers' rights" and would create "barriers for the sale of artisanal mezcals," by preventing mezcal producers outside the DO regions from including information about the percentage of agave used in their mezcal. The letter contended that if it became law, NOM 186 would make it almost impossible for consumers to evaluate the quality of agave spirits. Overall, the letter stipulated that by threatening thousands of small artisans' ability to sell their products, the proposals would lead to the extinction of traditional mezcals. Importantly, the petition argued that the proposals would also further reify the DOs for tequila and mezcal, leading to even starker hierarchies between those protected by the DOs and all of the mezcaleros who were excluded from them.

The conflict began to attract international attention. In February, the *New York Times* reported on the "fight over who owns the word 'agave.'"[35] A well-known spirits website published an official editorial stance, concluding that the proposals constituted "a blatant example of bullying and anti-competitive behavior" that "threaten[ed] to destroy centuries-old traditions."[36] On Facebook pages and blogs, the proposals' opponents railed against the big tequila companies' outright attempts to appropriate mezcal culture and squeeze out small producers. An article in the *Village Voice*, in turn, reflected a more pressing concern of many consumers: it warned that if the Mexican legislation passed, "our Mexican liquor options [could] be limited in the future."[37]

Partly in response to the widespread opposition, two governmental agencies issued official statements denouncing the proposal to copyright the word *agave*, declaring that such a copyright would generate unfair advantages for producers of spirits protected by DOs, to the detriment of producers outside the DO regions. However, NOM 186 remained on the table. Opponents convened two forums, one held Guadalajara in March 2012, and one in Mexico City in May 2012, which I attended. They invited representatives from the tequila industry and mezcaleros from across Mexico, as well as government officials, retailers, bartenders, and academics. The organizers of the forum emphasized that their main goal was to hear from people who had not been given a voice in the drafting of the original proposal. They collectively formulated an alternative proposal and held a press conference in which they shared their views with the public.

At the end of May, a second version of the NOM 186 proposal was published for public commentary. The revised proposal backed down on copyrighting the word *agave*, but in many ways remained unchanged. In response, in July 2012, opponents submitted a second petition and letter, signed by 3,212 people from thirty-seven countries. The letter, generated out of the discussion at the two forums, argued that the federal government had not consulted the producers who would be regulated by the new standard. It also maintained that the labels proposed in NOM 186 failed to provide "valid, clear, sufficient information" to consumers.[38] Signatories argued that it should be easy for consumers to distinguish pure agave distillates from products that contained generic (nonagave) sugars. They also proposed requiring that each label list the species of agave, the region(s) where the agave was grown, the names of all of the ingredients in the product, and the place where the mezcal was bottled.

In August 2012, a committee of the Mexican Congress recommended that the proposal for NOM 186 be withdrawn.[39] In October, the director of the Mexican Institute of Industrial Property publicly admitted that their attempt to brand the word *agave* had failed. "Legally, there is nothing left for me to do," he stated, while continuing to insist that the institute "had recognized and proved" that the existing DOs had a right to the exclusive use of the word *agave*.[40] An announcement on a Facebook page created by one of the opposition groups thanked "all the spirits professionals, academics, and agave lovers who showed support to stop NOM 186, and keep the word 'agave' uncensored." It continued: "Your care and attention . . . help keep the industry fair and interesting."

The failure of both proposals is remarkable. It represents one of the few instances when small producers have triumphed over the large tequila and mezcal distilleries and multinational liquor companies. According to Jorge Cruz, the pushback came as a surprise to the tequila companies, who were used to having "carte blanche" within the regulatory system. The small mezcaleros were victorious because they aligned with elites from Mexico and the United States, and because their rhetoric focused on the need to protect consumers. The proponents of NOM 186 had argued that the proposals would protect consumers from unsafe products and misleading information. Its opponents succeeded in part because they, too, emphasized consumer rights, although they framed their argument very differently. For example, at the Mexico City forum, several American bartenders gave presentations on the growing demand in the United States for artisanal spirits, warning of the danger of alienating this important market. Reflecting on the campaign, Jorge Cruz said that it was the perceived power of the (American) market that ultimately made the biggest difference. "We had an impact only when we started to speak their language—money and markets," he stated. He recalled meeting with some executives from the large tequila companies and their lawyers. "They were going on and on, explaining that this was a democratic process," he said. "And I said that we are also democratic, and our [constituents] want to boycott. When I said the word *boycott*, that is when they started to pay attention."[41] Thomas Evans reiterated the influence of the American market, explaining that "78 percent of tequila produced is exported; of that 75 percent comes to the United States." "What that means to us, to me," he continued, "is the opportunity to do some good. We have a voice and they do listen, whether they like it or not. They have to.[42]

In this case, American retailers and bartenders forged a crucial victory for small mezcal producers. The mezcal producers would never have been able to fight the huge tequila companies by themselves. Julio Ruíz, the owner of a mezcalería in Guadalajara, explained, "What is good is that [these American bartenders and retailers] are having a big influence on the decisions the big companies are making. . . . I could have gone to the same meeting, and they would have told me, 'Good-bye, you romantic idiot. You do not generate millions in sales.' The U.S. market is big, and they have to listen."[43] In addition to opening up new markets, American tastemakers have helped introduce new conversations about how to regulate and protect agave spirits. But at the same time, in their enthusiasm they have also largely shaped the terms of the debate. The debate has focused on consumers to the detriment of producers, communities, and the environment. New models of change, ones that come from mezcal producers themselves, provide another perspective.

FROM COLLECTIVE TRADITIONS TO COOPERATIVE STRATEGIES

In 1995, when very few people in the United States had even heard of mezcal, two nonprofit organizations, one based in Mexico City and one that worked with indigenous communities in Guerrero, began talking about how they might promote economic and social development through the sustainable use of natural resources. They decided to work with small mezcal producers in Guerrero. "When we arrived," recounted a researcher who had worked on the project since the beginning, "we found definitive evidence of mezcal [production] since the end of the 1700s, which had been passed down through oral tradition. . . . We thought when we arrived that they were going to be harvesting the wild agave without any thought or plan." After holding workshops to better understand how the indigenous communities in Guerrero were managing their agave, the nonprofits realized that there was already a complicated system in place. "There were indigenous communities . . . that had maintained their social fabric, . . . their community institutions, and who had a very interesting system of organizing to harvest the wild agave," the researcher explained. "Sometimes it was for public consumption, sometimes they used it for community celebrations. They made the decisions about how it would be divided up together, as a group."[44]

The project began as a combined effort between the two organizations and the mezcal producers and agave harvesters in communities in the highlands of rural Guerrero. Over a period of several years, staff members from the nonprofits held meetings with the maestros mezcaleros and others in the region, asking them how they made their mezcal, what practices were important to them, and what challenges they faced. The producers formed an association and began working to collectively determine a set of guidelines for how to manage their agave and produce their mezcal. Their goal was to create a label under which small producers from the region could sell their mezcal. In 2004, after years of hard work, they launched Mezcal Sanzekan.

I met up with Candelario Atlatenco and Alfonso Villanueva, both of whom worked with the association, at a festival celebrating mezcal and pozole (a traditional pre-Columbian corn stew found throughout Mexico) in Guerrero's capital city, Chilpancingo. As they poured samples of mezcal for the crowds of people at the festival, and then later, over bowls of Guerrero's famous green pozole, Atlatenco and Villanueva explained how the association and the label worked. All of the producers who sold their mezcal under the association's label agreed to adhere to a series of rules, which covered everything from when the agave was harvested to how the mezcal was aged. Villanueva walked me through the requirements that producers had to meet. "It starts with the cultivation of the agave," he said. All of their mezcal was made with *Agave cupreata*, a variety that is native to parts of Guerrero and Michoacán.[45] The members of the association decided that they would allow people to harvest only mature agave plants, and that the agave should be allowed to flower, to guarantee a supply of seeds. Villanueva explained that mature, flowering plants were "ideal for mezcal."[46] The association also takes part in other activities, such as reforesting areas with trees to be used for firewood, replanting agave, and creating reserves to prevent overgrazing by animals, in order to conserve environmental resources in their area.[47]

Once the agave has been harvested, producers must start roasting it within eight days to prevent fungi from forming. The agave is always roasted underground. After mashing the agave, they ferment the juices in wooden (instead of plastic or metal) vats. Members of the association are prohibited from adding yeasts or chemicals to accelerate fermentation. They distill their mezcal in wood-fired copper or stainless steel pot stills. The association agreed that all the mezcals sold under their label should be between 48 and 52 percent alcohol by volume, meaning that the mezcaleros cannot not water it down, as some producers do.

The association's guidelines are much more detailed than those outlined in the standard for mezcal, and I asked Villanueva if it was difficult for the mezcaleros to comply with them. "No," he said, "because this is what they do. This is how they have always made mezcal."[48] Instead of imposing harsh sanctions, the members of the group use regular tastings and a checklist to ensure that everyone is meeting the standards. They help people adjust their practices when necessary. Villanueva explained that although members of the association sometimes disagree about the rules, the mezcaleros do not have trouble adhering to them, because the rules reflect the practices that are valued by the people in the region. In contrast, because the regulations for tequila and mezcal introduce a lot of unfamiliar requirements, they are costly and difficult for small producers to meet.

For Atlatenco and Villanueva, one of the association's most important rules is that mezcal can be aged only in glass containers, stored in an underground cave. Because the official standard for mezcal requires that mezcal be aged in oak barrels, as tequila producers do, the association cannot label its mezcal as "reposado" or "añejo." Instead, all of their mezcal, no matter how long it is aged, must be labeled as "joven" (young). I asked Atlatenco and Villanueva why they had decided to age their mezcal in glass. "The rule came from the producers," said Atlatenco, explaining that this is "the way they aged their mezcal, and how their grandparents and their parents aged their mezcal: in big glass bottles, buried underground." The association decided to build an underground cave where all the members could age their mezcal. They wanted to stay true to the practices of their ancestors, even though they knew that many consumers, especially those in the United States, would pay more for reposados and añejos.

They said they also preferred the way their mezcal tasted. Pouring a sample of their mezcal into a plastic cup for me, Atlatenco described it as having "the scent of cooked agave," with a transparent color—"maybe a little yellowish, but very little."[49] Later, he walked over to the booth next to us. He brought back some of their mezcal, which had been aged in wooden barrels and had a deep caramel color. "This one tastes like wood," he told me, grimacing. Although Atlatenco and Villanueva preferred the taste of their mezcal, they knew that not everyone agreed. Atlatenco explained that mezcal aged in wooden barrels was sweeter and smoother, which might appeal to people who were not used to the strong, distinctive taste of (traditional) mezcals like theirs. But he hoped that the association would continue using the glass bottles, as they "had always done." "This is part of our culture, something that we shouldn't lose," he said. "This is precisely where the taste and the quality of the mezcal come from."[50]

Mezcal Sanzekan represents approximately thirty communities, twenty-seven small mezcal distilleries, and 150 agave farmers and harvesters. Their mezcal is still not available outside Mexico, but it is sold in mezcal bars in Guadalajara, Mexico City, and Oaxaca City, and the association's maestros mezcaleros have hosted tastings all over Mexico. At one recent tasting, at the posh Quinta Real in Puebla, guests compared the association's mezcals. Each mezcal was made from the same variety of agave, but by different mezcaleros, each identified by name. One of the most important aspects of the association is how it integrates and recognizes the mezcaleros. The producers themselves own the label, and they collectively decide on the price of their mezcal. The year I visited, they had agreed to sell their mezcal for seventy pesos, or a little over five U.S. dollars, per liter of bulk mezcal. That seemed low to me, but they said it was double what many mezcaleros in their region were getting. And unlike many producers who work with a private retailer, members aren't required to sell all of their mezcal to the association; they can sell part of it under the collective label, and sell some of it directly to consumers.

Finally, the association aims to recognize and promote the work of each individual maestro mezcalero. In Guerrero and Oaxaca, commercial mezcal is often homogenized. This means that a bottling plant buys mezcal in bulk from many small producers and then mixes it together, making adjustments to create a consistent, standard taste for each brand. Mezcal Sanzekan does not homogenize the producers' mezcal; instead, all of it is "differentiated," meaning that each bottle is linked to a particular mezcalero. "We have to respect the flavor of each producer," explained another member of association. "It's like when you make food. Each cook . . . gives a unique touch to the flavor of the food. [By keeping the mezcals separate,] we are preserving a part of our culture and also maintaining the flavor of each producer's mezcal."[51]

Each bottle of Mezcal Sanzekan bears the name, signature, and village of the mezcalero who made it, as well as a number representing the batch in which the agave was harvested and roasted. Atlatenco explained that consumers would come back and ask for a certain producer's mezcal. The taste varies considerably from producer to producer, and even from year to year. Atlatenco believed that the flavor of each mezcal was shaped by the location of the land where the agave was harvested and the water that was used to distill the mezcal—in other words, the terroir, although I never heard anyone use that word. In fact, most members of the association have probably never heard of terroir. However, by recognizing the way the taste of their mezcal varies from producer to producer and place to place, what they are doing is celebrating and protecting the link between their mezcal and the place where it originates.

The day after the festival, I boarded a bus. Our bus twisted around mountain roads until we arrived in the town where the association was based, about thirty kilometers from the capital city. I was met by three members of the association: Feliciano Padilla, Calixto Díaz, and Justino Peña. We all squeezed into Padilla's pickup truck, and for the next few hours they took me on a tour. We started at the association's nursery, where they had begun cultivating infant agave plants that could be transplanted into their native habitats. We then stopped to talk to a group of men harvesting wild agave along a steep hillside, and we finished by visiting several distilleries (known as *fábricas* in Guerrero), nestled into the woods and perched on the edge of mountain bluffs. We also visited the association's cave, in a beautiful new building with a colorful agave plant painted on the door. Padilla, Díaz, and Peña proudly showed me the underground aging room, where rows of large glass bottles were carefully labeled and lined up on metal shelves, as well as the bottling area upstairs. The bottling room was almost empty, with a lone folding table in the middle of the room, but the vast size of the room suggested a sense of possibility.

The mezcaleros I met were kind but reserved. They weren't used to talking about what made their mezcal special; they were just doing what people in this area had always done. But at every distillery we stopped at, they shared their mezcal with me, offering a hearty "Salud!" and smiling as I took my first sip. What struck me most was that for them, their attention to craft and the quality of their mezcal was self-evident, not something that needed to be articulated. As a result, I felt a little sheepish as I asked each person the same questions. What traditions matter the most? What qualities of mezcal are important to you?

As was the case for the small mezcaleros I talked to in Oaxaca and Michoacán, the producers in Guerrero believed that the taste of their mezcal resulted from the combination of the type of agave that they used (and where it was grown) and their own practices. As we stood looking out over a valley that had been planted with agave, Díaz explained, "The engineers say that in this area, because it is hotter, the agave has more sugars. It is sweeter." He added that in the region where he lived, further up in the highlands, the hillsides were covered with trees, and so the agave didn't produce as much sugar. The production practices and skills of each mezcalero—the "hand of the maker," as some people refer to it—were just as important. At each distillery, mezcaleros showed me the pits where they cooked their agave, their fermentation vats, and their stills, explaining how each step of the process contributed to the taste of their mezcal. One

Figure 20. Roasting agave piñas to make mezcal, Michoacán. Photo by David Suro.

mezcalero told me that people in Guerrero "had developed a palate, an idea, in our head and in our stomachs, of what a mezcal should be: with the flavor of smoke, and the flavor of earth, damp earth."

The mezcaleros in Guerrero didn't compare their methods to those employed by producers in other places, because most of them knew only how people in their region made mezcal. Toward the end of our tour, I asked Calixto Díaz what traditions were important to him. He replied that his relatives had taught him "that the tradition of mezcal is to always drink mezcal during good times, out of happiness, and out of courage." Feliciano Padilla interjected, "This is something old," referring to their region's mezcal heritage. "We don't know how it developed, but for us it is something historical, and we are not going to lose it," he said.

Padilla, Díaz, Peña, and the other mezcaleros in their cooperative hope that if the market for their mezcal continues to grow, they might be able to preserve their region's traditions. Their goal is to one day export their mezcal to the United States or even to China. At one distillery, the mezcalero explained that he had just recently joined the association in order to try to sell more mezcal. This, he said, would allow him to renovate his distillery. "We're going to pave this whole floor," he said, pointing to the dirt floor that we were standing on. He also hoped to build walls around the distillery, so everything wasn't out in the open air anymore. Padilla told me that he hoped that as the market developed, it would bring more jobs to the region and prevent people from having to emigrate to the United States to find work.

But new market opportunities also come with new conflicts. Some mezcaleros wondered if the association's guidelines were compatible with export markets, where consumers demanded a smoother product, like tequila. Others worried that the increased demand for mezcal would lead to a shortage of agave, despite the association's strict rules about harvesting and replanting agave. Finally, some people worried about the burdens the standard created for small producers. "We are going to continue participating in all of the discussions of the standards," Candelario Atlatenco told me. "We respect the standard, and the standard should respect us, right? Above everything, with the standard, we want to [preserve] good mezcal, and the culture above everything. We don't want to lose that."

A NEW ERA FOR MEZCAL

Mezcal Sanzekan's story gives me hope, and there are other stories like this in the mezcal industry. A new generation of producers and retailers has begun working with the older generation—their parents and grandparents, and older mezcaleros all over Mexico—in interesting ways. People are combining traditional practices with savvy marketing strategies; Mezcal Sanzekan has a Twitter account! And a growing group of retailers and consumers increasingly rejects the rigid classifications of the DO and the official standards and is instead trying to forge more direct connections with producers—by traveling to their distilleries, bringing producers to Mexico City or Oaxaca City for tastings, or simply using labels to make the production process more transparent.

I visited Carmela Robles, a fourth-generation mezcal producer, at her family's palenque in Oaxaca. Robles works with her father and brother; her brother has taken over as the maestro mezcalero, while Carmela handles most of the regulatory paperwork and marketing. Carmela's family still uses the clay pot stills that are typical in her village; she believes that this, along with the many varieties of wild and cultivated agave that they use, gives their mezcal a unique taste. The Robles family is one of the few I met who managed to get certified on their own, without an intermediary. When I visited them in 2009, they were selling their mezcal at several bars and restaurants in Oaxaca and Mexico City; a few years later, their mezcal had made it to the United States. Carmela was in graduate school at a university in Mexico City, and she worked actively with other small producers and nongovernmental organizations to advocate changes in the regulatory system and the promotion of traditional mezcals.

Julio Ruíz is another example of a person working to preserve traditional mezcals. He and his wife opened their mezcalería in 2009. The bar focuses on what he calls traditional mezcals: made only from mature agaves, roasted underground, mashed by hand or with a tahona, fermented naturally, and distilled without column stills. A few years after they opened the bar, they started a nonprofit organization dedicated to educating consumers about traditional mezcals. Ruíz explained that, as the bar became more popular, they often didn't have time to share information about the mezcal with their customers, so they opened up a separate space for tastings and educational demonstrations. The organization buys mezcal directly from about fifteen small mezcal producers in the surrounding region; they sell it by the copita in the bar and in bottles in the tasting room. "Many times [the producers] do not have the capacity for bottling," Ruíz told me. "It is a way of helping them, by providing a source of income." I asked him what he thought about the future of mezcal. "It's always going to be a fight," he said. He joked that he had put away some bottles of mezcal for his toddler son, in case traditional mezcals disappeared before his son became an adult. But Ruíz was optimistic; he saw promise in the fact that the mezcaleros in Michoacán had succeeded at petitioning for inclusion in the DO region, in the defeat of NOM 186, and in the younger generation's increasing demand for traditional mezcals.

The stories in this chapter, and the people who are part of them, offer a hopeful vision of the future of mezcal. Consumers are an important part of this story. By choosing to appreciate the diversity of mezcal, a new generation of consumers—especially in Mexico, but increasingly in the United

States as well—are rejecting the standardization, industrialization, and Americanization that characterizes the tequila industry. Marco Rivera, the manager of a mezcal bar in Mexico City, said that his goal was to create "a mezcal sanctuary." "It scares us to talk about mezcal, it scares us to talk about pulque, it scares us to talk about our own products," he explained. "Mexico has always been a little *malinchista* in this sense,[52] always [bringing] things from the outside . . . rejecting the Mexican. . . . Mexican is [seen as] corrupt, cheap, crappy. And in reality, to the contrary, we see that Mexican can be at the highest level . . . in terms of the complexity of the culture, the architecture, the gastronomy, the products, the history. So here, our intention is really to value [what is Mexican] and move away from this cliché of Mexico—[the idea] that Mexico is just mariachis and tequila."[53]

Rivera was in his early thirties, and he believed that the revaluing of indigenous Mexican culture was part of a growing trend among people of his generation. And I saw evidence of this, especially in Mexico City, where young, relatively wealthy consumers packed into mezcal bars and *pulquerías*, historically places for poor and working-class men. Claudia Vásquez, a graduate student writing her dissertation on mezcal, said that she and her friends consciously chose to drink mezcal, instead of tequila or beer, as a reflection of their indigenous roots.[54] Carmela Robles said she was fighting to change the industry's regulatory institutions because "mezcal [was] not folklore." She argued, "Folklore is the degradation of culture, from my point of view, and we represent culture, not folklore."[55] For people like Robles, who advocate revising the DO and the standards to better reflect the diversity of mezcals that are produced all over Mexico, protecting cultural traditions does not have to mean locking mezcaleros into "museums of production."[56]

7 Looking Forward

In January 2015, the online magazine *Drink Spirits* offered its predictions about the trends that would most shape the spirits market in the next year. This is "finally going to be the year that tequila has a run," declared Geoff Kleinman, the magazine's editor. "All the agave love could spill over to mezcal," he continued, forecasting that the combination of increased demand for agave spirits and mezcal's "compelling craft story" could be "just what the category needs to finally start breaking out."[1] Even if mezcal does not manage to "break out" in 2015, the last few years have been good ones for craft tequilas and mezcals, and for craft spirits more generally. A 2014 article on trends in the tequila industry noted that tequila brands are increasingly focusing on the "traditional, artisanal aspects" of production.[2] Another article asserted that because of the "new appreciation for small-batch, high-quality spirits and those who make them," we are in the midst of "a great mezcal awakening."[3]

Consumers increasingly recognize—and are willing to pay for—mezcals and tequilas that are tied to particular places and traditions. There are more tequila distilleries using tahonas today than there were when I started this project. Traditional and artisanal mezcals, including mezcals made from diverse varieties of agave and clay pot stills, are getting easier to find in the United States. While almost none of the people I interviewed in 2006 mentioned terroir, talk of terroir now pervades the tequila and mezcal industries. Tequila companies emphasize whether their agave comes from the highlands of Los Altos or the Amatitán-Tequila valley, and the idea of "estate-grown agave" has gained traction in recent years. One brand even started bottling tequila made with agave from a single field. A 2013 article in *Difford's Guide* concluded that "terroir no longer needs to remain [an] elusive concept," but is instead "being used to create unique products, tequilas which showcase the rich elements of their heritage."[4] For traditional mezcals, the links to terroir are even stronger. "Mezcal tastes like the place it was made," proclaimed one bartender.[5] Bars offer flights of mezcal that allow customers to compare, for example, mezcals from different varieties of agave or by different mezcaleros. The labels for artisanal mezcals detail a litany of distinguishing characteristics, including the variety (or varieties) of agave, method of roasting, type of still, name of the mezcalero, and village where it is produced.

These trends give me, and many of the people I interviewed, hope about the future of artisanal tequila and especially artisanal mezcal. When I asked mezcalería owner Julio Ruíz about his vision of the future, he said he believed that people would "keep making good mezcals." "The tradition is going to continue, with all the good efforts that are happening. . . . And every day there are more people involved, and that makes me happy," he stated.[6]

SHIFTING REGULATIONS

A recent series of events suggests that the trends in the market may be starting to influence the Mexican regulatory system in ways that will benefit small producers. In 2012, a proposal to brand the use of the word *agave* for producers in the registered denominations of origin (DOs) was defeated by a group of small mezcaleros who forged an alliance with academics, activists, retailers, and bartenders from the United States and Mexico.[7] The same year, producers from Michoacán learned that after six years of waiting, their petition for inclusion in the DO for mezcal had been approved, despite opposition from the National Chamber of the Tequila Industry and large mezcal producers from other states.[8] And in May 2014, the CRM announced that it was proposing a radical revision to the quality standard that regulates mezcal.

Among other things, the proposal stipulated that all mezcal should be made with 100 percent agave. Producers would be required to list the percentage and types of agave used to make their mezcal, as well as any flavors or additives, on their labels. The proposal eliminated the parameters for acidity, which, as I discussed in chapter 5, had been a problem for many traditional producers. Furthermore, the proposal differentiated, for the first time, between "mezcal" and "artisanal or traditional mezcal," which it defined according to specific production practices. For example, the agaves for artisanal mezcals would need to be roasted underground, while other mezcals could be made with a masonry oven or an autoclave. The proposal banned diffusers and column stills altogether.[9]

The proposal represented a radical break with the existing standard, a near duplicate of the standard that regulates the tequila industry. Just as revolutionary, the CRM, in the process of developing the proposal, actively sought public feedback. After releasing the first draft of the proposal, the CRM held eight public forums throughout the DO region. The CRM invited producers and other stakeholders to debate, comment, and suggest modifications to the proposal.

Although some people felt that the proposal didn't go far enough,[10] on the whole, it reflected many of the arguments that I had been hearing from small mezcaleros, retailers, and mezcal activists for years. For the industrial giants, the proposed revision represented a significant threat. In particular, by prohibiting diffusers and column stills, the new rules would require Casa Armando Guillermo Prieto, Mexico's biggest mezcal producer, to completely alter its methods. Not surprisingly, the company fought back, sending a team of representatives to the public forums.[11] Casa Armando Guillermo Prieto asserted that, given the investments they had already made in their production facilities, they didn't think any restrictions on methods were valid. In a letter submitted to the CRM, the company's legal representative argued against "limit[ing] innovations made for the benefit of consumers, the environment, [or] production efficiencies," or restricting investments that could "generate employment and the growth of the category." The letter reminded the CRM that there might be useful technological innovations that had not been considered yet. "It would be a shame if [these technologies] were thwarted due to the restrictions of the standard," the letter stated. It concluded by explicitly arguing against a democratic decision-making process. "We are not in agreement with the procedure that you [the CRM] are following," the letter stipulated. "It should not be [decided] by a majority of votes. . . . Numerically, there are many more small producers who are not affected by this proposal, than the companies that have invested very important sums of money in the production of large quantities of mezcal."[12]

Observers speculated that the company, in addition to lobbying publically, was behind the assault against the proposal that was waged in the Mexican press. One newspaper article claimed that the proposal aimed to "practically restrict the production of mezcal to exclusively artisanal methods." The article described the proposal's critics as "asking, more than anything," just to be allowed "to participate in the construction of the new standard."[13] It failed to mention that the process of debating the revised standard was by far the most democratic in the history of the regulation of tequila and mezcal. An editorial warned that the proposal could "set the industry back, limit the growth of production, and establish a legal precedent" that could be reproduced in industries like the tequila and beer industries, which "have given Mexico prestige, international renown, and foreign capital inflows associated with exports."[14]

Despite the attacks from the press, the CRM presented its revised version of the proposal barely a month after releasing the first draft, at a final meeting in Oaxaca City. One observer described a "standing-room-only gathering of over 200 mezcal producers, bottlers, brand owners, and agave growers from all eight states in the mezcal DO region."[15] The final proposal represented a consensus between the different stakeholder groups. It continued to define all mezcal as made from 100 percent agave and prohibit the use of diffusers. It outlined three categories: "mezcal," "artisanal mezcal," and "ancestral mezcal." Controversially, the proposal defined ancestral mezcal as made using only clay pot stills, even though some producers argued that mezcaleros in their regions had used copper stills for generations.[16] (According to the proposal, artisanal mezcal could be made with copper pot stills).

The specifics of the proposal—for example, the decision not to allow the use of copper pot stills in the production of ancestral mezcal, and the decision to prohibit diffusers altogether—are important. If the proposed standard passes, these decisions will have enduring impacts on mezcaleros throughout Mexico. Overall, however, what is most significant about the proposal is the fact that it represents a major break with the status quo: a recognition of the fundamental differences between mezcal and tequila, and an attempt to account for the diversity of the traditions and environments associated with the production of mezcal.

There are still many steps left before a new standard is passed. The CRM has reportedly submitted the final proposal to the federal government.[17] It must first be reviewed by the General Directorate of Standards (DGN), the federal agency charged with crafting and revising all the quality standards in Mexico. An advisory committee will consult with the DGN throughout the process, and the draft of the standard will be published in the *Diario Oficial* for sixty days. During this period, the public will be invited to comment on it. Afterward, the standard will be revised to incorporate "valid public concerns and comments."[18] It could be months or even years before anything is passed, and it's likely that the final version will be further watered down. But for people who have spent years advocating more inclusive standards, the CRM's proposal represents an unprecedented moment in the history of the mezcal industry. "Now we have a regulatory framework that is broader and more diverse and far-reaching, which will enable our drink to become a product that is more crafted and less industrialized," proclaimed the CRM's president.[19] Observers lauded the CRM's decision to break with the tequila model, which focuses on maximizing volumes of production. They argued that the proposal reflected a European (and more specifically, French) approach that aims to develop markets by preserving quality, thus allowing for higher prices.[20]

THE PERIL AND PROMISE OF THE MARKET

Looking back at the changes that have taken place in the mezcal and tequila industries over the last few years, it is tempting to think that things might be starting to change. Finally, people are talking about how to define traditional mezcals: in terms of the varieties of agave, and of the people, practices, and places that are part of them. What practices are worth trying to preserve, and how should that be done? What parameters are needed to guarantee the safety and quality of mezcal, and who do they exclude? In considering these questions, the CRM appears to be making a concerted effort to listen to the perspectives of all of the people involved with the production of mezcal; unlike in previous years, small mezcaleros have been fairly well represented. In March 2015, just a few weeks before I submitted the final version of this book, the CRM provided further evidence of its commitment to small producers. In its annual report, the CRM announced that it would be proposing lowering the tax rate for artisanal mezcal producers (to 10.07 percent, compared to 53 percent for industrial producers).[21] Given the evidence that high tax rates are one of the factors that prevent small producers from becoming certified, this proposal, which has a precedent in other industries in Mexico, represents another important step in the crafting of regulatory policies that consider the needs of small mezcaleros.

I am cautious with my optimism, however, because both the regulatory institutions that have historically stifled diversity and privileged multinational liquor companies, and the movements that have emerged to challenge them, are emblematic of the same process: neoliberalism. Discussions about how to define and protect the culture of Mexico's agave spirits are still primarily conducted within the parameters of the global marketplace. Arguments on all sides have focused on the imperative of responding to the demands of the market and protecting consumer rights.

In late 2014, I observed a discussion among a group of Americans that illuminates some of the risks inherent in a market-based system. The group was talking about the CRM's proposed revisions and how the group might influence them on behalf of small mezcal producers. Daniel Pérez, a Mexican academic who had joined us, raised a provocative point. The best thing the government could do, he said, would be to "leave them [the mezcal producers] in peace." "How can you standardize this great biodiversity, when each producer does things differently?" he asked. "I am tired of revising and revising and revising the standards."[22]

"But this could be problematic," said one spirits consultant. She felt that the group should show its support for the progress that had been made. Pérez disagreed. "All of the cases of regulation of agave distillates in this country have been a mistake," he said. "Every time they standardize, they leave all the richness [of these distillates] outside the standards." "[But] we have to be realistic," contended Jorge Cruz, the owner of a high-end tequila brand. "We dream of supporting standards that would truly be inclusive."[23] Most of the people around the table nodded.

Zach Johnson, the owner of a well-known mezcal bar in the United States, raised his hand. "I think that one thing we all think . . . is that we're entitled to mezcal being exported," he said. "We're assuming that the relationship we have, through our enthusiasm, is positive, because it's easy for us to enjoy the lifestyle we like so much, which [necessitates] standards. . . . So we want to turn the standards into something workable and positive, and it just might not be possible. Whether we're creating a better- or worse-case scenario, . . . it still may contribute to the extinction of the culture, through the exportation of mezcal." Another bartender objected. "There's not going to be mezcal without a standard," he said. "Of course it's not going to solve all the problems. But for now—it's a compromise. It's as good as we hope to get."[24] Others nodded in agreement.

"Is something better than nothing?" Essentially, this is the question that the group was debating, and one that anthropologist Sarah Besky asks at the end of *The Darjeeling Distinction,* an ethnography of how fair trade certification works in the context of large-scale tea plantations in India.[25] Her conclusion is that, while it is clear there is a market for justice, the market is not just. The fair trade and DO designations that she studied "involve a disciplined forgetting of the colonial histories, unequal power relations, and structural inequality that remain fundamental to the functioning of [tea] plantations," writes Besky. "The message of this book is that these simply cannot be willed away."[26] In a book about a very different topic— farmers' markets in Berkeley and Oakland, California—Alison Hope Alkon comes to a similar conclusion. She explains that proponents of the "green economy" embodied by farmers' markets and other alternative markets "attempt to redefine capitalism not as an exploitative system that must be overcome or restricted in order to protect people and the environment, but as a tool to create a more just and sustainable world."[27] However, Alkon finds that the marketplace does not treat environmentalism and social justice equally. In particular, affluent consumers are willing to pay premium prices for environmentally sustainable products, but social justice does not carry the same premium. "Working only through the market makes it difficult to address inequality," Alkon argues.[28]

MOVING BEYOND MARKETS

Besky's and Alkon's conclusions, like the questions raised by Zach Johnson, are unsettling. As educated and socially conscious consumers, we want to believe that our purchasing decisions—whether that means buying fair trade coffee, local produce, or traditional mezcals—can make a difference. Maybe they can. But it's also true that in a system based on "voting with your dollar," people with more dollars have more votes.[29]

This is true in the tequila and mezcal industries; the right to define what constitutes "tequila" and "mezcal" extends as much from market power as it does from a sense of tradition or justice. As Heather Paxson notes, notions of terroir and the "taste of place" have the potential to offer small producers a means of accounting for the "'spectrum of values' provided by their artisan labor" and the contributions of their environments. But as the concept of terroir has gained value in the global marketplace, it has become less certain that small producers will have the final say on what *terroir* signifies.[30] Instead, they will cede this power to affluent consumers and retailers. And the interests of wealthy consumers, no matter how committed those consumers are, are not always going to line up with what's best for producers, farmers, or workers.

Given that consumers do not necessarily value social justice, environmental sustainability, or the preservation of cultural traditions—and certainly do not prioritize them all equally—mechanisms for change must go outside the market. There is a need to move beyond market-based models in order to create more democratic, participatory, and inclusive ways of protecting, valuing, and preserving local foods and drinks and the people who make them. In Mexico, the system that protects and regulates DOs is based on a fundamentally neoliberal model: one that aims to protect markets for Mexican producers while creating as few barriers as possible. The representative of the DGN told me that the standards aim to "preserve the *minimum* characteristics that served to justify the DO."[31] In a context like this, it may be difficult, even for organizations like the CRM, to justify establishing rules to differentiate between industrial and traditional mezcals. My interview with a representative of the Mexican Institute of Industrial Property—a person who helped manage all of the DOs in Mexico—made the government's priorities clear. He told me that the factor that best predicted the success of a DO was "whether the product [had] a market presence, and whether the market was big enough." He explained that tequila was more successful "because it has a long time in the market, it has a big market, and it is consumed in many places and in great quantities."[32]

If we measure success in terms of market growth or the number of premium tequila brands, then the DO for tequila has indeed been very successful. But advocates of DOs argue that they also have the potential to protect the environment, sustain rural communities, and preserve cultural traditions. By these measures, the DO for tequila has failed. In the case of mezcal, there are indications that the regulatory institutions are evolving in a direction that might better protect traditional practices, largely because consumers value these practices. There is weaker evidence—in the case of tequila or mezcal—of a commitment to preserving environmental sustainability, and virtually no evidence of any efforts to ensure fair wages and just working conditions for workers or farmers.

Lasting change is unlikely without the involvement of the state. In *Beyond the Boycott*, a comparative analysis of transnational campaigns to monitor and address labor and human rights violations, sociologist Gay Seidman finds that "consumer pressure has been most successful when it is mobilized through institutions, not by appeals to individual consumers making decisions in supermarket aisles."[33] Further, she notes that states have generally played a greater role in successful campaigns than is generally acknowledged. In the cases of tequila and mezcal, we see evidence of this. The most consequential changes of the last several years—for example, the radical revisions that have been proposed for the mezcal standard, as well as the defeat of NOM 186—occurred when consumers, retailers, and activists in the United States and Mexico worked with producers to confront and influence the state institutions that regulate mezcal.

Of course, it's important not to idealize the state. As I write this, the public approval rating for Mexico's president is the lowest it has been since the mid-1990s, and 62 percent of Mexicans say that their country is on the wrong path.[34] More than one hundred thousand people have died in organized-crime-related violence since 2007, and hundreds of thousands of people took to the streets in the fall of 2014 after the disappearance of forty-three students in Ayotzinapa, Guerrero.[35] "Fue el estado" (the government did it) became a battle cry for protesters demanding justice, improved security, and greater accountability from their government. Many Mexican people have lost faith in their state. One of our most important roles as global citizens is to witness and make injustice known, whether this means exposing working conditions in the mezcal industry, violence and human rights violations in Mexico, or the way we treat migrant workers in the United States. As Seidman argues, strategies aimed at building state capacity and strengthening the institutions of democratic citizenship continue to hold the most promise for empowering workers and creating new possibilities for their voices and participation.[36]

What we drink and eat can make a difference. I believe that the growth of the market for traditional and artisanal mezcals and tequilas has, on the whole, helped empower small producers and shifted conversations around protecting Mexico's spirits in productive ways. But that's not enough. Saving mezcal won't save mezcaleros. And as long as the market dictates how to regulate and protect mezcal, it's always going to privilege mezcal over mezcaleros. We can—and should—choose mezcals and tequilas made from diverse, sustainably produced varieties of agave, according to the practices that have developed in particular places. But we also need to consider how agave farmers, workers, and small producers are treated. That means pushing companies to be more transparent about their labor practices and the prices they pay to agave farmers and mezcaleros. And it means advocating policy changes in the United States and in Mexico to support the people who make tequila and mezcal. These changes include revising the DOs and the quality standards, which have the potential to open up spaces for the protection of environments, people, and communities that help maintain the connections between specific products and places. But they also include revising agricultural policies that affect the price of agave and the structure of land ownership in Mexico, trade policies that have contributed to the flow of U.S. corn into Mexico and the flow of small farmers out of Mexico, and labor and migration policies that curtail workers' rights and abilities to organize on both sides of the border. Perhaps then, consumers and activists will be able to work alongside producers to preserve the quality and heritage of what so many have called "the legacy of all Mexicans."

METHODOLOGICAL APPENDIX

This project began over ten years ago, when, in 2004, I spent a semester working as a research assistant at the University of Guadalajara's campus in Autlán, a small city in southern Jalisco. In the wake of the agave shortage that began in 1999, the region surrounding the campus had witnessed dramatic land use changes, first as the tequila companies began renting land from small corn and bean farmers and planting it with agave, and then as the farmers and landowners in the region followed suit. Just in the municipality of Autlán, the amount of land planted with agave had increased from sixty-seven acres in 1995 to more than five thousand in 2004.[1] Researchers at the university were investigating the extent and implications of the changes and were looking for someone to interview the farmers in the region and see what factors were motivating their decisions to rent out their land or plant agave. Under the mentorship of Peter Gerritsen, a rural sociologist working in the Department of Ecology and Natural Resources, I interviewed twenty-five agave farmers and small landowners. Some of them were growing their own agave; others had rented their land to the tequila companies. In a context of low corn prices, insufficient (and unpredictable) rainfall, and a lack of access to cash or credit, many farmers had elected to rent their land to the tequila companies, even though the terms of the contracts were often unfavorable to the farmers. A smaller group of farmers had saved up enough money to grow their own agave and hoped that this would be a profitable investment. But even then, it was fairly clear to me that this wasn't likely to be a sustainable strategy for the region or the farmers; the agave supply had already started to recover, and prices were falling.

During my time in Autlán, I began contemplating the profound effects the tequila industry was having on the region, but at that point I had never even visited the town of Tequila, which was about four hours away by bus. Toward the end of my stay, a friend and I toured Cuervo's flagship distillery, La Rojeña, in downtown Tequila. La Rojeña, which Cuervo boasts is the oldest distillery in the Americas, offers an impressive tour, with its masonry ovens, gleaming copper stills, and thousands of stacked wooden barrels. But it was obvious that the glamour and glitz that I saw in Tequila were not trickling down to the farmers in southern Jalisco—nor, I suspected, to farmers, workers, and communities much closer to Tequila.

When I returned to Jalisco two years later to begin fieldwork for my dissertation, I hoped to better understand the impact of the institutions that regulated the tequila industry—the DO and the quality standard—on the people involved with the production, sales, and regulation of tequila. I started slowly, contacting the handful of people that my acquaintances could introduce me to. For example, at a party in the United States, I met a wine distributor who put me in touch with a small tequila distillery that his company worked with. This ended up being my first distillery tour and interview. As I did more interviews, I asked each person to recommend people that I should interview. Many people were willing to introduce me to their contacts in the industry. I also enrolled in a one-semester diploma program in tequila studies, offered by the University of Guadalajara. My classmates and I attended weekly lectures by industry experts, including representatives of the CNIT and CRT, archaeologists and tequila historians, film studies scholars, and biologists. I also did a lot of cold calling. Each time I approached a person I wanted to interview, I explained that I was a student from the United States and that I was studying the DO for tequila. I was initially surprised by how many people agreed to be interviewed, but 2006 was the height of the tequila boom. With the agave shortage over, distilleries were ramping up their production faster than ever. People seemed happy and proud to talk to me, an American, about how far the industry had come.

My interview experiences were shaped by gender, race, and class, as well as by my outsider status. I interviewed more men than women; for example, of the nineteen interviews I did with directors and owners of the tequila distilleries, only three were with women. Only one of the people I interviewed from governmental agencies and industry organizations was a woman. As noted in a recent study of the presence of women in the tequila industry, women's participation in the industry has grown, and women are represented in increasingly diverse positions: for example, as administrative assistants and accountants, lab technicians, and employees of organizations like the CRT and CNIT.[2] However, despite this progress, the vast majority of positions of power in the industry are still held by men; almost all the tequila companies are owned and managed by men, and men occupy almost all the positions on influential boards like those that advise the CRT and CNIT. The industry elites whom I interviewed—executives at the largest tequila companies, owners of the smaller and medium-sized companies, and top officials in governmental and industry organizations—lived in a world dominated by men, and they displayed their masculinity in specific ways. Other researchers have shown how men display masculinities during the interview process: for example, by emphasizing their heterosexuality, presenting themselves as powerful and busy, and positioning themselves as having expert knowledge.[3] The men I interviewed used different strategies to control the length and tempo of the interview: for example, by making me wait for a long period of time before the start of the interview, and by placing strict limits on the length of the interview. Many engaged in what Michael Schwalbe and Michelle Wolkomir call inappropriate sexualizing;[4] this often took the form of flirting, remarks about my appearance, or invitations for drinks or lunch. This meant that part of my job during an interview was to try to control these interactions: rejecting a lunch invitation, for example, or changing the subject. At the same time, I felt that this environment often gave me an advantage. The elite men I interviewed used flirting to establish their dominance; they did not perceive me, a young woman and a student at the time, as a threat or as someone with a lot of knowledge of the industry. This meant they were often willing to share politically controversial perspectives or what they considered to be "industry secrets"—for example, statistics about their company's sales or details about their business model—that I don't know they would have shared with someone they viewed as more of a contemporary.

My research experiences were mediated not just by gender but also by class, race, and age. The agave farmers I interviewed were also all men, but our class differences made these interactions very different from my interviews with the tequila elites. Some of the farmers adopted what Schwalbe and Wolkomir call "minimizing," giving terse answers that reveal little information.[5] This was likely partly just because they were not used to discussing their work or their opinions of the tequila industry. In order to draw more information from the farmers and make them more comfortable, I used a number of strategies, including offering not to use my recorder, accepting offers (from the farmers and especially from their wives and daughters) of coffee and snacks, and mentioning that I had talked to other farmers (without revealing their identities or the content of the interviews). I also made adjustments to my clothes and appearance. For my interviews with the tequila elites, which often took place in the morning, I wore business attire, including fitted skirts and high heels, which were the type of clothes worn by other women in the industry. I always changed my clothes before interviewing the farmers in the afternoons, instead wearing casual skirts and pants and carrying my interview materials (a simple notebook and my recorder) in a cotton bag instead of a briefcase.

The physical locations of the interviews were also very different, and this influenced their tone and content. While I interviewed the tequila elites in their offices, I met with the farmers in their homes. Although I asked many of the same questions, my conversations with the farmers tended to center on their daily work as farmers and their personal lives and livelihoods. Since the CRT had not given me the phone numbers of the farmers (and many of them didn't have phones anyway), I did not make appointments in advance, but instead went directly to people's houses. I interviewed most of the farmers in the late afternoon, when they were more likely to be home and done with their work for the day, which often started very early in the morning. After I knocked on people's doors, most people agreed to do the interview right then, although some requested that I come back another day. Through my clothes, my demeanor, and the way I approached the interviews (going door to door and starting with the most familiar types of questions, about farming practices), I tried to make myself seem less intimidating. Farmers regarded me with a mixture of intrigue and anxiety: intrigued that someone from the United States was studying what they did, and somewhat nervous about talking about it.

My interviews were also affected by the context of what was going on in the tequila industry and in Mexico. At the time, debates over immigration in the United States were focused on creating literal and virtual fences along the U.S.-Mexico border, and many people wanted to know what I thought about the fences: whether the proposals would go through, why "George Bush" insisted on putting up these fences, and what it all meant. In addition, as the price of agave continued to drop, farmers were becoming increasingly desperate. They hoped that I might be able to intervene on their behalf. Some asked me to advocate on behalf of the agave farmers in general, while others wondered if I could help them with more specific problems, such as contacting tequila companies that had broken contracts or otherwise failed to comply with their obligations. Throughout the process of doing (and then writing about) my research, I have felt the tension created by having started my project because I cared about the injustice and inequality in the tequila industry, yet feeling unable to have any concrete effect on the agave farmers and workers. I hope that by drawing attention to the experiences of the farmers and workers, this book may help them in some small way.

In 2009, I returned to Mexico to begin interviewing mezcal producers, retailers, and others involved with producing, promoting, selling, and regulating mezcal. These interviews took me from chic neighborhoods in Mexico City to the mountains of rural Guerrero and Oaxaca, but in many ways they paralleled the interviews I had done with the tequila executives and agave farmers. My interviews with the elites in the mezcal industry took place in fancy hotels and bars, and they signaled their masculinity and their class positions in subtle ways: in their interactions with hotel and restaurant staff and with their own employees, and in their references to other elites in the industry. By this point, however, I was a professor instead of a student, which shifted our interactions somewhat; although I was still an outsider, the people I interviewed treated me more as one of their colleagues or contemporaries.

My interviews with small mezcaleros were mediated by race and class and shaped by the fear and uncertainty over regulation that pervade the industry. Although I had approached the agave farmers directly, by knocking on their doors, I generally had to be introduced to the mezcal producers by an intermediary. This was partly because the mezcaleros tended to live in isolated, rural areas. In addition, I wanted to get more of a sense of how mezcal production varied from region to region, and so I interviewed mezcaleros in three states (Guerrero, Michoacán, and Oaxaca) instead of concentrating on one small town, as I had in Jalisco. Both women and men acted as my intermediaries; they included retailers who introduced me to the people who made mezcal under their labels, employees of NGOs and cooperatives, and academics. My interviews with the mezcaleros were shorter and less formal than all of my other interviews and generally centered on a tour of the distillery. The mezcaleros' responses to my more abstract questions—about what went into a quality mezcal, or what traditions were important—were succinct. Unlike the mezcal retailers, whose business models depended on their ability to convey the story of their mezcal to consumers, small mezcal producers weren't used to talking about their mezcal. Moreover, they didn't necessarily think of their work as a form of art or a valuable part of Mexican heritage, as the retailers framed it, but simply as how people in their families and their regions made mezcal.

Finally, my interviews with mezcal producers were shaped by differences related to class and ethnicity. I am white, and most of my intermediaries were mestizo (of combined European and indigenous descent), while many of the mezcaleros were indigenous. As I discuss in the book, the evolution of the tequila and mezcal industries is linked to their associations with mestizo and indigenous identities, respectively. For example, Marie Sarita Gaytán notes that the images of jimadores that are used in the tequila industry affirm "attributes of obedient mestizo masculinity" and help define the Tequila region "as an idealized site with workers whose ancestral lineages. . . tie them to the land [and] also to the product."[6] Within the tequila and mezcal industries, contemporary labor hierarchies are linked to class and ethnicity, with mestizo Mexicans occupying more

privileged positions, and with indigenous workers and mezcaleros working in the lowest-paying and most dangerous jobs. Indigenous people in
Mexico have long suffered from discrimination and exploitation. In 2012,
77 percent of Mexico's indigenous population lived below the poverty line,
compared to 43 percent of the general population.[7] Although we never
discussed these hierarchies during my interviews, they are pervasive in the
mezcal and tequila industries and in Mexico more generally.

In sum, this book is based on research conducted over a ten-year
period, from 2004 through 2014. I toured sixteen tequila distilleries and
eighteen mezcal distilleries. I also completed the first diploma program
in tequila studies at the University of Guadalajara, attended a two-day
conference sponsored by the CRT, observed two meetings of and one
demonstration by an agave farmers' union, participated in two official
tastings offered by the Mexican Tequila Academy, and attended two
mezcal tastings organized by mezcal education groups. I attended two
forums that brought together industry stakeholders and governmental
representatives to discuss changes in the institutions that regulate the
mezcal industry. I participated in a three-day tour of tequila distilleries
organized by a group of American aficionados, as well as a six-day tour of
mezcal and tequila distilleries organized by a group of American spirits
professionals.

I also interviewed people involved with the production, regulation, and
sale of tequila and mezcal. In Mexico, my research included 34 interviews
with owners and managers of the tequila companies and representatives
of industry organizations; 27 interviews with a group of randomly selected
agave farmers in Amatitán, Jalisco; 19 interviews with mezcal producers
and retailers and representatives of industry organizations; and 14 interviews with governmental officials. I also conducted short interviews with
17 small mezcal producers while touring their distilleries. Finally, I interviewed 9 retailers and bartenders in the United States and Europe, mostly
over the phone. In total, between 2006 and 2014, I interviewed 120 people from the tequila and mezcal industries, in addition to having informal
conversations with many others.

Tables 1 and 2 provide, for reference while reading, a brief description
of all of the research participants who are quoted in this book. The agave
farmers are described in table 2, while the other interview participants are

Table 1 Interviews with People Involved with the Production, Sales, and Regulation of Tequila and Mezcal

Pseudonym	Description	Location of residence	Year(s) of interview(s)
Felipe Aceves*	Jimador	Jalisco (Los Altos)	2014
Steven Adams	Owner of an artisanal mezcal brand	Oaxaca	2009
Víctor Álvarez	Production manager for an artisanal mezcal distillery	Oaxaca	2009
Candelario Atlatenco	Employee of an association of mezcal producers	Guerrero	2009
Gabriel Ávila	Large agave grower and owner of medium-sized tequila company	Jalisco (Los Altos)	2006
Sergio Calderón	Regional governmental official	Jalisco (Tequila)	2006
José Luis Camacho*	Jimador	Jalisco (Los Altos)	2014
Julieta Carrillo	Owner of a midrange, medium-sized tequila company	Jalisco (Los Altos)	2006
Emiliano Castro	High-level official at the CRM	Oaxaca	2009
Matt Clark	Bartender and co-owner of a mezcal bar	United States	2013
Gustavo Contreras	Secretary of Agriculture official	Jalisco (Guadalajara)	2006
Jorge Cruz	Owner of a high-end tequila brand	United States	2006, 2013
Santiago Delgado	Director of a high-end tequila company	Jalisco (Los Altos)	2006
Calixto Díaz	Small mezcal producer	Guerrero	2009
Alejandra Esquivel	Chemist at an artisanal mezcal distillery	Oaxaca	2009
Thomas Evans	Wine and spirits consultant	United States	2013
Luciano Fuentes*	Jimador	Jalisco (Los Altos)	2014
Eduardo Gallegos	Small mezcal producer	Michoacán	2010
Luis García	Director of agricultural operations for a large tequila company	Jalisco (Guadalajara)	2006

Name	Description	Location	Year
Fernanda Gutiérrez	Official at the General Directorate of Standards	Mexico City	2009
Hector Herrera*	Jimador	Jalisco (Los Altos)	2014
Zach Johnson	Bartender and co-owner of a mezcal bar	United States	2014
Jesús Martínez	Director of a midrange, medium-sized tequila distillery	Jalisco (Tequila)	2006
Curt Miller	Owner of a mezcal/tequila bar	United States	2013
Rodrigo Nuñez	Small agave farmer	Jalisco (Southern)	2004
Oscar Orozco	Owner of an artisanal tequila company	Jalisco (Los Altos)	2006
Feliciano Padilla	Small mezcal producer	Guerrero	2009
Daniel Pérez	Academic researcher	Colima	2014
Justino Peña	Small mezcal producer	Guerrero	2009
Martin Porras	Owner of an artisanal tequila brand	Europe	2013
Paulina Reyes	Researcher at an NGO focused on sustainable development	Mexico City	2009, 2012
Marco Rivera	Manager of a mezcal bar	Mexico City	2009
Carmela Robles	Codirector of an artisanal mezcal distillery	Oaxaca	2009
Manuel Romero	High-level official at the CRT	Jalisco (Guadalajara)	2006
Fernando Rosales	Founder of a midrange mezcal brand	Oaxaca	2009
Lindsay Ruhland	Brand ambassador and bartender	United States	2013
Julio Ruíz	Owner of a mezcal bar	Jalisco (Guadalajara)	2014
Javier Salcido	Small mezcal producer	Jalisco (Southern)	2012
Gerardo Silva	Director of agricultural operations for a large tequila company	Jalisco (Guadalajara)	2006
Diego Soto	Owner of an artisanal tequila company	Jalisco (Los Altos)	2006
Carlos Toledo	Small mezcal producer, leader in an association of mezcal producers	Michoacán	2009

(continued)

Table 1 (continued)

Pseudonym	Description	Location of residence	Year(s) of interview(s)
Ignacio Treviño	Researcher at the National Commission for the Knowledge and Use of Biodiversity	Mexico City	2009
Humberto Vargas	High-level official at the CRT	Jalisco (Guadalajara)	2006
Claudia Vásquez	Graduate student studying mezcal	Michoacán	2009
Alfonso Villanueva	Employee of an association of mezcal producers	Guerrero	2009
Eric Weber	Owner of an artisanal mezcal brand	United States	2013
Miguel Zamora	Plant manager for a medium-sized tequila company	Jalisco (Tequila)	2006
Ernesto Zepeda	Leader within the Mexican Tequila Academy	Jalisco (Guadalajara)	2006

* NOTE: These interviews (with the jimadores) were conducted in a group. All other interviews were conducted individually.

Table 2 Interviews with Farmers in Amatitán, 2006

	Household			Land (in hectares)			Income, 2005 (in Mexican pesos)		
PSEUDONYM	# OF ADULTS	# OF CHILDREN	PRIMARY ECONOMIC ACTIVITY	RENTED OR SHARED	OWNED	PLANTED WITH AGAVE	TOTAL HOUSEHOLD	PER CAPITA	FROM AGAVE CULTIVATION OR RENTAL OF LAND
Ernesto Castillo	4	0	farmer (plums)	6	7	1	37,400	9,350	−9,040
Ignacio Guzmán	3	0	bricklayer	0	1.5	1.5	68,875	22,958	1,000
Avellino López Rubio	7	2	agricultural day laborer (agave)	2	0	2	118,970	13,219	−9,230
Lucio Vega	5	0	agricultural day laborer (agave)	1	3.5	2	3,170	634	−16,975
Fidencio Mercado	2	3	jimador	3.5	0	2.5	39,338	7,868	−3,120
	3	1	agricultural day laborer (agave)	0	3	3	80,840	20,210	29,000
	3	3	municipal judge	0	3	3	—	—	−6,700
Fernando Quevedo	2	4	jimador	0	4	4	86,660	14,443	7,900
	3	3	agricultural day laborer (agave)	0	5	5	51,700	8,617	—
	1	0	retired	0	30	5	—	—	0
	3	1	agricultural day laborer (agave)	0	6	6	44,934	11,234	−4,001
Rigoberto Navarro	4	6	construction worker	0	6.5	6	165,769	16,577	−28,000
	2	0	agave grower	0	8	8	−21,000	−10,500	—
	2	3	pharmacist	0	8	8	—	—	—

(continued)

Table 2 (*continued*)

	Household			Land (in hectares)			Income, 2005 (in Mexican pesos)		
PSEUDONYM	# OF ADULTS	# OF CHILDREN	PRIMARY ECONOMIC ACTIVITY	RENTED OR SHARED	OWNED	PLANTED WITH AGAVE	TOTAL HOUSEHOLD	PER CAPITA	FROM AGAVE CULTIVATION OR RENTAL OF LAND
	5	0	agave grower	3	10	13	—	—	—
Alfonso Domínguez	2	0	agave grower	14	0	14	-21,338	-10,669	-24,938
	3	1	agave grower	0	19	14	38,208	9,552	-3,900
	2	0	agave grower	0	15	15	-1,252	-626	-3,202
	2	3	works for the family of one of the tequila companies	13	4	17	63,120	12,624	-60,000
José Guadalupe Ortega	3	0	retired	0	28	17	100,188	33,396	-80,000
	2	4	agave grower	24	0	24	—	—	—
Santiago Morales	2	3	agave grower	27.5	0	27.5	37,640	7,528	-35,060
	5	2	agave grower	5	40	35	311,371	44,482	94,706
	2	0	agave grower	0	48	48	—	—	—
Jaime Medina	2	0	agave grower	0	84	63	301,151	150,576	324,251
	1	0	agave grower	0	526	83	-47,175	-47,175	-17,300
	3	1	agave grower	56	100	156	265,111	66,278	459,778

described in table 1. I have included the agave farmers in a separate table because, unlike the other people I interviewed, the agave farmers were randomly selected from a population list of all of the registered agave farmers in the municipality of Amatitán. I have also included basic demographic information about all of the farmers interviewed, not just the ones who are quoted. All of the names in both tables are pseudonyms. In the book, I did occasionally use people's real names when citing a quote from a newspaper or another publicly available source.

Notes

1. THE PROMISE OF PLACE

1. Author fieldnotes (2012).

2. Author fieldnotes (2012).

3. Author fieldnotes (2012).

4. Zizumbo-Villarreal and Colunga-García Marín (2008); Zizumbo-Villar-real et al. (2009).

5. The finding of twenty species is from Larson and Aguirre (forthcoming). The finding of forty-two species is from Colunga-García Marín (2006); Colunga-García Marín et al. (2007).

6. Vigneaux (1863, 334).

7. De Barrios (1971, 46).

8. The original DO, published in 1974, restricted production to Jalisco and parts of Guanajuato, Michoacán, and Nayarit. Controversially, eleven municipalities in Tamaulipas were added in 1977.

9. The DO for mezcal originally included parts of Durango, Guerrero, Oaxaca, San Luis Potosí, and Zacatecas. Parts of Guanajuato, Tamaulipas, and Michoacán were added in 2001, 2003, and 2012, respectively.

10. Colunga-García Marín et al. (2007).

11. Petrini (2001, 28).

12. Friedmann (1993, 55).

13. McMichael (2000); McMichael (2005).

14. Kloppenburg et al. (1996, 34).

15. USDA (2013).

16. USDA (2014).

17. McMichael (2005, 287) used the notion of "food from nowhere," described by Bové and Dufour (2001), to discuss the "abstraction of agriculture through its incorporation and reproduction within global capital circuits," a fundamental characteristic of the corporate food regime.

18. Campbell (2009).

19. Campbell (2009, 312).

20. Robertson (1995).

21. Barham (2003, 131).

22. Renting et al. (2003, 398).

23. Feagan (2007).

24. At first, the cheese was made by a cheesemaker who would travel from farm to farm, collecting milk and then paying the farmers in cheese. Eventually, the system evolved into each village having a specialized building (Vernus 1998).

25. The term for denominations of origin differs from country to country. In this book, I use *denomination of origin* to refer to all the agreements that protect the link to terroir. When I am talking about specific laws in particular countries or institutions (e.g., appellations of origin in France or geographical indications in the World Trade Organization), I use the term adopted by that country or institution.

26. CIGC (2014a).

27. Colinet et al. (2006, 23–24).

28. CIGC (2014a).

29. Murray's Cheese (2014).

30. Author interviews (2007).

31. Author interviews (2007).

32. Boisard (2003).

33. Author interviews (2007).

34. CIGC (2014c).

35. Colinet et al. (2006).

36. Dupont (2002); Gerz and Dupont (2006, 83).

37. Dupont (2002); Gerz and Dupont (2006); Giovannucci et al. (2009).

38. CIGC (2014b).

39. Author interviews (2007).

40. Trubek (2008, 18–19).

41. Trubek (2008, 19).

42. Trubek (2008, 19).

43. Trubek (2008, 21–22).

44. Trubek (2008).

45. Parasecoli and Tasaki (2011).

46. As Kolleen Guy (2003) details in *When Champagne Became French: Wine and the Making of French Identity, 1820–1920*, champagne, the sparkling wine from northern France, had by this point gained tremendous symbolic and cultural capital and was being consumed around the world (including, ironically, in Mexico, where elites demonstrated their prestige by choosing champagne and other European products over tequila). But the wine producers in the Champagne region were powerless to stop producers in other parts of France and around the world from appropriating the name *champagne* for themselves. They turned to the French state for help.

47. Trubek (2008).

48. *Journal Officielle de la République Française* (1908, 5637).

49. *Journal Officielle de la République Française* (1919, 4726).

50. Gangjee (2012).

51. Trubek (2008).

52. Teil (2012, 481).

53. Moran (1993, 700).

54. Originally, the organization was called the Comité National des Appellations d'Origine. In 1947, the organization was transformed into the Institut National des Appellations d'Origine (Gangjee 2012).

55. Kireeva (2011, 39).

56. Kireeva (2011).

57. Kireeva (2011).

58. As Blakeney (2001) notes, the Lisbon Agreement was concluded in Lisbon in 1958. It was revised in Stockholm in 1967 and amended in 1979. The agreement defines appellations of origin as "the geographical denomination of a country, region, or locality, which serve to designate a product originating therein, the quality or characteristics of which are due to exclusively or essentially to the geographical environment, including natural and human factors" (Lisbon Agreement 1958).

59. Blakeney (2001, 638).

60. WIPO (2014).

61. Revel (2000).

62. Barham (2003).

63. Barham (2003, 132).

64. Gade (2004).

65. Gade (2004, 848).

66. Gade (2004).

67. Trubek (2008, 51).

68. Eurostat (2011).

69. European Commission (2014b).

70. Bodnár (2003).

71. Cohen (1999).

72. Waters (2010, 111–112).

73. Swarsdon (1999).

74. Waters (2010, 111–112).

75. I have borrowed the title of this section from Tim Josling's 2006 article "The War on Terroir: Geographical Indications as a Transatlantic Trade Conflict," published in the *Journal of Agricultural Economics*.

76. Kerr (2006). Parasecoli and Tasaki (2011, 109) argue that the status of geographical indications emerged as "one of the hot issues of the Doha Development Agenda (Doha Round) of the WTO multilateral trade negotiations," bringing agriculture to the forefront in issues of "global market accessibility, technical barriers to trade, export subsidies, domestic support to agriculture, and implementation of the WTO agreements by developing economies."

77. Article 22 of the agreement defines *geographical indications* as "indications which identify a good as originating in the territory of a Member, or a region or locality in that territory, where a given quality, reputation or other characteristic of the good is essentially attributable to its geographical origin" (WTO 1994). As Parasecoli and Tasaki (2011, 108) note, under this definition, references "to tradition, history, culture, or any other human factor [are] conspicuously absent."

78. Josling (2006).

79. Schultz (2014).

80. Calenda (2014).

81. Kerr (2006, 7).

82. For the first argument, see Menapace and Moschini (2012). For the second, see Scarpa et al. (2005).

83. Herrmann and Teuber (2011).

84. Economists argue that price premiums are necessary but not sufficient, given the more stringent production standards (and often, higher costs) associated with them, as compared to standard products. Moreover, they argue that price premiums could raise farmers' incomes and promote rural development (Josling 2006).

85. Deselnicu et al. (2013, 209).

86. Areté (2013).

87. Bessière (1998).

88. De Roest and Menghi (2000).

89. Controversially, although the ham must be processed in the hills around Parma, Italy, the pigs can be raised in a much larger region.

90. Bérard and Marchenay (2006).

91. Riccheri et al. (2006).

92. PDOs and PGIs are defined as names that identify a product "originating in a specific place, region, or, in exceptional cases, a country" (*Official Journal of the European Union* 2012, L 343/8). A PDO refers to a product whose "quality or

characteristics are essentially or exclusively due to a particular geographical environment with its inherent natural and human factors; and the production steps of which all take place in the defined geographical area." A PGI refers to a product whose "given quality, reputation, or other characteristic is essentially attributable to that geographical origin; and at least one of the production steps of which take place in the defined geographical area." The definition of a PDO is therefore more exclusive than that of a PGI.

93. Chever et al. (2012).

94. Chever et al. (2012).

95. oriGIn (2014).

96. Giovannucci et al. (2009) note that these countries fall into two groups: 111 nations with specific or sui generis systems of laws protecting DOs (referred to as "geographical indications" in the report), and 56 that use their own trademark systems.

97. Giovannucci et al. (2009) estimate that there are more than ten thousand geographical indications in the world. Approximately 70 percent come from Europe, with close to 20 percent coming from the United States, Canada, Australia, and New Zealand, collectively.

98. Giovannucci et al. (2009, 5).

99. This decision was made partly in response to contentions by the United States and Australia (and the subsequent WTO panel ruling) that Europe's strict regulations on DOs were discriminatory and in violation of the national treatment obligations and the most-favored-nation obligations of the Agreement on Trade-Related Aspects of Intellectual Property (Evans and Blakeney 2006). In 2007, Columbian coffee became the first non-European product to be granted PGI status in the European Union.

100. European Commission (2014a).

101. CIRAD (2013).

102. Larson (2007, 1).

103. Mara (2008).

104. Kerr (2006, 8).

105. Kerr (2006, 8).

106. Kerr (2006, 8).

107. DeSoucey (2010, 449).

108. Fourcade (2012, 526).

109. Fourcade (2012, 539).

110. MacDonald (2013).

111. Mutersbaugh (2005).

112. Rangnekar (2011, 2048).

113. Guthman (2007, 457).

114. Polanyi (1944); Guthman (2007, 473).

115. Robinson and Gibson (2011).

116. Besky (2013, 91).

117. Tregear et al. (2007).

118. Belletti and Marescotti (2002).

119. Tregear et al. (2007); Bowen and De Master (2011).

120. Besky (2013, 2014).

121. Parasecoli and Tasaki (2011, 112); see also Barrientos (2014); Besky (2013).

122. Areté (2013).

123. According to the study, clearly differentiated products—in other words, products with specific tastes or characteristics that made them notably different from their standard counterparts—and products with stricter production standards and fewer intermediaries, as well as those that were produced in greater volumes or that were more export-oriented, generally yielded higher premiums for farmers (Areté 2013).

124. Areté (2013).

125. Barjolle and Sylvander (2000, 33).

126. Mancini (2013).

127. Coombe and Aylwin (2011, 2034).

128. Coombe and Aylwin (2011).

129. Besky (2014, 84).

130. Besky (2014, 85).

131. Besky (2013, 2014).

2. FROM THE FIELDS TO YOUR GLASS

1. An añejo must be aged for at least one year in oak barrels that are no larger than six hundred liters; an extra añejo must be aged for at least three years in the same type of barrels.

2. Asimov (2010).

3. CRT (2015).

4. COMERCAM (2007); CRM (2015).

5. Gentry (1982 [2004]); Zizumbo-Villarreal and Colunga-García Marín (2007).

6. Valenzuela Zapata and Nabhan (2004, 3).

7. Chase et al. (2009).

8. Gentry (1982 [2004], 30).

9. Zizumbo-Villarreal and Colunga-García Marín (2008); Zizumbo-Villarreal et al. (2009).

10. The description is from *Relaciones Geográficas del Siglo XVI: Nueva Galicia* (1580), cited in Zizumbo-Villarreal and Colunga-García Marín (2008, 498).

11. From *Relaciones Geográficas del Siglo XVI: Michoacán* (1580), cited in Zizumbo-Villarreal and Colunga-García Marín (2008, 498).

12. This explanation of fermentation comes from Estes (2012, 127).

13. Bruman (1944), Walton (1977), and Zizumbo-Villarreal and Colunga-García Marín (2008) all trace the origin of agave spirits to the Colima volcanoes region.

14. Zizumbo-Villarreal, González-Zozoya, et al. (2009).

15. Bourke (1893); and Lumholtz (1902)

16. This quote, the first known description of agave spirits production, appeared in the writings of Domingo Lázaro de Arregui (1619), as cited in Zizumbo-Villarreal and Colunga-García Marín (2008, 502).

17. For a discussion of relations and trade between Mexico and the Philippines in colonial times, see Guevarra (2011). For a discussion of the use of the Filipino still in the production of mezcal, see Colunga-García Marín and Zizumbo-Villarreal (2007); Zizumbo-Villarreal and Colunga-García Marín (2008).

18. Jiménez Vizcarra (2013) differentiates between two stills of Arabic origin: the *alquitara* and the *alambique*. Both were typically made of copper. The primary difference between the two is that the *alambique* has a condenser with serpentine coils, while in the case of the *alquitara* the pot on top serves as the condenser.

19. Colunga-García Marín and Zizumbo-Villarreal (2007, 1664).

20. Zizumbo-Villarreal and Colunga-García Marín (2008).

21. As Zizumbo-Villarreal and Colunga-García Marín (2008) explain, the route followed the same path used by the Spanish beginning in 1524 for their northward explorations (documented by Sauer 1932, as cited in Zizumbo-Villarreal and Colunga-García Marín 2008). This route would have extended from Colima through western Jalisco, eventually reaching the Amatitán-Tequila valley, home of the town that tequila is named after. Carried along the route to mines in northern Jalisco and Zacatecas, distillation technology likely reached Bolaños (in northern Jalisco); following the southern route to Zacatecas, distillers would have arrived in Michoacán. Farther north, as West (1949) notes, seventeenth-century mine workers in Parral, in the northern Mexican state of Chihuahua, drank mezcal that was hauled overland from southern Durango. Bahre and Bradbury (1980) report evidence of a modified form of mezcal production in the mountains of Sonora.

22. Zizumbo-Villarreal and Colunga-García Marín (2008).

23. Gómez Arriola (2004, 362).

24. Luna Zamora (1991, 33).

25. Luna Zamora (1991).

26. Gómez Arriola (2004).

27. Jiménez Vizcarra (2008).

28. Gómez Arriola (2004).

29. Luna Zamora (1991).

30. Gómez Arriola (2004).

31. Luna Zamora (1991, 43).

32. Luna Zamora (1991, 43).

33. Luna Zamora (1991).

34. Gómez Arriola (2004).

35. Gómez Arriola (2004).

36. Walton (1977, 120–121).

37. Gómez Arriola (2004); Luna Zamora (1991).

38. Gómez Arriola (2004).

39. Luna Zamora (1991).

40. Luna Zamora (1991) assumes that the distillery would have operated for forty weeks out of the year; this yields a total annual volume of close to 1 million liters.

41. Payno (1864, 100).

42. Walton (1977).

43. Gómez Arriola (2004); Gómez Arriola (2010).

44. According to Gómez Arriola (2010), tahonas were used in the production of mezcal starting in the eighteenth century.

45. Gómez Arriola (2004).

46. Sánchez López (1989 [2005], 34).

47. Luna Zamora (1991); Huerta Rosas and Luna Zamora (forthcoming). The advertisement was published in *El Clamor Público*, a Spanish-language newspaper based in Los Angeles (*El Clamor Público* 1857).

48. Luna Zamora (1991, 80).

49. Rodríguez Gómez 2001: 154.

50. Regarding the Guadalajara–Mexico City Railway line, see Mitchell (2004). Luna Zamora (1991) argues that Tequila's strategic location and the completion of the railroad were critical to the expansion of the tequila industry.

51. Luna Zamora (1991).

52. Gómez Arriola (2010, 252).

53. This quote comes from *Informe y Colección de Artículos Relativos a los Fenómenos Geológicos Verificados en Jalisco en el Presente Año y en Épocas Anteriores*, 1875, p. 179, as cited by Huerta Rosas and Luna Zamora (forthcoming).

54. Luna Zamora (1991).

55. Gutiérrez González 2001

56. Gómez Arriola (2010).

57. Pérez (1887, 7).

58. Luna Zamora (1991, 79).

59. Gómez Arriola (2010).

60. Luna Zamora (1991).

61. Huerta Rosas and Luna Zamora (forthcoming); Luna Zamora (1991).

62. José María Guadalupe Cuervo was succeeded by his son-in-law Vicente Albino Rojas and then by Jesús Flores.

63. Gutiérrez González (2001).

64. Pérez (1887, 8).

65. Jiménez Vizcarra (2013, 35).

66. Jiménez Vizcarra (2013, 36).

67. Mitchell (2004); Gómez Arriola (2004).

68. Mitchell (2004).

69. Jiménez Vizcarra (2013).

70. Gómez Arriola (2004, 419).

71. Huerta Rosas and Luna Zamora (forthcoming).

72. The Cuervo family is an exception. According to Cuervo history, the family had 3 million agaves planted on their lands in 1868 (Mundo Cuervo 2014).

73. Luna Zamora (1991). *Hacienda,* the Spanish word for "estate," is an imprecise term but generally refers to large landed estates that often combined farming, cattle raising, and other income-generating activities. Van Young (2006, 107) notes that the haciendas were the most "highly visible social and economic institution in the late colonial countryside," dominating the factors of agricultural production (land, labor, and capital) and supplying the cities with most of their staple foodstuffs. People knew intuitively what a hacienda was, in contrast to other types of agricultural holdings. The amount of capital investment, the size of the landholding, and the variety of agricultural activities were the key factors that distinguished a hacienda from a farm or ranch.

74. Luna Zamora (1991, 102).

75. Luna Zamora (1991, 111).

76. Gómez Arriola (2004).

77. Gómez Arriola (2004, 406–407).

78. Mitchell (2004, 89).

79. From *Anuario de Estadística de la República Mexicana*, published in 1896, as cited in Walton (1977, 122). This does not include mezcal produced clandestinely in small distilleries for local sale or trade, which was not captured in the official statistics.

80. This quote from Pastor (1999), a traveler passing through Mexico, is cited in Rodríguez Gómez (2007, 155).

81. De Barrios (1971).

82. Mitchell (2004, 89).

83. Gaytán (2014, 44).

84. Luna Zamora (1991). This number includes tequila and mezcal distilleries in the state of Jalisco.

85. Luna Zamora (1991).

86. Luna Zamora (1991).

87. Torres (1998). Gentry (1982 [2004]) stated that blue agave plants typically required eight years to fully mature, but tequila companies have recently adopted new crop production and plant reproduction technologies in order to reduce the maturation time. Blue agave is now often harvested after five or six years.

88. Luna Zamora (1991, 169).

89. Luna Zamora (1991, 170).

90. Luna Zamora (1991).

91. Gutiérrez González (2001).

92. Mitchell (2004)

93. The first formal association of tequila distilleries had been formed back in 1923. The group pushed for the first law to regulate the tequila distilleries, the Regulation for Alcohol, Tequila, and Mezcals, established in 1928, but the law failed to prevent adulteration (Luna Zamora 1991).

94. *Diario Oficial* (1949). The standard actually allowed for the use of the other species of agave from the same genus; but by this point, *Agave tequilana* Weber was already dominant. Unlike its later iterations, the first standard did not allow for the use of generic sugars (e.g., sugarcane).

95. Luna Zamora (1991, 174).

96. Gutiérrez González (2001).

97. Luna Zamora (2005).

98. The 1968 revision expanded the territory in which the agave could be cultivated to include "regions within the adjoining states of Jalisco," as long as they exhibited "similar ecological characteristics" to those of Jalisco (*Diario Oficial* 1968, 7). The 1968 standard did not specifically define certain regions as appropriate or inappropriate for the cultivation of agave.

99. Gutiérrez González (2001).

100. Luna Zamora (1991, 175).

101. Luna Zamora (1991).

102. Luna Zamora (1991).

103. Cedeño Cruz and Alvarez-Jacobs (1999, 230); CRT (2014b).

104. Gutiérrez González (2001).

105. Luna Zamora (1991, 241).

106. Luna Zamora (1991); Funding Universe (2000).

107. Hernández López (2010); Instituto para el Fomento a la Calidad Total (2009). In 1994, Sauza's ownership transferred to Allied Domecq, the result of a merger between Pedro Domecq and Allied Lyons.

108. Luna Zamora (1991). Luna Zamora notes that the *maquila* trend started in the 1940s, when some of the distilleries in Los Altos began producing tequila for the large tequila companies in Tequila.

109. *Diario Oficial* (1974, 1977).

110. Luna Zamora (1991, 254).

111. The raw prices come from Luna Zamora (1991). With prices expressed in 2014 pesos, the real price of agave increased from about four pesos per kilogram in 1986 to more than ten pesos per kilogram in 1987 (calculations by Macías Macías 2015).

112. Luna Zamora (1991, 254).

113. Luna Zamora (1991); Funding Universe (2000).

114. Fourcade-Gourinchas and Babb (2002); Otero (2004).

115. Ibañez and Hernández (2006).

116. The CRT began at a meeting of all key stakeholders along the tequila supply chain on December 16, 1993. The organization began operating in 1994 (CRT 2014c).

117. Gutiérrez González (2001, 143).

118. Annex 313 of the North American Free Trade Agreement establishes bourbon whiskey and Tennessee whiskey, Canadian whiskey, and tequila and mezcal as "distinctive products" of the United States, Canada, and Mexico, respectively (NAFTA 1994). In 1997, the European Union and Mexico signed an agreement in which the European Union agreed to recognize Mexico's exclusive right to produce tequila and mezcal, in exchange for Mexico's recognition of a list of European spirits (*Diario Oficial* 1997a).

119. The process is complicated, however. When the CRT identifies a violation, it is unable to directly pursue prosecution; violations must be negotiated directly between the Mexican government and the government of the offending party (see CRT 2014a).

120. CRT (2004).

121. CRT (2015).

122. CRT (2015).

123. DISCUS (2013).

124. Sánchez López (1989 [2005], 34). Importantly, not all the distilleries outside of Jalisco were immune to processes of industrialization. As late as the mid-nineteenth century, the Pinos Hills region of western San Luis Potosí and southeastern Zacatecas may have produced more mezcal than the Tequila region (Walton 1977). Records from the early twentieth century indicate that in Pinos, Zacatecas, there were 25 million agave plants cultivated over a territory of about eighty thousand hectares, and that fifteen distilleries were producing more than 4 million liters of mezcal per year (Aguirre et al. 2001, as cited in Huerta Rosas and Luna Zamora forthcoming). The primary type of agave used in this region was (and still is) *Agave salmiana* subsp. *crassispina,* cultivated on large haciendas. In his thesis, Gabriel Somera (1952, as cited by Huerta Rosas and Luna Zamora forthcoming) noted that the distilleries in San Luis Potosí, Zacatecas, Nuevo León, and Tamaulipas were true industrial distilleries that could produce more than a hundred thousand liters per year. They also had modern technology and paid

employees. However, these distilleries did not achieve the fame or scale of the major tequila distilleries, and Huerta Rosas and Luna Zamora (forthcoming) note that despite the modernity of these distilleries, the majority continued to be powered by wood. Even today, many use masonry ovens to cook their agave and a tahona for crushing the piñas (Sistema Producto Maguey Mezcal Zacatecas 2012).

125. Gaytán (2014, 34); Taylor (1972, 8).

126. Gaytán (2014).

127. Gaytán (2014, 42).

128. Sánchez López (1989 [2005], 34).

129. This quote comes from Louis Lejeune, a French miner, as cited in Torrontera (2000, 134).

130. Illsley Granich (2009a).

131. Declaration published in Oaxaca, October 1922, as cited in Sánchez López (1989 [2005]).

132. Monterrosa Hernández (2005, 29).

133. Foote (1996, 5).

134. Illsley Granich (2009a).

135. Torrontera (2001, 135).

136. Bautista et al. (forthcoming).

137. Bautista et al. (forthcoming).

138. Bautista et al. (forthcoming).

139. Meixueiro et al. (1997); Monterrosa Hernández (2005).

140. Bautista et al. (forthcoming).

141. Meixueiro et al. (1997).

142. Bautista et al. (forthcoming).

143. Meixueiro et al. (1997).

144. Meixueiro et al. (1997).

145. Bautista et al. (forthcoming).

146. Sánchez López (1989 [2005]).

147. Monterrosa Hernández (2005).

148. Foote (1996, 5).

149. Bautista et al. (forthcoming).

150. Bautista et al. (forthcoming); Monterrosa Hernández (2005).

151. This estimate comes from a study by Díaz Montes (1980), as cited in Pool-Illsley and Illsley Granich (2012).

152. Foote (1996); Meixueiro et al. (1997). Gusano Rojo is the name of the brand of mezcal; the name of the company that sells it has changed over time. The company Nacional Vinícola began selling Gusano Rojo after it was established in 1970 (Meixueiro et al. 1997). More recently, the company Mezcales de Gusano is listed as the registered owner of Gusano Rojo (COMERCAM 2011).

153. Walton (1977).

154. Guerrero Gómez (1993).
155. Martin et al. (2011).
156. Bautista et al. (forthcoming).
157. Sánchez López (1989 [2005]).
158. Foote (1996, 6).
159. Foote (1996, 6).
160. Monterrosa Hernández (2005).
161. Bautista et al. (forthcoming).
162. Foote (1996).
163. Foote (1996, 12).
164. Foote (1996, 3, 14).
165. Sánchez López (1989 [2005], 168).
166. *Diario Oficial* (2012a).
167. In 2014, COMERCAM began referring to itself as the Mezcal Regulatory Council in official documents and on its website. In early 2015, when I finished writing this book, the name change had not yet been officially approved or published in the *Diario Oficial*. In my citations of documents produced by COMERCAM/the CRM, I use the name of the organization at the time that the document was published.
168. Mundo Cuervo (2008).
169. Gaytán (2014, 95).
170. Gaytán (2014, 99).
171. CRT (2012, 6).
172. Quezada Limón et al. (2014, 107).
173. On these distilleries' self-sufficiency, see Quezada Limón et al. (2014). On the percentage of agave in the tequila, see CRT (2012, 6).
174. CRT (2012, 6).
175. CRT (2012, 6).
176. Mixtos may be shipped in bulk and bottled outside the DO region (and even outside Mexico). Almost half of all tequila exports are bottled outside Mexico (CRT 2015). Tequilas made from 100 percent blue agave must be bottled within the DO region.
177. Quezada Limón et al. (2014, 129).
178. Tequila Fortaleza (2014).
179. Casa Dragones (2015).
180. CRT (2012, 6).
181. Holmes (2005).
182. *This American Life* (2002).
183. As discussed earlier in this chapter, Cuervo's story started in 1758, when a piece of land was deeded to José Antonio Cuervo for the cultivation of agave. After a brief period of prohibition, José Antonio's son was the first person to receive legal permission to begin producing mezcal, in 1795.

184. Alan (2011).

185. Author fieldnotes (2014).

186. Casas (2006).

187. Sauza (2014).

188. Casas (2006, 415).

189. Casas (2006).

190. Brown-Forman (2013, 4).

191. Edelstein (2013).

192. Ginley (2013).

193. Tequila Patrón (2014b, 194).

194. Patrón uses both tahonas and roller mills. Most of the company's tequila is a fifty-fifty blend of tequila made by the two methods, but for the Roca line it uses the tahona exclusively.

195. Patrón was originally produced by Siete Leguas, a long-standing Los Altos distillery with a reputation for using some of the most traditional practices in the industry. But in 2002, Patrón began shifting production to its own distillery; many of the aficionados I talked with said that the quality had declined since.

196. See also Gaytán and Bowen (2015).

197. CRT (2015).

198. Estes (2012, 137).

199. Author interviews (2009, 2013).

200. As noted earlier, Pedro Domecq eventually became Allied Domecq after being purchased by Allied Breweries.

201. In 1991, Heublein's Mexican affiliate, now owned by the British conglomerate Grand Metropolitan, acquired a 45 percent stake in Cuervo. When, in 1997, a merger between Grand Metropolitan and Guinness created Diageo, the Beckmann family (Cuervo's owners) claimed that the merger nullified the distribution contract that would allow Diageo to continue distributing Cuervo in the United States. In 2002, court battles ended in a settlement in which Diageo returned its share of the company to the Beckmann family and agreed to a new distribution contract that would end in June 2013. After Diageo severed ties with Cuervo in 2012 (reportedly to focus on premium tequilas), Cuervo announced that its brands would be distributed in North America by Proximo Spirits, which is owned by the Beckmann family.

202. In November 2014, Diageo announced that it had entered into an agreement with Jose Cuervo to take full control of Don Julio, in exchange for selling the Irish whiskey label Bushmills to Cuervo (Evans 2014).

203. See figure 1.2 in Valenzuela Zapata and Macías (2014).

204. Luna Zamora (1991); Casas (2006).

205. Luna Zamora (1991).

206. Molina Ramírez (2008).

207. The Spanish firm Osborne held a 25 percent stake between 2001 and 2004, when it sold its share back to the Romo family, who had established the company in 1870.

208. Preston (1996).

209. Author interviews (2013).

210. Janzen (2012).

211. Gentry (1982 [2004]).

212. Del Maguey (2014).

213. Author interviews (2009).

214. Author fieldnotes (2014).

215. Author interviews (2009).

216. Author interviews (2009).

217. Illsley Granich et al. (2009, 15).

218. Ginley (2013).

219. An exception is found in some villages in Michoacán, where people add small quantities of pulque to the mash before fermenting.

220. In between these two extremes is a group of producers in San Luis Potosí and Zacatecas who make mezcal in distilleries located in former haciendas (Illsley et al. 2009; Sistema Nacional 2006). The primary type of agave used is *Agave salmiana* subsp. *crassispina,* historically collected, and increasingly cultivated, by local ejidos from the common properties in the region (Sistema Producto Maguey Mezcal Zacatecas 2012). Their methods tend to resemble those of the most traditional tequila distilleries: they cook the agave in wood-burning stone ovens, chop the agave with a tahona, ferment the juices in stone or wooden tanks, and distill their mezcal in copper stills. These distilleries tout their long history—some have been producing mezcal for more than a hundred years—and their use of "the old production practices" (Sistema Producto Maguey Mezcal Zacatecas 2012). However, compared to the first group of mezcaleros, which constitutes the majority of producers in Mexico, these distilleries are considerably more industrial and concentrated, and they operate at a much larger scale. Many produce between ten thousand and twenty thousand liters per month (Sistema Nacional 2006), more than ten times what the smallest mezcaleros make annually.

221. This is still less than 15 percent of what Tequila Cuervo produced in its peak years. According to Impact Databank, Jose Cuervo's production increased from 3.2 million cases in 2002 to 3.9 million cases in 2007. Production volumes have decreased since then, to 3.5 million cases in 2012 (*Shanken News Daily* 2013).

222. Pool-Illsley and Illsley Granich (2012).

223. Pool-Illsley and Illsley Granich (2012).

224. Author interviews (2012).

225. Pool-Illsley and Illsley Granich (2012). Only producers in the DO region are allowed to certify and sell their product as mezcal; outside the DO boundaries, producers sell their mezcal as *destilados de agave* (agave distillates).

226. Author interviews (2009, 2013).
227. Black (2011).

3. WHOSE RULES RULE?

1. Gaytán (forthcoming, 1).
2. Preston (1996).
3. *Diario Oficial* (1991), my emphasis.
4. According to CRT records, total production of tequila increased from 104.3 million liters in 1995 to 190.6 million liters in 1999. In 2008, total production reached 312.1 million liters (CRT 2015).
5. Gaytán and Bowen (2015).
6. Marsden and Arce (1995); see also Guthman (2004a, 2004b, 2007); Renard (2005).
7. Freidberg (2004, 25).
8. Freidberg (2004).
9. *Diario Oficial* (1949).
10. *Diario Oficial* (1949, 3).
11. Valenzuela Zapata and Nabhan (2004).
12. Pérez (1887); Valenzuela Zapata and Nabhan (2004).
13. Valenzuela Zapata (2005); Valenzuela Zapata and Nabhan (2004).
14. Gutiérrez González (2001).
15. According to the World Intellectual Property Organization, Mexico became a party to the Lisbon Agreement in 1964, and the agreement entered into force in Mexico in 1966 (WIPO 2014). Rodríguez Cisneros (2001) states that Mexico established "denominations of origin" as a legal concept with a revision to the Industrial Property Law that went into effect in January 1973.
16. *Diario Oficial* (1974).
17. The request was made in 1976 (*Diario Oficial* 1977).
18. *Diario Oficial* (1977).
19. Fourcade-Gourinchas and Babb (2002); Otero (2004).
20. Ibañez and Hernández (2006).
21. On the 1994 standard, see *Diario Oficial* (1997b).
22. Author interviews (2006).
23. Author interviews (2006).
24. Author interviews (2006).
25. Author interviews (2006).
26. Author interviews (2006).
27. Freidberg (2004); Goodman (2004).
28. CRT (2005, 7).
29. Luna Zamora (1991, 168); Gutiérrez González (2001).

30. In practice, cane sugar, *piloncillo* (brown sugar loaf), cane molasses, and acid- or enzyme-hydrolyzed corn syrup are used, mainly because of cost considerations (Cedeño Cruz and Alvarez-Jacobs 1999).

31. Luna Zamora (1991, 171).

32. Gutiérrez González (2001).

33. Gutiérrez González (2001, 123).

34. Gutiérrez González (2001, 119).

35. Molina Ramírez (2008).

36. *Diario Oficial* (1974).

37. *Diario Oficial* (1974).

38. Chinaco (2014b).

39. Chinaco (2014b).

40. *Diario Oficial* (1974, 16).

41. *Diario Oficial* (1977).

42. *Diario Oficial* (1977).

43. *Diario Oficial* (1977).

44. Author interviews (2006).

45. Luna Zamora (1991).

46. According to Luna Zamora (1991), Cuervo and Sauza continued to bring in agave from Tamaulipas until 1986, owing to the agave shortage at the time.

47. Luna Zamora (1991, 222).

48. Chinaco (2014a). In an interview with the people who first imported Chinaco (published in Estes [2012]), they say that they launched in 1982 with their first distributor in Texas. But 1983 is widely reported (including by Chinaco itself) as the year Chinaco was introduced in the United States.

49. Author interviews (2013).

50. Chinaco (2014b).

51. Rodríguez Cisneros (2001).

52. Tequila may be aged in barrels made from *encino* or *roble;* both are translated as "oak" in English, but they represent different species. Reposado tequila must be aged for a minimum of two months; the size of the barrel is not specified. Añejo and extra añejo tequilas must be aged for a minimum of one year and three years, respectively, and the barrels cannot be bigger than six hundred liters (*Diario Oficial* 2012b).

53. Author interviews (2006).

54. Cedeño Cruz and Alvarez-Jacobs (1999); CRT (2014b).

55. Author interviews (2006).

56. Author interviews (2006).

57. Tequila Partida (2014).

58. Author fieldnotes (2014).

59. Author fieldnotes (2014).

60. Casas (2006, 415); Maxwell (2014).

61. Janzen (2012).

62. It is important to note that Herradura had gone on record as admitting that it used diffusers after cooking the agave. This is not nearly as controversial as the method employed by Cuervo and Sauza, in which diffusers are used before cooking. For some aficionados, any use of a diffuser is controversial, especially because it is impossible to verify how it is being used. Others may not understand the difference between the two methods.

63. Maxwell (2014).

64. The standard specifies that the added ingredients must not constitute more than 1 percent of the total weight of the tequila before it is bottled (*Diario Oficial* 1997b).

65. *Diario Oficial* (2006).

66. Author interviews (2007).

67. For example, Comté cheese producers, in France, created rules to limit growth and concentration among dairy farmers and preserve traditional cheese-making practices. Besides giving their particular DO cheese a reputation as one of the most traditional and authentic in France, the rules also represented an explicit strategy by the dairy farmers and small cheesemakers to resist cooptation by extralocal actors and ensure the industry's long-term sustainability; see Bowen (2011).

68. Author interviews (2006).

69. Author interviews (2013).

70. Author interviews (2013).

71. Author interviews (2013).

72. Author interviews (2013).

73. Author interviews (2006).

74. Tequila Partida (2014).

75. On F. Paul Pacult's reputation, see Forbes (2006); on Pacult's opinion of estate-grown agave, see English (2009).

76. Most of the tequila companies began to establish their own plantations in 2002 or 2003, during the agave shortage; thus, when the standard was passed in 2006, it allowed them to begin using their own three- or four-year-old agave to produce tequila.

77. Author interviews (2006).

78. CRT (2015).

79. Preston (1996).

80. Preston (1996).

81. Author interviews (2006).

82. Author interviews (2006).

83. Under the new agreement, a registry for all tequila bottlers in the United States was created (Office of the United States Trade Representative 2006). In addition, before any shipment of bulk tequila is permitted to leave Mexico, a form detailing the amount of tequila being shipped, the bottling company that it

is being shipped to, and the exporting company must be submitted to the CRT (author interviews 2006).

84. Author interviews (2006).

85. Ginley (2013).

86. *Technomic* (2012).

87. Tequila Patrón (2014a).

88. Author interviews (2006).

89. CRT 2005, 7.

90. This is the result of the Federal Law on Metrology and Standards, passed in 1992.

91. An advisory committee composed of representatives from the government, industry, and academic sectors consults with the DGN, and together they create a draft of the proposed standard, which is published in the *Diario Oficial*. The public has sixty days to comment on it. Afterward, the DGN committee revises the standard, taking into account valid public concerns and comments, and then the revised standard is published.

92. Author interviews (2009).

93. Author interviews (2009), my emphasis.

94. *Diario Oficial* (2012c).

95. Kinchy (2012); Harrison (2011).

96. Teil (2012, 478, 491).

97. The list of organizations that "participated" in the construction of the 1994 standard reflects the exclusivity of the process. Listed along with the CRT, the National Chamber of the Tequila Industry, and several governmental institutions (for example, the Mexican Institute of Industrial Property and the General Directorate of Standards) were twenty-seven private organizations, primarily medium and large tequila companies. The Distilled Spirits Council of the United States was also represented (despite the fact that the law is a Mexican law and the DO is owned by the Mexican state). With the exception of one distillery that is owned by a cooperative of farmers, the agave farmers were not represented. In the 2005 revisions, additional farmer representatives—including the Secretary of Agriculture and several farmer associations—are listed as having participated, but the tequila companies still dominated (and the Distilled Spirits Council of the United States, the trade association for the Canadian Distilled Spirits Industry, and the U.S. and Canadian embassies were included as well).

4. THE HEART OF THE AGAVE

1. Gaytán (2014).

2. As I discussed in chapter 2, most scholars believe that the production of mezcal originated in the Colima volcanoes region. From there, it spread throughout

western Mexico. A number of distilleries were established on haciendas in the Amatitán-Tequila valley in the eighteenth century. By the late eighteenth century, historical records indicate that mezcal was being produced in the valley in relatively large quantities.

3. Many people, especially in rural areas, use the word *mezcal* to refer to the agave that is used to make mezcal or tequila. Here, Castillo is referring to the agave plant.

4. Author interviews (2006).

5. Amatitán is a municipality in the state of Jalisco, and my list included farmers throughout the municipality, which encompasses both the town of Amatitán and several smaller villages.

6. Valenzuela Zapata and Macías Macías (2014). Three municipalities in Los Altos (Arandas, Tepatitlán, and Atotonilco) had more agave plants.

7. UNESCO (2015).

8. Gaytán (2014, 117).

9. Author interviews (2006).

10. Author interviews (2006).

11. With the land redistribution, portions of the land belonging to the haciendas were redistributed to smallholders organized into collective landholding units known as ejidos (Lewis 2002).

12. Author interviews (2006).

13. When adjusted for inflation, the prices are even more spectacular. Expressed in 2014 pesos, the price of agave ranged from twenty-seven to twenty-nine pesos per kilogram between 2000 and 2002 (calculations by Macías Macías 2015).

14. Author interviews (2006).

15. Author interviews (2006).

16. Wise (2010, 166).

17. Llamas (1999).

18. Author interviews (2006).

19. Author interviews (2006).

20. Bryson (2000).

21. Weiner (2000).

22. *Apoyos y Servicios a la Comercialización Agropecuaria* (2000).

23. Dalton (2005).

24. Solís-Aguilar et al. (2001).

25. Dalton (2005, 1071); Solís-Aguilar et al. (2001).

26. Author interviews (2006).

27. González (2002).

28. Calculations by Macías Macías (2015). See also Valenzuela Zapata and Macías Macías (2014, 35).

29. Author interviews (2006).

30. Velazco (2000).

31. CNIT (2010).

32. Weiner (2000).

33. Weiner (2000). It's not clear how a "rum-a-rita" is different from a daiquiri, but this is how they marketed it.

34. Solís-Aguilar et al. (2001).

35. See Aquino Bolaños et al. (2011) and Altuzar et al. (2007) for examples of this kind of research.

36. Dalton (2005).

37. Valenzuela Zapata and Nabhan (2004, 57).

38. Dalton (2005, 1070–1071).

39. Valenzuela Zapata and Nabhan (2004).

40. For example, as I discuss in Bowen (2011), at the time I visited producers of Comté cheese in France, the collective organization was limiting production through the sale of the rights to produce Comté cheese. These rights took the form of *plaques verts* (green plates), which were affixed to each round of cheese. The *plaques verts* were allocated to producers based on historical production volumes; they funded the collective organization and helped maintain stable and relatively high prices.

41. Bryson (2000).

42. Luna Zamora (1991, 128).

43. Luna Zamora (1991).

44. See Llamas (1999) for a discussion of historical relations between the agave farmers and tequila companies in Jalisco.

45. According to Luna Zamora (1991, 175), the price of agave never went above one peso per kilogram between 1960 and 1980.

46. Valenzuela Zapata (2005); Bowen and Valenzuela Zapata (2009).

47. Author interviews (2006). It is important to note that he was also referring to the fact that during periods of economic hardship, farmers often fail to fertilize their fields or adequately monitor for pest and disease infestation. This is a problem in the industry. However, he seemed to be advocating an overall shift away from labor-intensive cultivation practices, toward chemical-intensive methods of agave cultivation.

48. Author interviews (2006).

49. Author interviews (2006).

50. Macías Macías (2001).

51. SAGARPA (2000); SAGARPA (2005); SAGARPA (2010b).

52. As part of the decentralization of agricultural and rural policy in Mexico, Mexico is divided into 140 rural development districts; see De Janvry and Sadoulet (2007). Jalisco has 8 rural development districts. In quantifying the expansion of agave cultivation into southern Jalisco), I included the 2 districts in southeastern Jalisco, El Grullo and Ciudad Guzmán (SAGARPA 1999; SAGARPA 2010a).

53. Author interviews (2006).

54. Bowen and Gerritsen (2007, 477).

55. U.S. prices are expressed using the average exchange rate for 1996. Originally, the contracts usually offered the equivalent of the value of one ton of maize per hectare and 5 percent of the final harvest. By 2004, the contracting companies were frequently offering the value of two tons of maize per hectare but only 3 percent of the final harvest (Bowen 2004, 76). It is important to note that the Mexican government encouraged this shift by allowing farmers to also receive payments through the Program of Direct Support for the Countryside (PROCAMPO), an agricultural support program introduced in 1993. The program was originally designed to compensate farmers growing staple crops, which were expected to experience declining prices after the initiation of the North American Free Trade Agreement. When the program was first implemented, only growers of corn, dry beans, wheat, rice, sorghum, soybeans, safflower, cotton, and barley were eligible for support. However, in 1997, the program was expanded to include agave as well as other crops (Bowen and Gerritsen 2007).

56. During the first few years after the turn of the twenty-first century, when the tequila companies began moving into southern Jalisco, corn prices were very low. According to Wise (2010, 166), real corn prices in Mexico fell almost 70 percent between the early 1990s and 2005. Corn prices in Jalisco spiked in 2011 and particularly in 2012, likely owing to a number of factors, including increased production of biofuels in the United States and climate-related issues.

57. González (2002).

58. Zizumbo-Villarreal et al. (2013).

59. Bowen and Gerritsen (2007).

60. Betancourt (2003). In 2004, the complaint was rejected for lack of supporting evidence.

61. Calculations by Macías Macías (2015); see also Valenzuela Zapata and Macías Macías (2014, 35).

62. There is no clear consensus on how much it costs to produce a kilogram of agave, and costs vary over time. In 2005, a committee composed of representatives from the CRT, the major associations of agaveros, and the federal government (SAGARPA, SEDER) estimated the average costs of agave (over the entire cultivation cycle) to be 2.55 pesos per kilogram (author interviews 2006). A comparative analysis of seven municipalities (Valenzuela Zapata and Macías Macías 2014) estimated an average cost of production of 1.84 pesos per kilogram in 2010, with a cost of 3.05 pesos per kilogram in Amatitán. Expressed as real prices (in 2014 pesos), these estimations range from 2.12 pesos (the estimate by Valenzuela Zapata and Macías Macías) to 3.77 pesos per kilogram (the estimate by the CRT, farmers' associations, and federal government).

63. Author interviews (2006).

64. Author interviews (2006).

65. Author interviews (2006).
66. Author interviews (2006).
67. Author interviews (2006).
68. Author interviews (2006).
69. Llamas (1999, 20).
70. Author interviews (2006).
71. Author interviews (2006).
72. Author interviews (2006).
73. Author interviews (2006).
74. Author interviews (2006).
75. Author interviews (2006).
76. Calculations by Macías Macías (2015); see also Valenzuela Zapata and Macías Macías (2014, 35).
77. Hernández López and Porraz Gómez (2011).
78. Author interviews (2006).
79. Author interviews (2006).
80. SENASICA (2013).
81. CRT (2010, 4).
82. *El Economista* (2012).
83. Calculations by Macías Macías (2015); see also Valenzuela Zapata and Macías Macías (2014, 35).
84. *El Vigía* (2014).
85. CNIT (2013).
86. CNIT (2013).
87. *Revista Quo* (2014).
88. *El Economista* (2012).
89. Author interviews (2013).
90. Author interviews (2013).
91. Rodríguez (2014b).
92. Aragón (2014).
93. Matías (2014).
94. Valenzuela Zapata (2003) explains that agave plants generally begin to flower when they are about five years old. The quiote is removed in order to maximize the amount of sugar that stays in the agave plant. The removal of the quiote is done manually, with a coa or a machete, usually in the month of February or March.
95. CNIT (2005).
96. Gaytán (2014, 99).
97. This refers to metric tons, or a thousand kilograms.
98. Author interviews (2014).
99. Author interviews (2014).
100. One analysis calculated an average weight per piña of 50 kilograms, or 110 pounds (Saldaña Robles et al. 2012, 459). However, the size of each piña

varies widely, with some piñas weighing 120 kilograms (265 pounds) or more (Montañez et al. 2011, 4).

101. Hernández López and Porraz Gómez (2011).

102. The best-paying job is the *deshije*, the removal of the hijuelos, the vegetative offshoots of the agave plant. After about four years, an agave starts to send out shoots. Removing the hijuelos has two purposes: it helps maximize the growth of the agave plant, and it allows the hijuelos to be replanted. The workers we talked to in Los Altos in 2014 told us that they could earn seven hundred pesos per day doing this job, but that it lasted only one month out of the year (author interviews 2014).

103. The laborers I interviewed in Amatitán in 2006 reported daily wages of between 120 and 180 pesos (between 170 and 250 pesos when expressed in 2014 pesos) for their work preparing soils, pruning, and applying agricultural chemicals. Hernández López and Porraz Gómez (2011) report that agricultural workers received an average wage of 1,000 pesos per week, which translates to 166 pesos (182 pesos when expressed in 2014 pesos) per day if we assume that they were working six days per week. (This is not a guarantee, of course, but many of the laborers I interviewed in Amatitán said that they worked six days per week during periods when they could find work). Expressed in real terms, the wages reported by workers in Amatitán in 2006 and in Los Altos in 2011 and 2014 are all within the same range.

104. In the 1990s, as the "tequila boom" was just getting started, and given high rates of migration from Jalisco to the United States, the tequila companies faced a shortage of qualified workers. According to Hernández López and Porraz Gómez (2011), several tequila companies sent trucks down to Chiapas to bring a few dozen workers to Los Altos in 1998. The poverty rate in Chiapas, 75 percent, is the highest among all Mexican states (CONEVAL 2012).

105. Ríos (2008).

106. Hernández López and Porraz Gómez (2011, 174).

107. Hernández López and Porraz Gómez (2011).

108. Author fieldnotes (2014).

109. Hernández López and Porraz Gómez (2011, 171).

110. Hernández López and Porraz Gómez (2011, 171).

111. Holmes (2013).

112. Llamas (1999, 10).

113. Torres (1998, 78).

114. Luna Zamora (1991).

115. McMichael (2012).

116. Gravel (2007).

117. Gravel (2007, 83).

118. Driven by the structural adjustment policies adopted in the wake of Mexico's 1982 decision to default on its loans (and its subsequent bailout by the Interna-

tional Monetary Fund and foreign governments), and consolidated with the ratification of the North American Free Trade Agreement in 1993, neoliberal reforms focused on deregulating various sectors of the economy, privatizing state-owned enterprises, eliminating subsidies, and promoting foreign direct investment.

119. Appendini (1998); Fourcade-Gourinchas and Babb (2002); Gravel (2007); Hamilton (2002); McMichael (2012); Otero (2004).

120. La Porta and Lopez-de-Silanes (1999); Salas and Kikeri (2005).

121. Maldonado (2013).

122. Luna Zamora (1991, 120).

5. MAKING MEZCAL IN THE SHADOW OF THE DENOMINATION OF ORIGIN

1. It is difficult to estimate precisely the number of small producers in Michoacán or in any other state. The state registry includes three hundred producers, many of whom are uncertified (*Lo de Hoy en el Puerto* 2013). However, given producers' reluctance to step out of the shadows and risk being shut down or taxed by the state, there are likely many more.

2. Ward (2014).

3. Monterrosa Hernández (2005, 46–47).

4. Author interviews (2010).

5. At the time of my interview, the DO for mezcal did not include any parts of Michoacán; however, it was revised in 2012 and now includes his municipality.

6. Author interviews (2009).

7. On the DO, see *Diario Oficial* (1994b). On the quality standard, see *Diario Oficial* (1997c).

8. As I note in chapter 2, the organization's original name was the Mexican Regulatory Council for the Quality of Mezcal. In 2014, the organization changed its name to the Mezcal Regulatory Council. I refer to it by its current name, the Mezcal Regulatory Council, or the CRM, throughout the book.

9. Meixueiro et al. (1997).

10. Foote (1996); Meixueiro et al. (1997).

11. Walton (1977, 124).

12. Foote (1996, 6).

13. Pratt (2007, 291).

14. Meixueiro et al. (1997).

15. *Diario Oficial* (1994b); *Diario Oficial* (1997c).

16. Colunga-García Marín et al. (2007).

17. *Diario Oficial* (1997c).

18. The five species are: *Agave angustifolia* (maguey espadín); *Agave asperrima* (maguey de cerro, maguey bruto, or maguey cenizo); *Agave weberi* (maguey

de mezcal); *Agave potatorum* (maguey de mezcal, also known as tobalá); and *Agave salmiana* (maguey verde or maguey mezcalero) (*Diario Oficial* 1997c). Incredibly, the listings of the species in the standard contain several misspellings; these are the correct names, taken from Gentry (1982 [2004]).

19. CRM (2014d).

20. *Diario Oficial* (2012a).

21. *Diario Oficial* (2009).

22. COMERCAM (2007).

23. CRM (2015, 21).

24. CRM (2015, 37–44).

25. Author interviews (2009).

26. Author interviews (2009).

27. *Diario Oficial* (1994a).

28. Author interviews (2009).

29. The entire state of Jalisco is included in the territory of the DO for tequila. However, the costs and methods associated with tequila production are not viable for very small producers, so they cannot sell their products as tequila. Nor can they sell their products as mezcal, since they are outside the DO region for mezcal. Some parts of southern Jalisco have a well-established tradition of mezcal production (Zizumbo-Villarreal, Colunga-García Marín, et al. 2009).

30. Author fieldnotes (2009).

31. Author interviews (2013).

32. Author interviews (2009).

33. Author interviews (2010).

34. Although the tequila distilleries are not regulated by the DO for mezcal, they, like the mezcal producers in Oaxaca, had an interest in preventing producers from other states from being allowed to enter any of the DO regions.

35. Author interviews (2010).

36. Rosas (2012).

37. *Diario Oficial* (2003).

38. On species commonly used to make mezcal, see Larson and Aguirre (forthcoming). On species associated with the production of distilled spirits, see Colunga-García Marín (2006); Colunga-García Marín et al. (2007).

39. CRM (2015, 24).

40. Author interviews (2009).

41. Author interviews (2009).

42. A retailer who bought directly from many small mezcaleros estimated that fermentation times ranged from seven days to thirty-five (author interviews 2014).

43. Ward (2014).

44. Author interviews (2009).

45. Author interviews (2013).
46. Author fieldnotes (2014).
47. Mezcales Tradicionales (2011).
48. Author interviews (2010).
49. See, for example, Mezcaloteca (2014) and Mezonte (2014).
50. Diario Oficial (1997c).
51. Author fieldnotes (2009).
52. Vera Guzmán et al. (2012).
53. Author interviews (2013).
54. Author interviews (2009).
55. Author interviews (2013).
56. Lachenmeier et al. (2006).
57. García (2012).
58. Author interviews (2014).
59. Author interviews (2014).
60. Author interviews (2009).
61. The quantity of certified mezcal increased from just over four hundred thousand liters in 2005 to 1.6 million liters in 2011 (COMERCAM 2007; COMERCAM 2012).
62. CRM (2014a).
63. The standard specifies how many samples must be taken. The proportion of mezcal that is sampled declines as production volumes increase. For example, if a distillery produces fewer than 50 barrels of one type of mezcal, samples must be taken from two barrels (4 percent of the total). If the total production is between 51 and 500 barrels, samples from 3 barrels are required (as low as 0.6 percent of the total). If the total production is between 501 and 35,000 barrels, samples from 5 barrels are required (as low as 0.014 percent of total) (Diario Oficial 1997c).
64. Author interviews (2009).
65. Cost estimates are based on estimates provided on the CRM's website and were last updated in January 2013 (COMERCAM 2014). Estimates are for producers who are members of the CRM. The costs of certification are higher for nonmembers. Membership dues range from two thousand to ten thousand pesos per year. Conversions to U.S. dollars here are made using the average exchange rate for 2014.
66. Illsley Granich (2009b, 186).
67. Comparison is between bottled, certified mezcal and bottled, uncertified mezcal. Producers who sell their uncertified mezcal in bulk receive a lower price (Pool-Illsley and Illsley Granich 2012).
68. Castellanos (2009).
69. Author interviews (2009).
70. Luna Jiménez (2012); Zavala Lunes (2012).

71. The distilleries, located in the central Oaxaca valley, were reportedly not being used and had been abandoned (Zavala Lunes 2012).

72. Zavala Lunes (2012).

73. Barra Informativa (2013).

74. CRM (2015, 21).

75. CRM (2015, 23).

76. COMERCAM (2013).

77. Maillard (2013).

78. Author interviews (2009).

79. Author interviews (2009).

80. CRT (2015); CRM (2015).

81. Author interviews (2009).

82. Author interviews (2009).

6. HIPSTERS, HOPE, AND THE FUTURE OF ARTISANAL MEZCAL

1. Peabody (2009).

2. Fabricant (2013).

3. *Food and Wine* (2013).

4. Ginley (2013).

5. Steinhauer (2014).

6. Flannery (2013).

7. CRM (2015, 47).

8. In the mezcal industry and more generally, concepts like "artisanal" and "traditional" are fiercely debated. Throughout this book, I use *traditional* to refer to mezcal made by small producers employing the methods that are characteristic of their regions. This is similar to the definition used by many of the people I interviewed. I use *artisanal* to refer to mezcal that is made using somewhat traditional methods, but by larger producers, who often have made small adaptations to their production process. I use both terms somewhat loosely, because there is overlap between them.

9. Author interviews (2013).

10. Author interviews (2013).

11. Frizell (2009).

12. Nailey (2013).

13. English (2013).

14. Author interviews (2009).

15. Johnston and Baumann (2010, 92).

16. Johnston and Baumann (2010).

17. Paxson (2012, 6).

18. Paxson (2012, 7).

19. Author interviews (2013).

20. Author interviews (2013).

21. Author interviews (2013).

22. Author interviews (2009).

23. Author interviews (2009).

24. Author interviews (2013).

25. Author interviews (2013).

26. Author interviews (2013).

27. Author interviews (2013).

28. Matalon (2012).

29. Illsley Granich (2009b, 187).

30. Author interviews (2014).

31. Author interviews (2014).

32. Author interviews (2012).

33. Author interviews (2013).

34. Author interviews (2013).

35. Simonson (2012).

36. Cameron (2012).

37. Nader (2012).

38. Colunga-García Marín et al. (2012).

39. Terra (2012).

40. Leopo Flores (2012).

41. Author interviews (2013).

42. Author interviews (2013). Thomas Evans's statistics are very close, according to statistics from the CRT: in 2013, 76 percent of tequila was exported and 77 percent of tequila exports went to the United States (CRT 2015).

43. Author interviews (2014).

44. Author interviews (2009).

45. Martin et al. (2011).

46. Author interviews (2009).

47. Living on Earth (2004).

48. Author interviews (2009).

49. Author interviews (2009).

50. Author interviews (2009).

51. Author interviews (2009).

52. *Malinchista* is a pejorative term that refers to La Manlinche, the Indian mistress of Spanish conqueror Hernán Cortés, who betrayed her own people in exchange for new life. Here, *malinchista* is used to refer to Mexican people who reject their own heritage and culture in favor of foreign values, objects, or cultures.

53. Author interviews (2009)

54. Author fieldnotes (2009).

55. Author interviews (2009).

56. Bowen and De Master (2011, 81).

7. LOOKING FORWARD

1. Kleinman (2015).

2. Strenk (2014).

3. Ward (2014).

4. *Difford's Guide* (2013).

5. Ward (2014).

6. Author interviews (2014).

7. Bowen and Hamrick (2014).

8. *Diario Oficial* (2012a).

9. CRM (2014b).

10. For example, some people argued that the standard should not allow producers to use autoclaves or to age mezcal in wooden barrels.

11. Szczech (2014a).

12. Flores 2014.

13. *Al Momento* (2014).

14. *Diario El Fortín* (2014).

15. Szczech (2014b).

16. CRM (2014c).

17. Szczech (2014c).

18. Author interviews (2009). This is how the DGN representative whom I interviewed described the process.

19. Rodríguez (2014a).

20. Garrone (2014).

21. CRT (2015, 72).

22. Author fieldnotes (2014).

23. Author fieldnotes (2014).

24. Author fieldnotes (2014).

25. Besky (2013, 175).

26. Besky (2013, 176).

27. Alkon (2012, 145–146)

28. Alkon (2012, 153).

29. DeLind (2011); Alkon (2012).

30. Paxson (2012, 211).

31. Author interviews (2009), my emphasis.

32. Author interviews (2009).

33. Seidman (2007, 7). Seidman analyzes the antiapartheid movement and the development of the Sullivan Principles in South Africa, campaigns against child labor in India, and labor rights activism in Guatemala.

34. Case and Martin (2014).

35. On organized-crime-related violence, see *New York Times* (2014); see also Corchado (2013). On the students' disappearance, see Case and Martin (2014).

36. Seidman (2007).

METHODOLOGICAL APPENDIX

1. Bowen and Gerritsen (2007, 477).

2. Gaytán and Valenzuela Zapata (2012).

3. Pini (2005); see also Schwalbe and Wolkomir (2001). These researchers also note that in order to understand how gender shapes the interview process, we need to go beyond just looking at the genders of the interviewer and the interviewee and examine how gender intersects with differences along lines of race, class, and age, as well as the research topic and the context in which the interview takes place (meaning both the physical site of the interview and the broader field or context of the research).

4. Schwalbe and Wolkomir (2001).

5. Schwalbe and Wolkomir (2001).

6. Gaytán (2014, 100–101).

7. CONEVAL (2012).

Works Cited

Alan, David. 2011. "Trouble in Tequila-ville." *Edible Austin,* August 27, 2011. www.edibleaustin.com/index.php/food-2/beverages/909-trouble-in-tequila-ville.

Alkon, Alison. 2012. *Black, White, and Green: Farmers Markets, Race, and the Green Economy.* Athens: University of Georgia Press.

Al Momento. 2014. "Propone el Comercam Restringir a Métodos Artesanales la Producción de Mezcal." June 6. www.almomento.mx/propone-el-comercam-restringir-a-metodos-artesanales-la-produccion-de-mezcal/.

Altuzar, A., E.A. Malo, H. González-Hernández, and J.C. Rojas. 2007. "Electrophysiological and Behavioural Responses of *Scyphophorus acupunctatus* (Col., Curculionidae) to *Agave tequilana* Volatiles." *Journal of Applied Entomology* 131(2): 121–127.

Apoyos y Servicios a la Comercialización Agropecuaria. 2000. "De Nuestra Cosecha." *Revista Claridades Agropecuarios* 87 (November): 3–32. www.infoaserca.gob.mx/claridades/revistas/087/ca087.pdf.

Appendini, Kirsten. 1998. "Changing Agrarian Institutions: Interpreting the Contradictions." In *The Transformation of Rural Mexico: Reforming the Ejido Sector,* edited by Wayne Cornelius and David Myhre, pp. 25–38. San Diego: Center for U.S.-Mexico Studies, University of California, San Diego.

Aquino Bolaños, T., J. Ruíz Vega, S. Girón Pablo, R. Pérez Pacheco, S.H. Martínez Tomas, and M.E. Silva Rivera. 2011. "Interrelationships of the Agave Weevil *Scyphophorus acupunctatus* (Gyllenhal), *Erwinia carotovora*

(Dye), Entomopathogenic Agents and Agrochemicals." *African Journal of Biotechnology* 10(68): 15402–15406.

Aragón, Evlin. 2014. "Mezcaleros Tiran Producto para Protestar por Falta Apoyo." *El Financiero,* September 4. www.elfinanciero.com.mx/economia /mezcaleros-tiran-producto-para-protestar-por-falta-apoyo.html.

Areté Research and Consulting in Economics (Areté). 2013. *Study on Accessing the Added Value of PDO/PGI Products.* http://ec.europa.eu/agriculture /external-studies/2013/added-value-pdo-pgi/exec-sum_en.pdf.

Asimov, Eric. 2010. "Mezcal, Tequila's Smoky, Spicy Cousin." *New York Times.* August 16. www.nytimes.com/2010/08/18/dining/reviews/18wine.html.

Bahre, Conrad, and David Bradbury. 1980. "Manufacture of Mescal in Sonora, Mexico." *Economic Botany* 34(4): 391–400.

Barham, Elizabeth. 2003. "Translating Terroir: The Global Challenge of French AOC Labeling." *Journal of Rural Studies* 19(1): 127–138.

Barjolle, Dominique, and Bertil Sylvander. 2000. "Protected Designations of Origin and Protected Geographical Indications in Europe: Regulation or Policy? Recommendations." *PDO and PGI Products: Market, Supply Chains, and Institutions.* FAIR 1-CT 95–0306, Final Report, June 2000. Brussels: European Commission.

Barra Informativa. 2013. "COMERCAM Va por el Relanzamiento del Mezcal." http://barrainformativa.com/index.php?option=com_content&view=article &id=4499:comercam-va-por-el-relanzamiento-del-mezcal&catid=39:oaxaca &Itemid=58.

Barrientos, Stephanie. 2014. "Gendered Global Production Networks: Analysis of Cocoa-Chocolate Sourcing." *Regional Studies* 48(5): 791–803.

Bautista, Juan Antonio, Javier Ramírez Juárez, and Mascha Smit. Forthcoming. "Origen, Auge, y Crisis de la Industria del Mezcal en Oaxaca." In *Aguas de las Verdes Matas: Tequila y Mezcal,* edited by José Luis Vera Cortés and Rodolfo Fernández, pp. 107–121. Mexico City: Artes de México.

Belletti, Giovanni, and Andrea Marescotti. 2002. *Link between Origin-Labeled Products and Rural Development.* WP Report 3. Le Mans, France: Development of Origin-Labeled Products: Humanity, Innovations, and Sustainability (DOLPHINS).

Bérard, Laurence, and Philippe Marchenay. 2006. "Local Products and Geographical Knowledge: Taking Account of Local Knowledge and Biodiversity." *International Social Science Journal* 58(187): 109–116.

Besky, Sarah. 2013. *The Darjeeling Distinction: Labor and Justice on Fair-Trade Tea Plantations in India.* Berkeley: University of California Press.

———. 2014. "The Labor of Terroir and the Terroir of Labor: Geographical Indication and Darjeeling Tea Plantations." *Agriculture and Human Values* 31(1): 83–96.

Bessière, Jacinthe. 1998. "Local Development and Heritage: Traditional Food and Cuisine as Tourist Attractions in Rural Areas." *Sociologia Ruralis* 38(1): 21–34.

Betancourt, José Díaz. 2003. "Acusan de Erosión a Empresa José Cuervo, en Jalisco." *La Jornada*, October 23. www.jornada.unam.mx/2003/10/24 /038n1est.php?printver=0&fly=1.

Black, Kent. 2011. "Toby Keith, Mezcal Endorsement Pioneer." *Businessweek*. November 17. www.businessweek.com/magazine/toby-keith-mezcal-endorsement-pioneer-11172011.html.

Blakeney, Michael. 2001. "Proposals for the International Regulation of Geographical Indications." *Journal of World Intellectual Property* 4(5): 629–652.

Bodnár, Judit. 2003. "Roquefort vs. Big Mac: Globalization and Its Others." *European Journal of Sociology* 44(1): 68–79.

Boisard, Pierre. 2003. *Camembert: A National Myth*. Berkeley: University of California Press.

Bourke, John G. 1893. "Primitive Distillation among the Tarascoes." *American Anthropologist* 6: 65–70.

Bové, José, François Dufour, and Gilles Luneau. 2001. *The World Is Not for Sale: Farmers against Junk Food*. London: Verso.

Bowen, Sarah. 2004. "The Road to Margaritaville: Expansion of Agave Cultivation and Power Dynamics in Southern Jalisco, Mexico." Master's thesis. Madison: University of Wisconsin-Madison.

———. 2011. "The Importance of Place: Re-territorialising Embeddedness." *Sociologia Ruralis* 51(4): 325–348.

Bowen, Sarah, and Kathryn De Master. 2011. "New Rural Livelihoods or Museums of Production? Quality Food Initiatives in Practice." *Journal of Rural Studies* 27(1): 73–82.

Bowen, Sarah, and Marie Sarita Gaytán. 2012. "The Paradox of Protection: National Identity, Global Commodity Chains, and the Tequila Industry." *Social Problems* 59(1): 70–93.

Bowen, Sarah, and Peter Gerritsen. 2007. "Reverse Leasing and Power Dynamics among Blue Agave Farmers in Western Mexico." *Agriculture and Human Values* 24(4): 473–488.

Bowen, Sarah, and Danny Hamrick. 2014. "Defining Mexico's Spirit." *Gastronomica* 14(4): 26–33.

Bowen, Sarah, and Ana Valenzuela Zapata. 2009. "Geographical Indications, Terroir, and Socioeconomic and Ecological Sustainability: The Case of Tequila." *Journal of Rural Studies* 25(1): 108–119.

Brown-Forman. 2013. *Proof: 2013 Annual Report*. Louisville, KY: Brown-Forman.

Bruman, Henry J. 1944. The Asiatic Origin of the Huichol Still. *Geographical Review* 34: 418–427.

Bryson, Lew. 2000. "Hard Up in Jalisco: Shortage of Blue Agave Plants, Tequila's Raw Material, Drives Up Prices." *Chicago Tribune,* March 22. http://lewbryson.com/tribteq.htm.

Calenda, Carlo. 2014. "Real Parmesan Cheese and Geographical Indications." *Wall Street Journal,* April 1. www.wsj.com/articles/SB100014240527023033 25204579467553826945522.

Cámara Nacional de la Industria Tequilera (CNIT). 2005. *Informe Estadístico 2005.* Guadalajara: Cámara Nacional de la Industria Tequila (previously posted online; no longer available).

———. 2010. *Informe Estadístico 2010.* www.tequileros.org/stuff/file_estadistica /1310142683.pdf (no longer available online).

———. 2013. *Estadísticas a Diciembre 2013.* www.tequileros.org/stuff/file_ estadistica/1393350128.pdf.

Cameron, Ian. 2012. "NOM-186: Our Editorial Stance." *Diffords Guide,* January 24. www.diffordsguide.com/class-magazine/read-online/en/2012-01-24 /page-8/nom-186:-what-class-thinks?force_issue=41&.

Campbell, Hugh. 2009. "Breaking New Ground in Food Regime Theory: Corporate Environmentalism, Ecological Feedbacks and the 'Food from Somewhere' Regime?" *Agriculture and Human Values* 26(4): 309–319.

Casa Dragones. 2015. "Modern Process." http://casadragones.com/sipping-tequila/modern-process/.

Casas, Rosalba. 2006. "Between Traditions and Modernity: Technological Strategies at Three Tequila Firms." *Technology in Society* 28(3): 407–419.

Case, Brendan, and Eric Martin. 2014. "Mexico President's Approval Drops to Lowest since Taking Office." *Bloomberg Business Week,* December 1. www .businessweek.com/news/2014-12-01/ mexico-president-s-approval-drops-to-lowest-since-taking-office.

Castellanos, Montserrat. 2009. "Alerta Canaimez sobre Aumento en Venta de Mezcal Adulterado por IEPS." *Voz del Sur.* November 6. http://vozdelsur .com.mx/oaxaca/2303-alerta-canaimez-sobre-aumento-en-venta-de-mezcal-adulterado-por-ieps.html.

Cedeño Cruz, M., and J. Alvarez-Jacobs. 1999. "Production of Tequila from Agave: Historical Influences and Contemporary Processes." In *The Alcohol Textbook,* 4th ed., edited by K. A. Jacques, T. P. Lyons, and D. R. Kelsall, pp. 225–241. Nottingham, U.K.: Nottingham University Press.

Centre de Coopération Internationale en Recherche Agronomique pour le Développement (CIRAD). 2013. "The First African 'Protected Geographic Indication.'" Centre de Coopération Internationale en Recherche Agronomique pour le Développement. February 22. www.cirad.fr/en/news /all-news-items/press-releases/2013/geographic-indications.

Chase, Mark W., James L. Reveal, and Michael F. Fay. 2009. "A Subfamilial Classification for the Expanded Asparagalean Families Amaryllidaceae,

Asparagaceae and Xanthorrhoeaceae." *Botanical Journal of the Linnean Society* 161(2): 132–136.

Chávez, Daniel. 2006. "Globalizing Tequila: Mexican Television's Representations of the Neoliberal Reconversion of Land and Labor." *Arizona Journal of Hispanic Cultural Studies* 10: 187–203.

Chever, Tanguy, Christian Renault, Séverine Renault, and Violanie Romieu (AND-International). 2012. *Value of Products and Foodstuffs, Wines, Aromatized Wines and Spirits Protected by a Geographical Indication (GI)*. European Commission. http://ec.europa.eu/agriculture/external-studies/2012/value-gi/summary_en.pdf.

Chinaco. 2014a. "Accolades." www.chinacotequila.com/landing.php?p=accolades.

———. 2014b. "Legacy of the Warrior Spirit." www.chinacotequila.com/landing.php?p=chinaco.

Cohen, Roger. 1999. "The World: Heartburn; Fearful over the Future, Europe Seizes on Food." *New York Times*. August 29. www.nytimes.com/1999/08/29/weekinreview/the-world-heartburn-fearful-over-the-future-europe-seizes-on-food.html.

Colinet, Pierre, Marion Desquilbet, Daniel Hassan, Sylvette Monier-Dilhan, Valérie Orozco, and Vincent Réquillart. 2006. *Case Study: Comté Cheese in France*. Toulouse, France: Institut Nationale de la Recherche Agronomique. http://ec.europa.eu/agriculture/quality/certification/docs/case3_en.pdf.

Colunga-García Marín, Patricia. 2006. *Base de Datos de Nombres Técnicos o de Uso Común en el Aprovechamiento de los Agaves en México*. Final report, SNIB-CONABIO Project Number CS007. Mérida: Centro de Investigación Científica de Yucatán, A.C. www.conabio.gob.mx/institucion/proyectos/resultados/InfCS007.pdf.

Colunga-García Marín, Patricia, Catarina Illsley Granich, Alejandro Calvillo, and David Suro-Piñera. 2012. Oposición y Propuestas al PROY-NOM-186-SCFI-2012, Bebidas Alcohólicas, Bebidas Alcohólicas Elaboradas a Partir de Agave, July 6. http://207.248.177.30/expediente/v99/_B001203212.pdf.

Colunga-García Marín, Patricia, Alfonso Larqué Saavedra, Luis E. Eguiarte, and Daniel Zizumbo-Villarreal. 2007. *En Lo Ancestral Hay Futuro: Del Tequila, Los Mezcales, y Otros Agaves*. Mérida, Mexico: Centro de Investigación Científica de Yucatán, A.C.

Colunga-García Marín, Patricia, and Daniel Zizumbo-Villarreal. 2007. "Tequila and Other Agave Spirits from West-Central Mexico: Current Germplasm Diversity, Conservation and Origin." *Biodiversity and Conservation* 16(6): 1653–1667.

Comisión Nacional para el Conocimiento y el Uso de la Biodiversidad (CONABIO). 2006. *Mezcales y Diversidad*. 2nd. ed. Mexico City: Comisión Nacional para el Conocimiento y Uso de la Biodiversidad. www.conabio.gob.mx

/informacion/metadata/gis/mmezcales_gw.xml?_httpcache=yes&_xsl=/db
/metadata/xsl/fgdc_html.xsl&_indent=no.

Comite Interprofessionel du Gruyère du Comté (CIGC). 2014a. "La Filière Comté en Bref." Last updated September 17, 2014. www.comte.com /decouvrir/une-filiere-organisee-et-solidaire/la-filiere-comte-en-bref.html.

———. 2014b. "On the Farm." www.comte-usa.com/about-comte/on-the-farm/.

———. 2014c. "Rapide Portrait d'un Grand Fromage." Last updated September 17, 2014. www.comte.com/decouvrir/rapide-portrait-dun-grand-fromage .html.

Consejo Mexicano Regulador de la Calidad del Mezcal (COMERCAM). 2007. *Informe Anual de Actividades, Febrero 2006–Febrero 2007*. Oaxaca, Mexico: COMERCAM.

———. 2011. *Informe Anual, Consejo Directivo, Abril 2010–Abril 2012*. Oaxaca, Mexico: COMERCAM.

———. 2012. *Informe Consejo Directivo, Abril 2009–Abril 2012*. Oaxaca, Mexico: COMERCAM.

———. 2013. *Informe de Actividades, Consejo Directivo, 2012–2015* (published April 2013). Oaxaca, Mexico: COMERCAM. www.crm.org.mx/PDF /INFORMES/INFORME2012.pdf.

———. 2014. "Cuotas Vigentes." www.crm.org.mx/PDF/CUOTAS.pdf.

Consejo Nacional de Evaluación de la Política de Desarrollo Social (CONEVAL). 2012. "Pobreza en México." www.coneval.gob.mx/Medicion/Paginas /Medici%C3%B3n/Pobreza%202012/Pobreza-2012.aspx.

Consejo Regulador del Mezcal (CRM). 2014a. "Diagramas del Proceso de Certificación." www.crm.org.mx/PDF/PROCESO_CERTIFICACION.pdf.

———. 2014b. "Propuesta de Modificación de la NOM 070, Borrador para Discusión," May 19. www.crm.org.mx/PDF/DENOMINACION/PROPUESTA_ %20NOM_070_DISCUSION.pdf.

———. 2014c. "Propuesta de Modificación de la NOM 070, Propuesta Consesada," June 23. www.crm.org.mx/PDF/DENOMINACION/PROPUESTA_ CONSENSADA_23JUN2014.pdf.

———. 2014d. "Quienes Somos." www.crm.org.mx/index.php?option=com_cont ent&view=article&id=44&Itemid=57.

———. 2015. *Informe 2015*. Oaxaca City: Consejo Regulador del Mezcal. http:// www.crm.org.mx/PDF/popup/informe.pdf.

Consejo Regulador del Tequila (CRT). 2004. "El CRT-Creando Alianzas: Pro Defensa del Tequila." *Gaceta* 4: 18–19.

———. 2005. "Miguel Ángel Domínquez, Nuevo Presidente del Consejo Regulador del Tequila A.C." *Gaceta* 5: 4–7.

———. 2010. *Actualización de la Base de Datos y Diagnóstico Fitosanitario*. Guadalajara: CRT. www.crt.org.mx/images/documentos/inventarioagave2010b .pdf.

————. 2012. *Información Estadística, Enero-Junio 2012.* Guadalajara: CRT.

————. 2014a. "Asuntos Internacionales." www.crt.org.mx/index.php?option= com_content&view=article&id=274&Itemid=200&lang=es.

————. 2014b. "Elaboration." www.crt.org.mx/index.php?option=com_content& view=article&id=92&Itemid=174&lang=en.

————. 2014c. "Events 20 Aniversario 1994–2014." www.tequila.org.mx/.

————. 2015. "Información Estadística." Consejo Regulador del Tequila. www .crt.org.mx/EstadisticasCRTweb/.

Coombe, Rosemary J., and Nicole Aylwin. 2011. "Bordering Diversity and Desire: Using Intellectual Property to Mark Place-Based Products." *Environment and Planning* 43: 2027–2042.

Corchado, Alfredo. 2013. *Midnight in Mexico: A Reporter's Journey through a Country's Descent into Darkness.* New York: Penguin.

Dalton, Rex. 2005. "Saving the Agave." *Nature* 428 (December 22–29, 2005): 1070–1071.

De Barrios, Virginia. 1971. *A Guide to Tequila, Mezcal, and Pulque.* Mexico City: Editorial Minutiae Mexicana.

De Janvry, Alain, and Elisabeth Sadoulet. 2007. "Toward a Territorial Approach to Rural Development." *Journal of Agricultural and Development Economics* 4: 66–98.

DeLind, Laura. 2011. "Are Local Food and the Local Food Movement Taking Us Where We Want to Go? Or Are We Hitching Our Wagons to the Wrong Star?" *Agriculture and Human Values* 28(2): 273–283.

Del Maguey. 2014. "Tobala. Del Maguey: Single Village Mezcal." http://mezcal .com/tobala/.

De Roest, Kees, and Alberto Menghi. 2000. "Reconsidering 'Traditional' Food: The Case of Parmigiano Reggiano Cheese." *Sociologia Ruralis* 40(4): 439–451.

Deselnicu, Oana, Marco Costanigro, Diogo Souza-Monteiro, and Dawn Thilmany McFadden. 2013. "A Meta-Analysis of Geographic Indication Food Valuation Studies: What Drives the Premium for Origin Based Labels?" *Journal of Agriculture and Resource Economics* 38(2): 204–219.

DeSoucey, Michaela. 2010. "Gastronationalism: Food Traditions and Authenticity Politics in the European Union." *American Sociological Review* 75(3): 432–455.

Diario El Fortín. 2014. "En Riesgo La Industria Mezcalera." May 29, 2014. www.elfortindiario.info/slider/en-riesgo-la-industria-mezcalera/.

Diario Oficial de la Federación. 1949. "Norma Oficial de Calidad para Tequila, DGN R9–1949." June 14. http://mezcalestradicionales.mx/mezcales_herencia_ cultural_y_bio/Ponencias%20PDF/27%20NOM%20Tequila%201949.pdf.

————. 1968. "Norma Oficial de Calidad para Tequila, DGN R-9–1968." March 29. www.dof.gob.mx/nota_to_imagen_fs.php?codnota=4806925&fecha=29 /03/1968&cod_diario=206897.

———. 1974. "Declaración General de la Protección a la Denominación de Origen 'Tequila.'" December 9. http://dof.gob.mx/nota_to_imagen_fs.php?codnota=4731635&fecha=09/12/1974&cod_diario=203903.

———. 1977. "Declaración General de Protección a la Denominación de Origen 'Tequila.'" October 13. www.wipo.int/wipolex/en/text.jsp?file_id=220989.

———. 1991. "Ley de la Propiedad Industrial." June 27. www.wipo.int/wipolex/es/text.jsp?file_id=264465.

———. 1994a. "Extracto de la Solicitud de Declaración de Protección de la Denominación de Origen Mezcal." September 5. http://dof.gob.mx/nota_detalle.php?codigo=4735479&fecha=05/09/1994.

———. 1994b. "Resolution Mediante la Cual Se Otorga la Protección Prevista a la Denominación de Origen Mezcal, Para Ser Aplicada a la Bebida Alcohólica del Mismo Nombre." November 11. http://dof.gob.mx/nota_detalle.php?codigo=4768551&fecha=28/11/1994.

———. 1997a. "Acuerdo entre los Estados Unidos Mexicanos y la Comunidad Europea sobre el Reconocimiento Mutuo y la Protección de las Denominaciones de Origen en el Sector de las Bebidas Espirituosas." July 21. www.economia.gob.mx/files/marco_normativo/A108.pdf.

———. 1997b. "Norma Oficial Mexicana, NOM-006-SCFI-1994, Bebidas Alcohólicas—Tequila—Especificaciones." August 14. www.colpos.mx/bancodenormas/noficiales/NOM-006-SCFI-1994.PDF.

———. 1997c. "Norma Oficial Mexicana, NOM-070-SCFI-1994, Bebidas Alcohólicas—Mezcal—Especificaciones." June 12. http://dof.gob.mx/nota_detalle.php?codigo=4883475&fecha=12/06/1997.

———. 2003. "Modificación a la Declaración General de Protección de la Denominación de Origen Mezcal, Publicada el 28 de Noviembre de 1994." March 3. http://dof.gob.mx/nota_detalle.php?codigo=698211&fecha=03/03/2003.

———. 2006. "Norma Oficial Mexicana, NOM-006-SCFI-2005, Bebidas alcohólicas-Tequila—Especificaciones." January 6. www.ordenjuridico.gob.mx/Federal/PE/APF/APC/SE/Normas/Oficiales/NOM-006-SCFI-2005.pdf.

———. 2009. "Modificación del Inciso 6.1.1 de la Norma Oficial Mexicana NOM-070-SCFI-1994, Bebidas Alcohólicas-Mezcal-Especificaciones, Publicada el 12 de Junio de 1997." August 5. http://dof.gob.mx/nota_detalle.php?codigo=5101711&fecha=05/08/2009.

———. 2012a. "Modificación a la Declaración General de Protección de la Denominación de Origen Mezcal." November 22. www.dof.gob.mx/nota_detalle.php?codigo=5278677&fecha=22/11/2012.

———. 2012b. "Norma Oficial Mexicana NOM-006-SCFI-2012, Bebidas Alcohólicas—Tequila—Especificaciones." December 12. http://dof.gob.mx/nota_detalle.php?codigo=5282165&fecha=13/12/2012.

————. 2012c. "Respuesta a los Comentarios Recibidos al Proyecto de Norma Oficial Mexicana PROY-NOM-006-SCFI-2012, Bebidas Alcohólicas—Tequila—Especificaciones." June 15. http://dof.gob.mx/nota_detalle_popup .php?codigo=5279239.

Difford's Guide. 2013. "Science vs. Soul? Evidence for Terroir Finally Revealed." December 17. www.diffordsguide.com/magazine/2013–12–17/6 /terroir.

Dupont, Franck. 2002. *Impact de l'Utilisation d'une Indication Géographique sur l'Agriculture et le Développement Rural.* Paris: Ministère de l'Agriculture, de l'Alimentation, de la Pêche, et des Affaires Rurales.

Edelstein, Ilana. 2013. *The Patrón Way: From Fantasy to Fortune; Lessons on Taking Any Business from Idea to Iconic Brand.* Columbus, OH: McGraw-Hill Professional.

El Clamor Público. 1857. "Anuncios." 2(57) (June 27): 3. http://digitallibrary.usc .edu/cdm/compoundobject/collection/p15799coll70/id/508.

El Economista. 2012. "Productores del Tequila Advierten Déficit Agavero." May 3. http://eleconomista.com.mx/estados/2012/05/03/productores-tequila-advierten-deficit-agavero.

El Vigía. 2014. "Reducen Productores Inventario de Agave." December 1. www .elvigia.net/general/2014/12/1/reducen-productores-inventario-agave-179912 .html.

English, Camper. 2009. "The Trouble with Tequila." February 10. www .alcademics.com/2009/02/the-trouble-with-tequila.html.

————. 2013. "Ten Cool Things about Houston Bar The Pastry War." Alcademics, August 26. www.alcademics.com/2013/08/ten-cool-things-about-houston-bar-the-pastry-war.html.

Estes, Tomas. 2012. *The Tequila Ambassador.* London: Odd Firm of Sin Limited.

European Commission. 2014a. "DOOR Database." http://ec.europa.eu/agriculture /quality/door/list.html;jsessionid=pL0hLqqLXhNmFQyFl1b24mY3t9dJQPflg 3xbL2YphGT4k6zdWn34!-370879141.

————. 2014b. "Member States Fact Sheets: European Union." http://ec.europa .eu/agriculture/statistics/factsheets/pdf/eu_en.pdf.

Eurostat. 2011. "Food: From Farm to Fork Statistics." *Eurostat Pocketbooks.* http://epp.eurostat.ec.europa.eu/cache/ITY_OFFPUB/KS-32–11–743/EN /KS-32–11–743-EN.PDF.

Evans, G. E., and Michael Blakeney. 2006. "The Protection of Geographical Indications after Doho: Quo Vadis?" *Journal of International Economic Law* 9(3): 575–614.

Evans, Peter. 2014. "Diageo to Take Full Control of Don Julio." *Wall Street Journal,* November 3. www.wsj.com/articles/diageo-to-take-full-control-of-don-julio-1414999566.

Fabricant, Florence. 2013. "Go Deeper into Mexico with Mezcal." *New York Times*, September 26. www.nytimes.com/2013/10/02/dining/go-deeper-into-mexico-with-mezcal.html.

Feagan, Robert. 2007. "The Place of Food: Mapping Out the 'Local' in Local Food Systems." *Progress in Human Geography* 31(1): 23–42.

Flannery, Nathaniel Parish. 2013. "Mexico's Exports: Beer, Tequila, and Now Mezcal." *Forbes*, October 30. www.forbes.com/sites/nathanielparishflannery/2013/10/30/mexicos-exports-beer-tequila-and-now-mezcal/.

Flores, Javier. 2014. Personal communication to COMERCAM. www.experiencemezcal.com/wp-content/uploads/CAGP-Letter-.pdf.

Food and Wine. 2013. "2013 Cocktail Trends." www.foodandwine.com/slideshows/2013-cocktail-trends/11.

Foote, William. 1996. "The Resurrection of Oaxacan Spirits: Modernizing the Mescal Industry in Southern Mexico." *Institute of Current World Affairs Letters* WF-11 (August 31): 1–15. www.icwa.org/txtArticles/WF-11.htm.

Forbes. 2006. "F. Paul Pacult." February 21. www.forbes.com/2006/02/21/cx_0221wine9.html.

Fourcade, Marion. 2012. "The Vile and the Noble: On the Relation between Natural and Social Classifications in the French Wine World." *Sociological Quarterly* 53(4): 524–545.

Fourcade-Gourinchas, Marion, and Sarah Babb. 2002. "The Rebirth of the Liberal Creed: Paths to Neoliberalism in Four Countries." *American Journal of Sociology* 108(3): 533–579.

Freidberg, Susanne. 2004. *French Beans and Food Scares: Culture and Commerce in an Anxious Age*. Oxford: Oxford University Press.

Friedmann, Harriett. 1993. "The Political Economy of Food: A Global Crisis." *New Left Review* 197 (January–February): 29–57.

Frizell, St. John. 2009. "Mezcal: National Spirit." *Saveur*, November 12. www.saveur.com/article/Wine-and-Drink/National-Spirit.

Funding Universe. 2000. "Casa Cuervo, S.A. de C.V. History." www.fundinguniverse.com/company-histories/casa-cuervo-s-a-de-c-v-history/.

Gade, Daniel. 2004. "Tradition, Territory, and *Terroir* in French Viticulture: Cassis, France, and Appellation Contrôlée. Annals of the Association of American Geographers 94: 848–867.

Gangjee, Dev. 2012. *Relocating the Law of Geographical Indications*. Cambridge: Cambridge University Press.

García, Juan Pablo. 2012. "Peligra Credibilidad del Buen Mezcal por Corrupción en COMERCAM: Diputada." *RIOaxaca*. www.rioaxaca.com/estado/123-politica/44345-peligra-credibilidad-del-buen-mezcal-por-corrupcion-en-comercam-afirma-campos-orozco.

Garrone, Max. 2014. "The Debate over COMERCAM's Rules Continues." Mezcalistas. http://mezcalistas.com/the-debate-over-comercams-rules-continues/.

Gaytán, Marie Sarita. 2014. ¡Tequila!: Distilling the Spirit of Mexico. Stanford, CA: Stanford University Press.

————. Forthcoming. "The Transformation of Tequila: From Hangover to Highbrow." Journal of Consumer Culture. http://joc.sagepub.com/content /early/2014/11/04/1469540514556169.full.pdf+html.

Gaytán, Marie Sarita, and Sarah Bowen. 2015. "Naturalizing Neoliberalism and the De-Mexicanization of the Tequila Industry. Environment and Planning A 47(2): 267–283.

Gaytán, Marie Sarita, and Ana Valenzuela Zapata. 2012. "Más Allá del Mito: Mujeres, Tequila y Nación." Mexican Studies/Estudios Mexicanos 28(1): 183–208.

Gentry, Howard. 1982 [2004]. Agaves of Continental North America. Tucson: University of Arizona Press.

Gerz, Astrid, and Franck Dupont. 2006. "Comté Cheese in France: Impact of a Geographical Indication on Rural Development." In Origin-Based Products: Lessons for Pro-Poor Market Development, edited by Petra van de Kop, Denis Sautier, and Astrid Gerz, pp. 75–88. Bulletin 372. Amsterdam: KIT Publishers.

Ginley, Mike. 2013. "U.S. Beverage Alcohol Trends." PowerPoint presentation at the U.S. Beverage Alcohol Forum. www.usdrinksconference.com/assets /files/agenda/U.S.%20 Beverage%20Alcohol%20Trends.pdf.

Giovannucci, Daniele, Tim Josling, William Kerr, Bernard O'Connor, and May Yeung. 2009. Guide to Geographical Indications: Linking Products and Their Origins. Geneva: International Trade Center. http://legacy.intracen .org/publications/Free-publications/Geographical_Indications.pdf.

Gómez Arriola, Ignacio. 2004. El Paisaje Agavero y las Antiguas Instalaciones Industriales de Tequila, México. Guadalajara: Instituto Nacional de Antro-plogía e Historia (Jalisco).

————. 2010. "La Arquitectura del Tequila." PhD thesis, Universidad Michoa-cana de San Nicolás de Hidalgo, Morelia, Mexico.

González, Marco Antonio. 2002. "Blue Agave Producers in the Tequila Agro-Industry in Jalisco, Mexico: The Beginning of Production Alliances in the Context of the End of Land Reform." PhD thesis, University of Oxford, Oxford.

González Escárcega, Oscar. 2012. "Mezcal, la Bebida Ancestral de Moda." El Universal, July 11. www.eluniversal.com.mx/articulos/72019.html.

Goodman, David. 2004. "Rural Europe Redux? Reflections on Alternative Agro-Food Networks and Paradigm Change." Sociologia Ruralis 44(1): 3–16.

Gravel, Nathalie. 2007. "Mexican Smallholders Adrift: The Urgent Need for a New Social Contract in Rural Mexico." *Journal of Latin American Geography* 6(2): 77–98.

Guerrero Gómez, Gerardo. 1993. *Elaboración del Mezcal en Una Comunidad Nahuatl: Atliaca, Guerrero.* Chilpancingo, Guerrero: Dirección General de Culturas Populares.

Guevarra, Rudy. 2011. "Filipinos in Nueva España: Filipino-Mexican Relations, Mestizaje, and Identity in Colonial and Contemporary Mexico." *Journal of Asian American Studies* 14(3): 389–416.

Guthman, Julie. 2004a. *Agrarian Dreams? The Paradox of Organic Farming in California.* Berkeley: University of California Press.

———. 2004b. "Back to the Land: The Paradox of Organic Food Standards." *Environment and Planning A* 36(3): 511–528.

———. 2007. "The Polanyian Way? Voluntary Food Labels as Neoliberal Governance." *Antipode* 39(3): 456–478.

Guy, Kolleen. 2003. *When Champagne Became French: Wine and the Making of a National Identity.* Baltimore: Johns Hopkins University Press.

Gutiérrez González, Salvador. 2001. *Realidad y Mitos del Tequila: Criatura y Genio del Mexicano a Través de los Siglos.* Guadalajara: Editorial Agata.

Hamilton, Sarah. 2002. "Neoliberalism, Gender, and Property Rights in Rural Mexico." *Latin American Research Review* 37(1): 119–43.

Harrison, Jill Lindsey. 2011. *Pesticide Drift and the Pursuit of Environmental Justice.* Cambridge, MA: MIT Press.

Hernández López, José de Jesús. 2010. "El Vino Mezcal de Tequila: Entre El Pulque, El Aguaradiente de Caña, y El Vino de Uva." In *Vinos de Europa y de América,* edited by Frédéric Duhart and Sergio Antonio Corona Páez, pp. 25–42. Paris: Éditions Le Manuscrit.

Hernández López, Rafael Alonso, and Iván Francisco Porraz Gómez. 2011. "¿De Paisano a Paisano? Explotación Laboral y Exclusión Social de Jornaleros Chiapanecos en Jalisco." *Nómadas* 34: 167–185.

Herrmann, Roland, and Ramona Teuber. 2011. "Geographically Differentiated Products." In *Oxford Handbook of the Economics of Food Consumption and Policy,* edited by Jayson Lusk, Jutta Roosen, and Jason Shogren, pp. 811–843. Oxford: Oxford University Press.

Holmes, Paul. 2005. "Cuervo Nation." *The Holmes Report.* May 7. www .holmesreport.com/casestudy-info/4547/Cuervo-Nation.aspx.

Holmes, Seth. 2013. *Fresh Fruit, Broken Bodies: Migrant Farmworkers in the United States.* Berkeley: University of California Press.

Huerta Rosas, Rogelio, and Rogelio Luna Zamora. Forthcoming. "Los Caminos del Mezcal y el Tequila." In *Agua de las Verdes Matas: Tequila y Mezcal,* edited by José Luis Vera Cortés and Rodolfo Fernández, pp. 43–67. Mexico City: Artes de México.

Ibañez, José Alberto, and Yessika Hernández. 2006. "The Role of Regulatory Improvement Programs in the Strengthening of the Rule of Law in Mexico." Working Paper Series, Justice in Mexico Project, Issue No. 3. San Diego, CA: Center for U.S.-Mexico Studies.

Illsley Granich, Catarina, Daniele Giovannucci, and Claudia Bautista. 2009. *La Dinámica Territorial de la Zona Mezcalera de Oaxaca: Entre la Cultura y el Comercio*. Mexico City: Grupo de Estudios Ambientales, A.C.

Illsley Granich, Catarina. 2009a. "Biodiversidad, Campesinos y la Tradición Mezcalera Mexicana." *Boletín Biblio Mezcalófilo* 2 (February): 16–22. www .mezcalpedia.com/attachments/054_Boletin%20BiblioMezcalofilo%20 2%20febrero%202009%20comprimido.pdf.

———. 2009b. "The Case of Mezcal, Mexico." In *Guide to Geographical Indications: Linking Products and Their Origins*, edited by Daniele Giovannucci, Tim Josling, William Kerr, Bernard O'Connor, and May Yeung. pp. 183–196. Geneva: International Trade Center. http://legacy.intracen.org/publications /Free-publications/Geographical_Indications.pdf.

Institut National de l'Origine et de la Qualité (INAO). 2014a. *Les Fondements de l'Appellation d'Origine des Vins Fins*. www.inao.gouv.fr/public/home .php?pageFromIndex=textesPages/Les_fondements_de_l_appellation391 .php~mnu=391.

———. 2014b. *Guide du Demandeur d'une Appellation d'Origine (AOC/AOP)*. www.inao.gouv.fr/repository/editeur/pdf/divers/Guide_du_demandeur_ AOC.pdf.

Instituto para el Fomento a la Calidad Total. 2009. "Organizaciones Ganadores 2009." http://competitividad.org.mx/images/stories/PNCganadoras_09_2_ bookmarks.pdf.

Janzen, Emma. 2012. "From Agave Fields to Your Glass: What's Going On with Tequila These Days." *Austin American Statesman*, May 15. www.statesman .com/news/lifestyles/food-cooking/from-agave-fields-to-your-glass-whats- going-on-w-2/nRnk2/.

Jiménez Vizcarra, Miguel Claudio. 2008. "El Origen y Desarrollo de la Agroindustria del Vino Mezcal Tequila." Guadalajara: Benemérita Sociedad de Geografía y Estadística del Estado de Jalisco. www.museocjv.com /LIBROSDECLAUDIO/monografias/origenagroindustriatequila.pdf.

———. 2013. *El Vino Mezcal, Tequila, y la Polémica sobre la Destilación Prehispánica*. Guadalajara: Benemérita Sociedad de Geografía y Estadística del Estado de Jalisco. www.museocjv.com/librodestilacion.html.

Johnston, Josée, and Shyon Baumann. 2010. *Foodies: Democracy and Distinction in the Gourmet Foodscape*. New York: Routledge.

Josling, Tim. 2006. "The War on Terroir: Geographical Indications as a Transatlantic Trade Conflict." *Journal of Agricultural Economics* 57(3): 337–363.

Journal Officielle de la République Française. 1908. "Loi Modifiant l'Article 11 de la Loi de 1er Août 1905 sur la Répression des Fraudes dans la Vente des Marchandises et des Falsifications des Denrées Alimentaires et des Produits Agricoles et Complétant Cette Loi par un Article Additionnel." August 11. http://gallica.bnf.fr/ark:/12148/bpt6k6253207k/f1.image.r=Journal%20 officiel%20de%20la%20R%C3%A9publique%20fran%C3%A7aise.langFR.

———. 1919. "Loi Relative a la Protection des Appellations d'Origine." May 8. http://gallica.bnf.fr/ark:/12148/bpt6k6372770j/f2.image.r=Journal%20 officiel%20de%20la%20R%C3%A9publique%20fran%C3%A7aise.langFR.

Kerr, William. 2006. "Enjoying a Good Port with a Clear Conscience: Geographic Indicators, Rent Seeking and Development." *Estey Centre Journal of International Law and Trade Policy* 7(1): 1–14.

Kinchy, Abby. 2012. *Seeds, Science, and Struggle: The Global Politics of Transgenic Crops.* Cambridge, MA: MIT Press.

Kireeva, Irina, comp. 2011. *European Legislation on Protection of Geographical Indications: Overview of the EU Member States' Legal Framework for Protection of Geographical Indications.* European Union–China Project for the Protection of Intellectual Property Rights. www.ipr2.org/storage /European_legislation_on_protection_of_GIs1011.pdf.

Kleinman, Geoff. 2015. "2015 Spirit and Alcohol Trends Predictions." *Drink Spirits*, January 5. www.drinkspirits.com/general-spirits/2015-spirit-alcohol-trends-predictions/.

Kloppenburg, Jack, John Hendrickson, and G. W. Stevenson. 1996. "Coming in to the Foodshed." *Agriculture and Human Values* 13(3): 33–42.

La Botica. 2010. "La Botica." http://labotica.com.mx/.

Lachenmeier, Dirk, Eva-Maria Sohnius, Rainer Attig, and Mercedes López. 2006. "Quantification of Selected Volatile Constituents and Anions in Mexican Agave Spirits (Tequila, Mezcal, Sotol, Bacanora)." *Journal of Agricultural and Food Chemistry* 54(11): 3911–3915.

La Porta, Rafael, and Florencia Lopez-de-Silanes. 1999. "The Benefits of Privatization: Evidence from Mexico." *Quarterly Journal of Economics* 114(4): 1193–1142.

Larson, Jorge. 2007. *Relevance of Geographical Indications and Designations of Origin for the Sustainable Use of Genetic Resources.* Rome: Global Facilitation Unit for Underutilized Species.

Larson, Jorge, and Xitlali Aguirre. Forthcoming. "Normas de Etiquetado y Dilución de Significados en la Comercialización de Mezcal y Otros Destilados de Maguey en México." In *Agua de las Verdes Matas: Tequila and Mezcal*, pp. 167–187. Mexico City: Artes de México.

Leclert, Lucie. 2007. "Who Benefits from the 'Denominación de Origen' Tequila?" Master's thesis, Wageningen University, Wageningen, the Netherlands.

Leopo Flores, Marcela. 2012. "Ganan Opositores de la Marca 'Agave' Batalla al IMPI." Nuestro Tequila. October 23. www.nuestrotequila.com/verSeccion .php?t ipo=noticia&idElemento=227.

Lewis, Jessa. 2002. "Agrarian Change and Privatization of *Ejido* Land in Northern Mexico." *Journal of Agrarian Change* 2(3): 401–419.

Lisbon Agreement for the Protection of Appellations of Origin and Their International Recognition (October 31, 1958, as revised on July 14, 1967 and as amended on September 28, 1979). 1958. World Intellectual Property Organization. www.wipo.int/export/sites/www/lisbon/en/legal_texts /lisbon_agreement.pdf.

Living on Earth. 2004. "Bottoms Up for Once Lowly Mezcal." October 22. www .loe.org/shows/segments.html?programID=04-P13-00043&segmentID=3.

Llamas, Jorge. 1999. "La Política del Agave." *Estudios Agrarios* 13: 9–29.

Lo de Hoy en el Puerto. 2013. "La Producción Tradicional de Mezcal Genera en Michoacán Más de Tres Mil Empleos Directos." October 28. www .lodehoyenelpuerto.com/noticias/index.php?option=com_k2&view= item&id=5315:la-producci%C3%B3n-tradicional-de-mezcal-genera-en- michoac%C3%A1n-m%C3%A1s-de-tres-mil-empleos-directos.

Lumholtz, Carl. 1902. *Unknown Mexico: A Record of Five Years' Exploration among the Tribes of the Western Sierra Madre; In the Tierra Caliente of Tepic and Jalisco; and among the Tarascans of Michoacán.* Vol. 2. New York: Charles Scribner's Sons.

Luna Jiménez, Rebeca. 2012. "Denuncia Corrupción de Ex Directivos de la COMERCAM." *Diario Despertar de Oaxaca,* May 29. www.despertardeoaxaca .com/?p=3432.

Luna Zamora, Rogelio. 1991. *La Historia del Tequila, de sus Regiones y sus Hombres.* Mexico City: Conaculta.

Luna Zamora, Rogelio. 2005. "Disyuntivas del Patrimonio del Tequila en el Era Neoliberal." In *Bebidas y Regiones: Historia e Impacto de la Cultura Etílica en México,* edited by Camilo Contreras Delgado and Isabel Ortega Ridaura, pp. 21–38. Mexico City: Plaza y Valdés.

MacDonald, Kenneth. 2013. "The Morality of Cheese: A Paradox of Defensive Localism in a Transnational Cultural Economy." *Geoforum* 44: 93–102.

Macías Macías, Alejandro. 2001. "El Cluster en la Industria del Tequila en Jalisco, Mexico." *Agroalimentaria* 13: 57–72.

———. 2015. "Precio de Agave, 1985–2014." Personal communication, January 3, 2015.

Maillard, Tatiana. 2013. "La Ley y El Orden de los Mezcalier." *Emeequis.* August 18. www.m-x.com.mx/xml/pdf/309/58.pdf.

Maldonado, Salvador Y. 2013. "La Nueva NOM del Tequila Obliga a la Agricul- tura por Contrato." *El Informador,* February 7. www.informador.com.mx

/economia/2013/435675/6/la-nueva-nom-del-tequila-obliga-a-la-agricultura-por-contrato.htm.

Mancini, Maria Cecilia. 2013. "Localised Agro-Food Systems and Geographical Indications in the Face of Globalisation: The Case of *Queso Chontaleño.*" *Sociologia Ruralis* 53(2): 180–200.

Mara, Kaitlin. 2008. "Advocates Say Geographic Indications Will Benefit Developing Nations." *Intellectual Property Watch.* www.ip-watch.org/2008/07/11/advocates-say-geographical-indications-will-benefit-developing-nations/.

Marsden, Terry, and Alberto Arce. 1995. "Constructing Quality: Emerging Food Networks in the Rural Transition." *Environment and Planning A* 27(8): 1261–1279.

Martin, Meredith, Charles Peters, Matthew Palmer, and Catarina Granich Illsley. 2011. "Effect of Habitat and Grazing on the Regeneration of Wild *Agave cupreata* in Guerrero, Mexico." *Forest Ecology and Management* 262: 1443–1451.

Matalon, Lorne. 2012. "Mezcal Production Drawing Mexicans Back Home." *NPR Fronteras Desk.* December 11. http://lornematalon.com/2012/12/11/mezcal-production-drawing-mexicans-back-home/.

Matías, Pedro. 2014. "Oaxaca: Existen Productores de Mezcal Frenar Compra Indiscriminada de Maguey." *Proceso,* September 4. www.proceso.com.mx/?p=381353.

Maxwell, Khrys. 2014. "There May Be Too Much Agave in Your Tequila or Mezcal." MuchoAgave. www.muchoagave.com/the-difusor---there-may-be-too-much-agave-in-your-tequila-or-mezcal.html.

———. 2000. "Global Food Politics." In *Hungry for Profit: The Agribusiness Threat to Farmers, Food, and the Environment,* edited by Fred Magdoff, John Bellamy Foster, and Frederick H. Buttel, pp. 125–144. New York: Monthly Review Press.

———. 2005. "Global Development and the Corporate Food Regime." In *Research in Rural Sociology and Development.* Vol. 11: *New Directions in the Sociology of Global Development,* edited by Frederick Buttel and Philip McMichael, pp. 269–303. Amsterdam: Elsevier.

———. 2012. *Development and Social Change: A Global Perspective.* 5th ed. Thousand Oaks, CA: Sage Publications.

Meixueiro, Anselmo Arellanes, Andrés Henestrosa, Cora Franchini, Jorge Pablo de Aguinaco, Alexander Pepping, and María Eugenia Valles. 1997. *Mezcal: Elixir de una Larga Vida.* Oaxaca, Mexico: CVS Publications.

Menapace, Luisa, and GinoCarlo Moschini. 2012. "Quality Certification by Geographical Indications, Trademarks and Firm Reputation." *European Review of Agricultural Economics* 39(4): 539–566.

Mezcal El Cortijo. 2014. "Nuestra Historia." www.mezcalelcortijo.com/acerca /historia/.

Mezcales Tradicionales de los Pueblos de México. 2011. "¿Qué Son Los MT?" http://mezcalestradicionales.mx/mezcales-tradicionales/%C2%BFque-son-los-mt/.

Mezcaloteca. 2014. "Mezcal Tradicional." www.mezcaloteca.com/.

Mezonte. 2014. "Guía/Guide." http://mezonte.com/guia/.

Mitchell, Tim. 2004. *Intoxicated Identities: Alcohol's Power in Mexican History and Culture*. New York: Routledge.

Molina Ramírez, Tania. 2008. "En Materia de Tequila a Granel, La Ley es Perversa: Sólo Se Refiere a Territorio Nacional." *La Jornada*, March 24. www.jornada.unam.mx/2008/03/24/index.php?section=gastronomia&articl e=a19n1gas.

Montañez, José, Juan Victoria, Rebeca Flores, and María Vivar. 2011. "Fermentación de los Fructanos del Agave Tequilana Weber Azul por Zymomonas Mobilis y Saccharomyces Cerevisiae en la Producción de Bioetanol." *Información Tecnológica* 22(6): 3–14.

Monterrosa Hernández, Cornelio. 2005. *Ayer y Hoy del Mezcal: Breve Historia del Mezcal en Luá (Oaxaca)*. Oaxaca, Mexico: Union de Palenqueros de Oaxaca de Mezcal Artesanal.

Moran, Warren. 1993. "The Wine Appellation as Territory in France and California." *Annals of the Association of American Geographers* 83(4): 694–717.

Mundo Cuervo. 2008. "What Is Mundo Cuervo?" http://mundocuervo.com.

———. 2014. "250 Años de Historia." www.mundocuervo.com/en/sobre-cuervo /250-anos-de-historia.html.

Murray's Cheese. 2014. "Comte Saint Antoine." www.murrayscheese.com/comte-saint-antoine.html.

Mutersbaugh, Tad. 2005. "Fighting Standards with Standards: Harmonization, Rents, and Social Accountability in Certified Agrofood Networks." *Environment and Planning A* 37(11): 2033–2051.

Nader, Alexia. 2012. "Booze News: A Quarrel over Agave in Mexico." *Village Voice*, February 14. http://blogs.villagevoice.com/forkintheroad/2012/02 /booze_news_a_qu.php.

Nailey, Richard. 2013. "The EYE: Mezcal, Hold the Worm." *Forbes Life*, March 28. www.forbes.com/sites/richardnalley/2013/03/28/the-eye-mezcal-hold-the-worm/.

North American Free Trade Agreement (NAFTA). 1994. "Annex 313: Distinctive Products." www.sice.oas.org/trade/nafta/chap-034.asp#an313.

Official Journal of the European Union. 2012. "Regulation (EU) No 1151/2012 of the European Parliament and of the Council of 21 November 2012 on Quality Schemes for Agricultural Products and Foodstuffs." December 12,

L 343/1—L 343/29. http://eur-lex.europa.eu/legal-content/EN/TXT/PDF /?uri=CELEX:32012R1151&from=en.

Office of the United States Trade Representative. 2006. "United States and Mexico Reach Agreement on Tequila." Press release, January 17. www.ttb .gov/pdf/tequila-agreement-press-release.pdf.

Oxfam International. 2003. *Dumping without Borders: How US Agricultural Policies Are Destroying the Livelihoods of Mexican Corn Farmers.* Washington, DC: Oxfam International.

Organization for an International Geographical Indications Network (oriGIn). 2014. "Background." www.origin-gi.com/index.php/en/about-us/background .html.

Otero, Gerardo. 2004. *Mexico in Transition: Neoliberal Globalism, the State, and Civil Society.* London: Zed Books.

Parasecoli, Fabio, and Aya Tasaki. 2011. "Shared Meals and Food Fights: Geographical Indications, Rural Development, and the Environment." *Environment and Society: Advances in Research* 2(1): 106–123.

Paxson, Heather. 2012. *The Life of Cheese: Crafting Food and Value in America.* Berkeley: University of California Press.

Payno, Manuel. 1864. *Memoria sobre El Maguey Mexicano y Sus Diversos Productos.* Mexico: Imprenta de A. Boix, a cargo de Miguel Zornoza.

Peabody, W. 2009. "Mezcal Free Spirit." *LA Times Magazine,* November. www .latimesmagazine.com/2009/11/mezcal.html.

Pérez, Lázaro. 1887. *Estudio sobre el Maguey Llamado Mezcal en el Estado de Jalisco.* Guadalajara: Imprenta Ancira y Hermano.

Petrini, Carlo. 2001. *Slow Food: The Case for Taste.* New York: Columbia University Press.

Pini, Barbara. 2005. "Interviewing Men: Gender and the Collection and Interpretation of Qualitative Data." *Journal of Sociology* 41(2): 201–216.

Polanyi, Karl. 1944. *The Great Transformation.* Boston: Beacon Press.

Pool-Illsley, Emilia, and Illsley Granich, Catarina. 2012. "El Papel de los Activos Culturales en las Dinámicas Territoriales Rurales: El Caso de Tlacolula y Ocotlán en Valles Centrales de Oaxaca, México." *Grupo de Estudios Ambientales A.C.* www.rimisp.org/wpcontent/files_mf/1378403544dtricmezcalmay o29finalcompletochico.pdf.

Pratt, Jeff. 2007. "Food Values: The Local and the Authentic." *Critique of Anthropology* 27(3): 285–300.

Preston, Julia. 1996. "Drinking Tequila but Thinking Cognac, Maybe?" *New York Times,* January 4. www.nytimes.com/1996/01/04/business/international-business-drinking-tequila-but-thinking-cognac-maybe.html.

Quezada Limón, Fabiola, Aglae Lazcarro Rivera, and Jorge Velázuqez Nuñez. 2014. *La Micro y Pequeña Empresa Tequilera, Una Alternativa en la Globalización: El Caso Amatitán.* Guadalajara: Universidad de Guadalajara.

Rangnekar, Dwijen. 2011. "Re-making Place: The Social Construction of a Geographical Indication for Feni?" *Environment and Planning A* 43(9): 2043–2059.

Renard, Marie-Christine. 2005. "Quality Certification, Regulation, and Power in Fair Trade." *Journal of Rural Studies* 21(4): 419–431.

Renting, Henk, Terry Marsden, and Jo Banks. 2003. "Understanding Alternative Food Networks: Exploring the Role of Short Food Supply Chains in Rural Development." *Environnent and Planning A* 35(3): 393–411.

Revel, Jacques. 2000. "Histoire vs. Mémoire en France Aujourd'hui." *French Politics, Culture and Society* 18(1): 1–12.

Revista Quo. 2014. "El Tequila Está en Peligro de Extinción." Reprinted at *CNN Expansion,* April 12. www.cnnexpansion.com/especiales/2014/04/02 /el-tequila-esta-en-peligro-de-extincion.

Riccheri, Mariano, Benjamin Görlach, Stephanie Schlegel, Helen Keefe, and Anna Leipprand. 2006. *Assessing the Applicability of Geographical Indications as a Means to Improve Environmental Quality in Affected Ecosystems and the Competitiveness of Agricultural Products: Impacts of the IPR Rules on Sustainable Development Contract No. SCS8-CT-2004-503613.* Ecologic Institute. www.ecologic.eu/download/projekte/1800–1849/1802/wp3_final_report.pdf.

Ríos, Julio. 2008. "Explotados . . . Como en EU." *Proceso Edición Jalisco,* no. 1636, March 9. www.proceso.com.mx/?p=91895.

Robertson, Roland. 1995. "Glocalization: Time-Space and Homogeneity-Heterogeneity." In *Global Modernities,* edited by Mike Featherstone, Scott Lash, and Roland Robertson, pp. 25–44. Thousand Oaks, CA: Sage Publications.

Robinson, Daniel, and Chris Gibson. 2011. "Governing Knowledge: Discourses and Tactics of the European Union in Trade-Related Intellectual Property Negotiations." *Antipode* 43(5): 1883–1910.

Rodríguez, Oscar. 2014a. "Cambio de Reglas para el Mezcal." *Milenio,* June 24. www.milenio.com/estados/mezcal-norma-nuevas_reglas-cada_5_anos_ 0_323367790.html.

———. 2014b. "Industria del Mezcal, al Borde de Crisis por Escasez de Agave." *Milenio,* March 3. www.milenio.com/negocios/Industria-mezcal-crisis-escasez-agave_0_255574683.html.

Rodríguez Cisneros, Esperanza. 2001. "The Protection of Geographical Indications in Mexico." Paper presented at the Symposium on the International Protection of Geographical Indications, Montevideo, Uruguay.

Rodríguez Gómez, Guadalupe. 2001. "La Denominación de Origen del Tequila: Pugnas de Poder y la Construcción de la Especificidad Sociocultural del Agave Azul." *Nueva Antropología* 20(67): 141–171.

Rosas, Tania. 2012. "Mezcal Michoacano Entrará a la Zona de DO." *El Economista,* November 21. http://eleconomista.com.mx/estados/2012/11/21 /mezcal-michoacano-entrara-zona-do.

Saldaña Robles, Alberto, Ryszard Jerzy Serwatowski Hlawinska, Noé Saldaña Robles, César Gutiérrez Vaca, José Manuel Cabrera Sixto, and Salvador García Barrón. 2012. "Determinación de Algunas Propiedades Físicas de Agave Tequilana Weber para Mecanizar la Cosecha." *Revista Mexicana de Ciencias Agrícolas* 3(3): 451–465.

Salas, Fernando, and Sunita Kikeri. 2005. *Regulatory Reform: Institution Building: Lessons from Mexico.* Public Policy for the Private Sector, Note Number 282. Washington, DC: World Bank.

Sánchez López, Alberto. 1989 [2005]. *Oaxaca: Tierra de Maguey y Mezcal.* Oaxaca, Mexico: CONACYT.

Sauza Tequila. 2014. "Welcome." http://us.sauzatequila.com/tequilas.

Scarpa, Riccardo, George Philippidis, and Fiorenza Spalatro. 2005. "Product-Country Images and Preference Heterogeneity for Mediterranean Food Products: A Discrete Choice Framework." *Agribusiness* 21: 329–349.

Schultz, Rob. 2014. "Say Cheese? Europeans Would Prefer We'd Call It Something Else." *Wisconsin State Journal,* February 9. http://host.madison.com /news/local/say-cheese-europeans-would-prefer-we-d-call-it-something /article_ffa27ae0-50c5-5825-a7da-d457754a9e3b.html.

Schwalbe, Michael, and Michelle Wolkomir. 2001. "The Masculine Self as Problem and Resource in Interview Studies of Men." *Men and Masculinities* 4: 90–103.

Secretaría de Agricultura, Ganadería, Desarrollo Rural, Pesca, y Alimentación (SAGARPA). 1999. "Cierre de la Producción Agrícola por Distrito, 1999 (Agave, Estado Jalisco)." www.siap.gob.mx/index.php?option=com_wrapper &view=wrapper&Itemid=351.

———. 2000. "Cierre de la Producción Agrícola por Estado, 2000 (Agave)." www.siap.gob.mx/index.php?option=com_wrapper&view=wrapper&Ite mid=351.

———. 2005. "Cierre de la Producción Agrícola por Estado, 2005 (Agave)." www.siap.gob.mx/index.php?option=com_wrapper&view=wrapper&Ite mid=351.

———. 2010a. "Cierre de la Producción Agrícola por Distrito, 2010 (Agave, Estado Jalisco)." www.siap.gob.mx/index.php?option=com_wrapper&view= wrapper&Itemid=351.

———. 2010b. "Cierre de la Producción Agrícola por Estado, 2010 (Agave)." www.siap.gob.mx/index.php?option=com_wrapper&view=wrapper&Ite mid=351.

Seidman, Gay. 2007. *Beyond the Boycott: Labor Rights, Human Rights, and Transnational Activism.* New York: Russell Sage Foundation.

Servicio Nacional de Sanidad, Inocuidad, y Calidad Agroalimentaria (SENASICA). 2013. "Plagas Reglamentadas del Agave." www.senasica.gob.mx /?id=5491.

Shanken News Daily. 2013. "Proximo's New Mission: Revitalizing Jose Cuervo in the US Market." *Shanken News Daily,* March 1. www.shankennewsdaily. com/index.php/2013/03/01/5240/proximos-new-mission-revitalizing-jose-cuervo-in-the-u-s-market/.

Simonson, Robert. 2012. "Mexican Distillers Fight over the Word 'Agave.'" *New York Times,* February 10. http://dinersjournal.blogs.nytimes.com/2012/02/10/mexican-distillers-fight-over-the-word-agave/?_php=true&_type=blogs&_r=0.

Sistema Nacional Maguey Mezcal. 2006. *Plan Rector Sistema Nacional Maguey Mezcal.* San Luis Potosí, Mexico: SAGARPA. www.sientemezcal.com/pdf/PlanRector.pdf.

Sistema Producto Maguey Mezcal Zacatecas. 2012. *Plan Rector Comité Estatal Sistema Producto Maguey Mezcal.* Juchipila, Mexico: SAGARPA. http://dev.pue.itesm.mx/sagarpa/estatales/ept%20comite%20sistema%20producto%20maguey%20mezcal%20zacatecas/plan%20rector%20que%20contiene%20programa%20de%20trabajo%202012/pr_maguey_mezcal_zacatecas_2012.pdf.

Solís-Aguilar, Juan Fernando, Héctor González-Hernández, Jorge Luis Leyva-Vázquez, Armando Equihua-Martínez, Francisco Javier Flores-Mendoza, and Ángel Equihua-Martínez. 2001. "*Scyphophorus acupunctatus* Gyllenhal, Plaga del Agave Tequilero en Jalisco, México." *Agrociencia* 35: 663–670.

Spivak, Mark. 2012. *Iconic Spirits: An Intoxicating History.* Guilford, CT: Lyons Press.

Steinhauer, Jennifer. 2014. "Budget Problems? Kentucky and Elsewhere Find Answer in Bottle." *New York Times,* November 28. www.nytimes.com/2014/11/29/us/budget-problems-kentucky-and-elsewhere-find-answer-in-bottle.html.

Strenk, Tom. 2014. "Tequila's Rising Star." *Beverage Dynamics,* May 12. www.beveragedynamics.com/2014/05/12/tequilas-rising-star/2118/.

Swarsdon, Anne. 1999. "Something's Rotten in Roquefort: A New U.S. Tariff; French Town Retaliates with a Tax on Coca-Cola." *Washington Post,* April 21.

Szczech, Clayton. 2014a. "Battle Lines Drawn over Mezcal Rule Changes." Experience Mezcal. June 18. www.experiencemezcal.com/2014/06/mezcal-norm-changes-pt2/.

———. 2014b. "Mezcaleros United around Improved Norm." Experience Mezcal. June 26. www.experiencemezcal.com/2014/06/mezcal-norm-changes-pt3/.

———. 2014c. "What's Next for the Mezcal Norm?" Experience Mezcal. December 8. www.experiencemezcal.com/2014/12/december-2014-update-on-mezcal-norm-revisions/.

Taylor, William. 1972. *Landlord and Peasant in Colonial Oaxaca.* Stanford, CA: Stanford University Press.

Technomic. 2012. "Technomic Identifies Top 250 Spirit Brands." April 9. http://
technomic.tm00.com/u/Technomic/0FXUmBU7gznvxmB/Technomic-
Identifies-Top-250-Spirit-Brands-headline---longdate.htm.

Teil, Geneviève. 2012. "No Such Thing as Terroir?: Objectivities and the
Regimes of Existence of Objects." *Science, Technology, & Human Values*
37(5): 478–505.

Tequila Fortaleza. 2014. "The History of Tequila Fortaleza." http://tequilafortaleza
.com/the-history-of-tequila-fortaleza/.

Tequila Partida. 2014. "Our Tequila." www.partidatequila.com/our-tequila/.

Tequila Patrón. 2014a. "Patrón XO Café." www.patrontequila.com/xocafe-
flavors#cafe.

———. 2014b. "The Process of Making Patrón Tequila." www.patrontequila.
com/perfection.

Terra. 2012. "Exhorta Comision Permanente de la SE Retirar Proyecto de
Norma Sobre Bebidas Elaboradas de Agave." August 2. http://economia
.terra.com.mx/noticias/noticia.aspx?idNoticia=201208021835_AGE_
81464656.

New York Times Editorial Board. 2014. "Law and Order in Mexico." *New York
Times,* November 11. www.nytimes.com/2014/11/12/opinion/murder-in-
mexico.html?_r=0.

This American Life. 2002. "205: Plan B." February 1. www.thisamericanlife.org
/radio-archives/episode/205/plan-b?act=1.

Torres, Gabriel. 1998. "The Agave War: Toward an Agenda for the Post NAFTA
Ejido." In *The Future Role of the Ejido in Rural Mexico,* edited by Richard
Snyder and Gabriel Torres, pp. 73–100. La Jolla: Center for U.S.-Mexican
Studies, University of California, San Diego.

Torrontera, Ulises. 2001. *Mezcalería.* 2nd ed. Oaxaca, Mexico: Farolito
Ediciones.

Tregear, Angela, Filippo Arfini, Giovanni Belletti, and Andrea Marescotti.
2007. "Regional Foods and Rural Development: The Role of Product
Qualification." *Journal of Rural Studies* 23(1): 12–22.

Trubek, Amy. 2008. *The Taste of Place: A Cultural Journey into Terroir.*
Berkeley: University of California Press.

United Nations Educational, Scientific, and Cultural Organization (UNESCO).
2015. "Agave Landscape and Ancient Industrial Facilities of Tequila." http://
whc.unesco.org/en/list/1209.

United States Department of Agriculture (USDA). 2013. "National Count of
Farmers Market Directory Listing Graph: 1994–2013." USDA Agricultural
Marketing Service. www.ams.usda.gov/AMSv1.0/ams.fetchTemplateData
.do?template=TemplateS&leftNav=WholesaleandFarmersMarkets&page=W
FMFarmersMarketGrowth&description=Farmers%20Market%20Growth.

———. 2014. "Know Your Farmer, Know Your Food." www.usda.gov/wps/portal /usda/knowyourfarmer?navid=knowyourfarmer.

Valenzuela Zapata, Ana. 2003. *El Agave Tequilero: Cultivo e Industria de México*. Mexico City: Ediciones Mundi-Prensa.

———. 2005. "Indicaciones Geográficas y Sustentabilidad: El Caso del Tequila." PhD diss. Universidad Autónoma de Nuevo León, Monterrey, Mexico.

Valenzuela Zapata, Ana, and Alejandro Macías Macías. 2014. *La Indicación Geográfica Tequila: Lecciones de la Primera Denominación de Origen Mexicana*. Mexico City: CONABIO.

Valenzuela Zapata, Ana, and Gary Paul Nabhan. 2004. *¡Tequila!: A Natural and Cultural History*. Tucson: University of Arizona Press.

Van Young, Eric. 2006. *Hacienda and Market in Eighteenth Century Mexico*. 2nd ed. Lanham, MD: Rowman and Littlefield.

Velazco, Jorge. 2000. "Paran 30% de las Tequileras." *Reforma*, September 25. http://reforma.vlex.com.mx/vid/paran-30-tequileras-81057326.

Vera Guzmán, A., Mercedes Guadalupe López, and José Luis Chávez-Servia. 2012. "Chemical Composition and Volatile Compounds in the Artisanal Fermentation of Mezcal in Oaxaca, Mexico." *African Journal of Biotechnology* 11(78): 14344–14353.

Vernus, Michel. 1998. *Une Saveur Venue des Siècles: Gruyère, Abondance, Beaufort, Comté*. Saint-Gingolph, France: Editions Cabédita.

Vigneaux, Ernest. 1863. *Souvenirs d'un Prisonnier de Guerre au Mexique, 1854–1855*. Paris: Imprimerie de Ch. Lahure et Cie.

Walton, Mylie. 1977. "The Evolution and Location of Mezcal and Tequila in Mexico." *Revista Geográfica* 85: 113–132.

Ward, Logan. 2014. "Mexico's Old Soul." *Garden and Gun* (June–July). http:// gardenandgun.com/article/mezcals-old-soul.

Waters, Sarah. 2010. "Globalization, the Confédération Paysanne, and Symbolic Power." *French Politics, Culture & Society* 28(2): 96–117.

Weiner, Tim. 2000. "The Tequila Crisis: Take It with a Grain of Salt." *New York Times*, September 20.

West, Robert C. 1949. *The Mining Community in Northern New Spain, the Parral Mining District*. Berkeley: University of California Press.

Wise, Timothy. 2010. "The Impacts of U.S. Agricultural Policies on Mexican Producers." In *Subsidizing Inequality: Mexican Corn Policy since NAFTA*, edited by Jonathan Fox and Libby Haight, pp. 163–171. Santa Cruz, CA: Woodrow Wilson International Center for Scholars.

World Intellectual Property Organization (WIPO). 2014. "Contracting Parities— Lisbon Agreement." www.wipo.int/treaties/en/ShowResults.jsp?lang= en&treaty_id=10.

World Trade Organization (WTO). 1994. "Agreement on Trade-Related Aspects of Intellectual Property Rights," pt. 2, sec. 3: "Geographical Indications." www.wto.org/english/docs_e/legal_e/27-trips_04b_e.htm#3.

Zavala Lunes, Juan Carlos. 2012. "Mezcal, Industria Adulterada." *Estado 20*, September 3. www.estado20.com/mientrastantoen/oaxaca/88-mezcal-industria-adulterada.html.

———. 2013. "Se Dispara Exportación de Mezcal en 371%." Ipoaxaca.mx. May 29. http://ipoaxaca.mx/extensions/components/content-component/article-category-list/565-se-dispara-exportacion-de-mezcal-en-371.

Zizumbo-Villarreal, Daniel, and Patricia Colunga-García Marín. 2007. "La Introducción de la Destilación y el Origen de los Mezcales en el Occidente de México." In *Lo Ancestral Hay Futuro: Del Tequila, Los Mezcales, y Otros Agaves*, edited by Patricia Colunga-García Marín, Alfonso Larqué Saavedra, Luis Eguiarte, and Daniel Zizumbo-Villarreal, pp. 85–112. Mérida, Mexico: Centro de Investigación Científica de Yucatán, A.C.

———. 2008. "Early Coconut Distillation and the Origins of Mezcal and Tequila Spirits in West-Central Mexico." *Genetic Resources and Crop Evolution* 55: 493–510.

Zizumbo-Villarreal, Daniel, Patricia Colunga-García Marín, Ofelia Vargas-Ponce, Jesús Juan Rosales-Adame, and Roberto Carlos Nieto Olivares. 2009. "Tecnología Agrícola Tradicional en la Producción de Vino Mezcal (Mezcal y Tequila) en el Sur de Jalisco, México." *Revista de Geografía Agrícola* 42: 65–82.

Zizumbo-Villarreal, Daniel, Fernando González-Zozoya, Angeles Olay-Barrientos, Laura Almendros-López, Patricia Flores-Pérez, and Patricia Colunga-García Marín. 2009. "Distillation in Western Mesoamerica before European Contact." *Economic Botany* 63(4): 413–426.

Zizumbo-Villarreal, Daniel, Ofelia Vargas-Ponce, Jesús J. Rosales-Adame, and Patricia Colunga-García Marín. 2013. "Sustainability of the Traditional Management of *Agave* Genetic Resources in the Elaboration of Mezcal and Tequila Spirits in Western Mexico." *Genetic Resources and Crop Evolution* 60(1): 33–47.

Index

CALIFORNIA STUDIES IN FOOD AND CULTURE

Darra Goldstein, Editor